MW00912841

From Crip to Christ

Change from the Inside Out

From Crip to Christ

Change from the Inside Out

Eric M. West

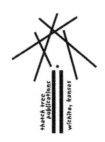

thatch tree
publications

wichita, kansas

From Crip to Christ   Change from the Inside Out

Library of Congress Control Number: 2013933257

ISBN: 978-0-9801940-4-3

Printed in the USA by Signature Book Printing, www.sbpbooks.com

Thatch Tree Publications, Wichita, Kansas

Editing, cover design, graphics, photo restoration, and page design by
    Kathy Alba, Ph.D.
    Author of *Across the Soul's Boundary, An Epic in Seven Volumes.*

For information or to order or to communicate with the author:

    Thatch Tree Publications
    2250 N. Rock Road, Suite 118-169
    Wichita KS 67226
        email: thatchtreepub@aol.com

"Therefore if any man be in Christ, he is a new creature;
old things are passed away;
behold, all things are become new"
(2 Corinthians 5:17 KJV).

Dedication

Without shame or hesitation, I first and foremost dedicate this book to the God of Abraham, Isaac, and Jacob. He is solely responsible for giving me life and a reason to hope. As the old gospel song says, "Where would I be if He didn't care?" I thank my Lord and Savior Jesus Christ for being willing to suffer by having His blood shed for me and for countless others that I may have reconciliation with God. He is the only reason I can hope. I can't say it enough: Jesus Christ has placed the highest value on me by paying a price that I could never pay. I praise and thank Him for loving me in a way that only He can as well as putting the dream of writing this book in my heart and not letting me give up over the long years of getting ready to find the right time. I am forever grateful to my Lord.

I also dedicate this book to my wife, Andrea, and to my kids, Ashley and Isaiah, whom God has given to me. I am grateful to you. I especially appreciate my wife for pressing forward with me, even though it was not always easy as we both tried to heal. I have learned many things from you about hospitality and giving, about how to deal with the business side of life. Being married to you has forced me to grow up in many ways.

I thank God for my kids. You mean so much to me, and I enjoy you thoroughly. It is my hope that if you have learned anything from me, it's how much I love you, even when I discipline you. I hope you will come to realize that I put boundaries around you and have to say "no" at times because your mom and I care; it has always been for your long-term good. But even more, I hope you have seen in me a willingness to obey Christ, who commands me to guide and care for you. You have my permission to follow my example only when I am being obedient to Christ Jesus our Lord. This is the legacy I hope to leave for you.

My biological father, "Big William," is no longer with us, but I thank God for giving him to me for the short time that He did. Although I didn't have the opportunity to grow up knowing my dad, I always desired him as any kid would his father. I'm grateful we got to know each other for a brief time. He met the thug but came to know the young man. I miss him and wish I could have enjoyed him more. I dedicate this book to your memory, Pop!

To my mother, Marie, I thank God for choosing you to be my mom. In spite of the past, I love you, Momma, for being my friend today. I thank you for the many times you sacrificed for me. I don't remember you looking me in the eyes and saying "I love you, son" while I was growing up, but in other ways, you did say it; and I thank you for that. Since I've been married, you've never once put your nose in our business but respected us both by letting us handle our own marriage. In the best way you've known how, the legacy you're leaving me is that you've tried to be the mom to me now that wasn't always so easy back then. And as far as I'm concerned, you've more than made up for the past as I've watched you slowly change. I love you.

As for my grandmother, "Momma Mag," what can I say about her? She was my first caretaker, the first love I ever knew. It was from her that I first heard the word "God." She taught me to honor Him and to respect authority. She showed me by her kind example to value all people, whether black or white. She taught me to say "yes ma'am" and "yes sir." I first learned to laugh with my grandma.

To my mother-in-law, Momma Stine, you have been the best mother-in-law in the world. You too have respected our marriage and have always been there for us, never taking any sides. You and the rest of the family have accepted me from day one, and I have seen no let up. I want to say thanks. I love you all!

To my sisters and brothers on both sides: I love you all, and I am privileged to have the distinction of being called your big brother.

To my stepmother Louise: in the beginning, I didn't feel like you accepted me and didn't know what to make of it. But that changed, and I soon felt I was like your own. You mean a lot to me, and I am proud to be called your stepson. And to my family on both the Douglas and Owens sides: you are too many to name, but you know who you are. I'm glad to be a member of your families.

To those in the Christian faith who supported me at the moment of my change and since that time, including Kim and Yvonne Seeback, Fred and Jolene Stoesz, Andy and Lisa Entz, Jerry and Ruth Peters, Al and Ruth Ewert, Joe and Sue Graham and the rest of the ranch staff, all from World Impact: you became the models for me in how to be a committed couple in marriage. I watched you closely, learning from you, as you loved and respected one another and made the necessary sacrifices for your families. Even in the tough times, Christ remained the final say.

To the former Wichita mayor, Bob Knight and his wife, Jane; also to George and Marjean Fooshee as well as Al and Ruth Ewert, World Impact missionaries; and to my Central Christian Church family and the school faculties of Central Christian Academy Ministries and their families for their encouragement to my family over the years.

To Edward, you have been a true friend to me since the day we met at the age of nine. We cut our hands and bonded our blood to forge a friendship that has continued to this day. After surviving the streets, we are both walking with Christ today. I thank God for you, homey. Brothers forever!

I thank the Lord for bringing people along side me in the long journey of writing this book. A number of you supported it when it was just an idea, a dream. You test-read it for me and gave me encouragement and good counsel when sometimes I wanted to drop the whole thing as God had to stretch and heal me. And you further supported me with financial gifts to keep the project going. Further, to Paula Morgan for helping with the rough draft, Melissa Scapa who took the time to type all 110,226 words, and to Ellen Myers who inspired me for Christ and recommended my story to the radio drama program "Unshackled." You are all too many to name, but God knows who you are—and so do I. Thank you for being the Body of Christ to me.

To Dr. Kathy Alba for coming along side me and following God's lead, for your willingness to honor Christ in helping me when I was discouraged from going forward with this pursuit: you have been a true answer to my prayers. I thank you and your company, Thatch Tree Publications, for your outstanding service and commitment to me in editing, designing, and publishing my book. May God continue to bless you.

To the many kids I've had the honor of leading, loving through listening, being available in the late night hours during phone calls, spending time on the basketball court or over lunch—whatever was called for. You mean as much to me as I hope I've meant to you, and I hope you saw Christ's love in me. You know who you are, though you are far too many to name. Thanks for letting me be a part of your lives.

Last, I dedicate this book to those in Watts and the surrounding areas in south central Los Angeles. To those whom I grew up with in the PJs (the Imperial Courts Housing Projects) and in the Jordan Downs, I will always remember you. Not that many of us made it out of the hood, dead or alive.

I remember the broken homes, the tough times, and the good days I shared with many of you—especially those I went to school with at Grape Street Elementary, Edwin Markham Jr. High, and David Star Jordan High School. I went through many things with you and remember the times when I put my life on the line for some of you as some of you did for me.

Many of our homeboys are dead now, and many are serving the rest of their lives in prison. But to those who are still alive, I just want to say how much you mean to me; and until my dying day, I will never, ever, forget you. There was a time when I had no hope, no dream, and no feel for how I fit into this thing we call life. I am one of only a few who do have hope beyond the hood. I want to be a living example for you that there is hope and that change is possible. God has not abandoned you but is more than willing to show you His purpose for you. He has placed great value on your life, even if society and the system have not. May my story be a light for you; I pray that you will come to know the future that God wants to give you.

I didn't wake up one day and decide I needed to change my life. Gang banging was all I knew. It meant everything to me, and I was more than willing to give up my life for Grape Street Watts Crips. But God chose to allow some hard things to take place in my family— if that is what it took to shake me and get my attention. And my life has not been the same since that time. That is my hope for you. Keep your heads up because there is One who cares. As a former member of the Crip family, you will always be in my prayers.

Introduction

Finally, the bell had rung! I couldn't wait to go out to recess. My friends, Albert and Chris—who were among my best friends at the time—and I went out to find Jill. All the guys liked Jill and often made fools of themselves around her—including me! She was beautiful, well dressed, and very classy. Albert and Chris knew I liked her but was too scared to tell her. I was ashamed of my speech impediment and had very, very little self-confidence. But they decided to push me anyway.

My buddies finally talked me into stepping up to the plate, insisting, "If you like her, then stop talking about it and tell her!" So they convinced me to write her a letter. I did that with the words,

Dear Jill, I like you. Do you like me? Yes ___ No___.

And to top it off, I think I put a dime in with the letter to impress her, and Albert took it to her.

I can remember having mixed emotions about it. A part of me was excited about telling her, even though it was in letter form; but a part of me feared that she would reject me. To my utter amazement, Jill checked the "Yes" box; and I became the first kid from the ghetto to go to space. That blew me away! It gave me a confidence that I hadn't felt since leaving Arkansas.

Pretty soon word began to spread that Jill liked me, and that made some of the bad boys despise me even more it seemed. I had become their punching bag and a laughing stock. Before moving to

California, my stuttering condition was not that much of an issue, but now it had become a big one. I was given the name "Stutter-Box," even though I hadn't asked for it. I was not used to people hating me; but for whatever reason, I was treated by some as though they really did. For what? I hadn't offended anyone or talked about anybody's momma. They gave me no explanation, and I dared not ask for one. I had been living in Watts for about three years and had been made a victim throughout that time. I felt like I had to figure out a way to get those bullies to like me if I was going to get through it.

Somehow I got the idea that if I just stood there and let them mock me and spit all kinds of jokes at me and if I could just laugh along with them, then they would eventually stop and accept me. So I found a way to slip into their circles and let my stuttering be the topic of choice.

One day at recess, this was never more true. We were playing on the monkey bars when I glanced up and saw Jill and her friend coming in our direction. I had a gut feeling of what was about to happen, but I knew I had to stick with my game plan.

True enough, the guys saw that moment as an opportunity to humiliate me in front of Jill and her friend. They started saying things like, "Man, why you be talking like that? You sound retarded, homeboy! You be like, 'Uh! Uh! Uh!' Spit it out, nigga! Stutter-Box!" They said stuff like that, which destroyed any shred of confidence and self-worth in me. Yet I could not let them see how they had humiliated me.

As Jill walked by, she heard all this; and seeing through her eyes, I felt like she was telling me to stop them. It was as if she were asking me without saying a word, *"Are you going to just stand there and let them talk about you like that?"* And what was my response? Laughter!

I was willing to turn on myself and join in with my so-called friends, to laugh along at myself with them. And I stood there chuckling as Jill and her friend strolled on by. I felt ashamed of myself and just wanted to die. And that day, I believe I did die inside to the person I had been. It was like taking the only picture of me on planet earth and cutting it to pieces.

Finally I couldn't take it anymore, so I pretended—lied—and told the guys that I had to use the restroom. I jogged my way in that direction; but the closer I got, the more I began to cry. I picked up my speed so that no one would see the tears fall. Once I arrived, I ran into the restroom and just started to weep—and I'm talking crocodile tears. I kept thrusting my middle fingers into my face and chest, wishing I were dead. I turned my attention to God and asked, *"Why did you make me like this? Why don't you make them leave me alone? And why do my momma have to stutter too?"*

My mind kept telling me that God didn't care or that He didn't really have the power to stop people from messing with me. I should just leave Him alone. I stood there waiting on God to answer me audibly, but He didn't. So I dried my tears and decided to believe in the deepest parts within me that Jesus couldn't help me; my only answer was to let Him go. It was that day that I rebelled in my heart—at the ripe old age of eleven.

Hello. I want to thank you for taking the time to read my book. It is my story and my life, and it is my joy to share it with you. I don't pretend to be an expert in sociology or in any other –ology, but it is my desire to share my life exactly how it was and show what drove me into gang activity in the first place. But even more than that, I want to explain who was responsible for bringing me out of that destructive life that was heading to a head-on collision with death, prison, or at the very least, a hopeless life, empty of any dream or direction.

People often wonder what makes a gang-banger—or anyone for that matter—simply walk up to someone for senseless reasons and just shoot that person without any justifiable cause. People aren't born bitter or angry at the world, but there *is* just that inborn potential to become that way if their hearts aren't loved and protected.

It is definitely a heart issue. And this is the point of my story. I just want to share with you how it was for me and how Jesus Christ turned around my destructive lifestyle and, even more, how He has given me an unshakable hope for today and beyond.

It is also my hope that you will enjoy the story and that maybe, just maybe, you will be encouraged through it. I am so glad to open up my life and show how God has changed what could have been a sad story into one of victory. Thank you so much for taking the time to read my book. I hope it will be a blessing to you.

Chapter One

I was born to teenage parents on October 28, 1965, at the Jefferson County Hospital in Pine Bluff, Arkansas. My mother was three months into her seventeenth year, and my father was about eighteen. His name was William Douglas, and my mother's name is Marie Owens.

The two of them began dating in high school. I'm told that he was a star running back in football, and she was just your typical young girl, looking for her own place in life. She fell in love with him in those years and some time later became pregnant with me.

Unfortunately, she wasn't the only one. Another young lady also became pregnant by him. When my mother found out about it, she was obviously devastated. She decided she couldn't stay in that situation and decided to drop their relationship.

But she took it even further. She told him he couldn't be a part of my life and was only allowed to see me immediately after my birth. He and his family, I'm told, did come to visit me. But it did not continue since my mother had prohibited it.

It was the middle of the sixties, and America was going through turbulent times. Prayer and the Bible were declared "unconstitutional" by the Supreme Court of the United States. President John F. Kennedy had been assassinated by the alleged Lee Harvey Oswald. A national split in our nation was underway over the Vietnam War, and a national rebellion by the Baby Boomer generation was in full swing. They were the teenagers of the day, just wanting to break away from their parents' generation and its authority. And my mother was no different. She had decided to leave home just to do what she wanted to do.

14

My father decided to join the U.S. Army and was shipped off to war as a combat soldier instead of going to college to play football. He would later become one of the first soldiers to be affected by the chemical "Agent Orange" which was not supposed to hurt human life.

That was not the end of trials in that incredible decade, though. The Civil Rights movement would struggle for our basic civil rights as black people, which would result in civil rights laws for not only blacks but for all Americans of color. There were national riots in big cities, including probably the most famous, the Watts riots of 1965. This would culminate in the assassinations of Dr. King, Malcom X, Attorney General Robert F. Kennedy, and NAACP leader, Medger Evers.

Shortly after I was born, my young mother, who had just turned seventeen, decided to not only leave home but to leave the state of Arkansas itself. But because we were living in my grandparents' home, she knew I was in good hands. And after a few months of my birth, she left and went to Chicago, Illinois.

But again, I was in a safe place. My grandparents, Robert and Maggie Owens, were more than willing to raise me even though they would have preferred that my mom had stayed. She was their last child. With them, I was the only youngster in the home, so I would imagine they had to adjust to a new lifestyle quickly. They had not had a baby around in seventeen years—when they had my mother.

My earliest memory goes back to when my Uncle Sonny, my mother's oldest brother, used to let me follow him to the backyard to get water from our pump. He would let me carry a tin bucket and would put water into it, and I would carry that back inside. I was about a year old or so.

I had gotten really sick when I was about a year and a half. Somehow I had developed meningitis and pneumonia and was given a slim chance of living. It would become my first brush with death.

My mother was contacted in Chicago; but as I understand it, she was unable to leave immediately because their area was having a snow storm, and all transportation was held up. Still, she came home as soon as she could to be with me. When she returned, she did not come alone. She was pregnant with my sister Charmaine, whose father was a member of the Black Panther Party.

My first traumatic experience came when my Uncle Sonny

was killed. As I've heard it told, my mother was on one side of him and his mother—my grandmother—was on the other side when he was shot to death. He and a cousin were gambling at the time, and he won. His cousin got upset and started a fight with him. That led to his being shot to death.

At the funeral, though I was not yet two years old, I watched my grandmother weep for her first born son. At one point she even tried to grab the casket. I started crying because I had to watch her cry, the only caretaker I knew. It was very tough for me to have my world shaken at that age. And even then, as God is my witness, somehow I knew he was gone for good.

On October 28, 1967, later that same year, my sister Charmaine was born. It was also my second birthday. I was told that she was my birthday present. I remember the day she came home, I was filled with excitement. When she arrived, I went right to her. All I could think of was that I had to hold her in my arms; any resistance to my will was unacceptable. I yelled and screamed for her; and finally, I was shown respect: those grown-ups finally heard my cry. I was instructed to sit down on the bed, up against the wall, and was shown how to hold her in my lap.

My mother stayed around, I've heard, for a little while and then decided to go back to Chicago. Before she left, she made arrangements with our god-grandparents, residing next door to us, to let my sister live with them. At least that gave us the chance to grow up together.

Some of the greatest moments of my life occurred with my sister. We didn't have a TV in our home, but my sister had one in theirs. We would sit down in front of the television, with peanut butter and jelly sandwiches and juice or whatever, watching those old black and white cartoons, like "Popeye the Sailor Man." One of my particular favorites featured some Indians doing a rain dance.

I was about four at this time, and my sister was about two. Charmaine and I went outside in the front yard one day and did a rain dance while patting our mouths and trying to sound like Indians. That day the sky was gray; and as I look back in hindsight, I know it was going to rain anyway. But when it finally started raining, we swore up and down that we'd caused it. That was one of the most innocent and sweetest times in my young life.

But something emerged during that time that I realized later was not a good thing. My grandfather, who loved me dearly, did something that wasn't the kindest thing to do. One day my sister Charmaine and I were sitting on the porch playing when he came outside with a big red apple that looked to me like a huge red volleyball. I took it from my grandpa's hand as he told me intensely not to give Charmaine any of it. It sounded fine with me, so I bit into it. She started crying because I didn't share it with her. I didn't understand it at the time, obviously; but apparently he though she was a white man's baby because she was light skinned.

My mother, who had come back to town after about a two-year span, was in the house with my grandmother when she heard the sound of crying. When she came out to investigate what Charmaine was upset about, my grandfather told her what he had done. The two argued a little, and then my mom took the apple and cut it in half between us.

My grandfather, as I understand it, had had bad experiences with white people in his past; and because of my sister's light complexion, he assumed she was a white man's child. His bias was not personally against her but against white people in general. Unfortunately, though, she was in the middle of it.

My grandfather, who had a huge presence in our home, said what he meant and meant what he said. I can recall him saying he didn't believe in God and my grandmother responding that he was crazy to admit such a thing. He could be very tough, but I can remember him loving me very much; he was quite gentle to me as well. But for reasons he must have felt deeply, he would not show that same love for Charmaine. It was absolutely no fault of her own.

For the most part, I was sheltered from outside things. As I've mentioned, we didn't own a TV in our home. If I got the chance to watch any programs, I did so at my sister's or my friend Ricky's place (two houses down). I recollect a time when I was watching "Batman" at his house when Dr. King was assassinated. We didn't understand it all, but it affected us because we noticed the adults in our families and in the community crying and upset.

Still, I was quite sheltered and well loved and protected. I had the absolute freedom to crawl up in my grandparents' laps and knew that love would be waiting for me. I can't say enough about how they loved me—especially my grandmother who made me laugh, dried my tears when I cried, and told me what I needed to hear.

I rarely ever got spankings. This was probably because I was the only kid in the home, so I didn't have any siblings to compete with or fight with. And, though I was spoiled, I was not spoiled rotten. They began teaching me manners early on: to say "Yes Ma'am," "Yes Sir," "Thank you," and "You're welcome."

My grandmother and I used to sit out on the porch at night, enjoying the great Arkansas panorama of darkness when stars would be flung across the sky. She often made plenty of sweets such as cakes, pies, and T-cakes and provided quantities of fruit around our home. We would sit out there and eat snacks while wrapped up in one of her homemade quilts, and we would just laugh and talk.

I first heard about God from her. And she would tell me stories about her childhood, slavery, and other things. I can't explain thoroughly enough how peaceful it was to be in my grandmother's arms.

But no one can be so protected as to not be affected negatively at all. It was a terribly rainy night. They called those upheavals "electrical storms" because lightening would flash across the sky, followed by piercing thunder that seemed to split open the heavens. My cousin had come over to spend a night with us, and he ended up sharing a bed with me. I guess he was just as afraid as I was. Normally, I would be in bed with my grandparents at a time like that. But on this occasion, when I finally went to sleep, I was suddenly awakened because I felt my cousin up against me. What he was trying to do to me was not natural since it gave me a bad feeling. I told him to stop; he had been molesting me from behind. It made me feel dirty inside. He kept begging me not to tell anyone, but thank God I did.

I got up and ran into my grandparents' room and told them what my cousin was trying to do. My grandfather was very angry that one of his grandsons would attempt something like that with another. Instead of killing him, he just made him leave. And as far as I can remember, that cousin was never allowed in our home again.

At that time people didn't talk about incest in public like you would about the weather or sports today; it was handled more within the family. Likewise, I wasn't taken to a psychologist or abuse counselor to talk about it. My grandparents handled the situation as best they could and continued to love and protect me with all their hearts. Because of that, the event was just a bump in the road for me. I bounced back and continued to experience the happy life I had always lived.

When I was five, my grandpa's life would change dramatically. I guess he had been having some health problems, among them asthma, and was being watched by a physician. On this particular day, he had an appointment with his doctor. As I understand it, after the appointment, he was walking down the stairs and suddenly collapsed. He had had an asthma attack and could not recover. He died in my grandmother's arms.

That was devastating to me. He was such a towering figure in our family, and he was now gone from it.

By this time, my mother had come back to help bury my grandfather and gave birth to another child, my baby sister, Tonya. My mom stayed for a couple of months or so, then left after having made arrangements for Tonya to live with my sister Charmaine.

After my grandfather's death and my mother's departure, my grandmother and I were left alone in the home. Still, this situation gave us time together, which was good. She was such an excellent example for me: a constant picture of what it means to value those around you. My grandma was never one to shy away from an opportunity to reach out to people. I believe watching her during my early years gave me a sense of how to make people feel welcome in my world, and God uses that today.

I remember vividly that my grandmother and I were sitting and talking on the porch one day when a guy walked by. My grandmother yelled something out to him, got his attention, and made him laugh. She made him feel happy and then invited him to come in and enjoy some dessert with us. He ate and chatted with us a little while and then went on his way.

I recall another day my grandmother and I walked to a store at a time when racism was still in the air; and when we got inside, she asked for a particular product. The white cashier told her that they were out of it. Coincidentally, another person—a white man—entered the store and asked for the same item. At once, he was shown where to get it. I looked up at my grandma as if to say, *"What's going on?"* She glanced down at me and gently said, in effect, "That's all right; God will take care of it."

This was the character of this wonderful lady, my grandma. Everyone in our neighborhood loved her because she was consistently genuine and kind. People wanted to greet her, in large part, I believe, because she was greeting them. These were both whites and blacks, the individuals who knew her up close.

I loved sitting at her feet when she had company over. She and her lady friends would be laughing and talking about various topics, and I had the privilege of listening. Usually kids were told to run and play and not to be staring into people's mouths, but I was welcome to either listen or to play. And many times I chose to stay and listen.

My grandmother and I usually went everywhere together. Yet on one particular day, I was not able to go because she had a doctor's appointment. A cousin was in town, staying at our Aunt Tommie's house; so my grandmother asked her if she would watch me while Aunt Tommie took her to the doctor's office.

This cousin was about sixteen or so, and she and I were the only ones in the house. After a while, she asked if I wanted to learn how to play "the birds and the bees." I didn't know what that meant, so she proposed to "teach" me. She told me to follow her into the restroom, where she then proceeded to take off my clothes. As a six-year-old boy, who was pretty sheltered from stuff like that, this naturally made me feel uncomfortable and uneasy about what she was doing. By then she too was shedding her clothes and told me to get in the tub with her, all the while calling it "the birds and the bees game," making it sound innocent. She lay down in the tub, pulled me on top of her, and began fondling me.

And once again, I felt that same dirty feeling inside. Somehow I knew it was wrong, so I told her to stop. Then suddenly Aunt Tommie came home without our hearing her. The restroom was clear to the back of the house, and the bathroom door was shut. Even still, Aunt Tommie broke open the door and yelled at her in horror. My cousin started trying to make excuses; but Aunt Tommie, who treated me like the grandson that she didn't have, went crazy on her. She told me to get dressed; and I was scared to death, thinking I was going to get in trouble as well. So I started crying. But Aunt Tommie assured me that it wasn't my fault.

My cousin's vacation was cut short, obviously; she was sent back to wherever she had come from, and I never saw her again. When

I visited Aunt Tommie in the mid '90s, she asked me if I remembered that occurrence. I thanked her for confirming it for me, for her loving me in spite of the event, and that I had indeed remembered and had to face it. My wife was present for that conversation.

Aunt Tommie

It was no surprise how my grandmother reacted when she finally found out about it. I would imagine that she blamed herself for putting me in that situation, though she had absolutely no guilt to claim. It had not been her fault.

After that, life continued on as it had. My world-view did not crumble because of incestuous events, nor did I question my identity. My grandmother's love covered those dirty feelings, so I didn't have to spend time wondering about any of it.

Even though my mom was not in the picture, my sisters certainly were. Charmaine and Tonya and I spent a lot of time together daily. Having them living next door made things much easier as far as keeping us together. By this time, Poppa Kimbrogh, who was helping to raise my sisters, had died, leaving Momma Rena to care for the girls alone.

Chapter Two

That summer before my seventh birthday, my mother showed up again. Even then, I didn't know or believe she was my mother. I had always seen my grandmother as my mom because she had been the only one who had cared for me up to this point. I remember somebody telling me that my grandmother's daughter, Marie, was my mother. I resisted that notion quickly. I had had no bonding experience with her at all, so I simply had nothing tangible I could relate to.

My mother stayed for a couple of weeks before leaving again. She had mentioned to my grandmother that she wanted to come back and get me so that I could live with her. She was still recognized as my legal guardian, though she had never been my caregiver. My grandmother reluctantly agreed. Gradually she began to prepare me for the change by reminding me every now and then of what was about to happen to me in terms of my going to live with my mom. I think I denied it in my mind up until the moment it came.

For that remaining summer, I continued as the happy little kid I had always been. My best friends, Ricky and Victor H., and I continued to climb trees, play Batman and Robin, and do the things little boys do. I found time every day to play with my sisters as well.

One of the things I enjoyed during those months was going out to Aunt Tommie's family farm with her during watermelon season. They had rows and rows of melon vines, and little did I understand I would be picking my last great watermelon.

Then that day finally arrived. Two strange men showed up in our front yard. I was playing outside when I saw them pull up and get out of the car. They went up on the porch and knocked. My grand-mother came to the door; and after she spent a few minutes with them, I started walking toward them with curiosity see who they were and what they wanted. My grandmother was calling me at the same time.

My grandmother introduced me to these two unfamiliar peo-ple and told me that one of them, Charles, was my mother, Marie's, friend and that he had come to take me to her. He tried to talk to me, but I wasn't hearing it. Instantly, I grabbed my grandma by her waist and clung as tight as a six year old could. Keep in mind that she was the only mom I had ever known; she was my caregiver, the one who got up late at night with me when I cried. Grandma was the one who prayed with me on the side of my bed, who fed me, clothed me, bathed me, and taught me right from wrong. And now, the very thought of be-ing torn from her was devastating to me. To leave her was unthinkable.

By then she was crying as well while trying to calm me and assure me that it would work itself out. Again, we didn't own a TV in our home, so I had no exposure to the outside world of such horrors as suicide or murder. But as I was crying, a car came in sight from down the road. Suddenly I got a thought: *"Run out in the street and lie down in front of the car and die!"* The idea suggested that at least I wouldn't have to leave my grandmother. So I pushed off of her, ran into the street, and lay down. Fortunately, Big Charles rushed out there after me and signaled for the car to slow down; then he picked me up and walked back into the yard.

Before leaving, I was allowed to go around to the houses of my friends Ricky and Victor and Gale to say goodbye. Victor was more like a big brother to me. He was probably a year older than I was. For sure I was going to miss him, his sister Gale, and their parents a lot because I spent most of my time playing at his house.

Aunt Tommie was like my second grandma. It was hard to say bye to her as well. She had bought me my first pair of cowboy boots and gave me the nickname "boots." I finally went to my sisters and Momma Rena's house, next door, and gave them hugs and said my goodbyes.

My grandmother had already been packing my clothes before this dreadful day. We cried together and finally had to part our ways. Reluctantly, I got in the car and could not take my eyes off of her until she was out of sight. And neither did she leave that spot until I was out of hers.

I can't begin to explain how flattened I felt that day and how that affected me emotionally. Big Charles and Uncle James tried to make some small talk—to make it easier for me, I guess. But I didn't want to talk. The ride took a couple of hours or so. When we got to Hot Springs, my mother came outside to greet me. At least she was a familiar face. Still, I didn't have much to say to her either because I felt she was the cause of my being taken away from my grandmother in the first place. These people kept on trying to make conversation with me; but at that point, it felt like I was dying inside. I just didn't want to be part of their chatter. But a small turn in events would make things a little easier in my transition.

I can't remember if it was the same day or the next, but the three of us went over to Big Charles' sister's house so I could meet them. His sister's name was Ruthie Maye. She was the wife of James, who had come with Big Charles to Pine Bluff to get me.

They had two kids, Jean and Patricia. They were about ages four and two. My first impression of Ruthie Maye was as a woman seeming very pleasant and warm. With her sweet spirit, she reminded me somewhat of my grandmother. Right away she welcomed me to her home and into her family. She then invited me—when I was ready—to call her "Auntie." I smiled and nodded. And James encouraged me to call him "Uncle."

Aunt Ruthie Maye and her family became my favorites quickly, and I looked forward to going over there as often as I could. I found that whenever I would visit them, it gave me a break from having to worry about my grandmother back home in Pine Bluff.

That school year I was enrolled at Goldstem Elementary in Hot Springs. School was different for me, which is probably typical for most kids who enter a classroom for the first time. One of their breakfast items was those Suzy Q-like cakes. We had a choice between chocolate or banana flavor and then chocolate or white milk. That was always a treat.

One of the first peer pressures I would face at my new school was very strange. True, I met some very kind kids, both white and black, and I got along well. But soon I would meet my first bully.

That particular white kid had decided he didn't like me, and no amount of appeasement could win him over. I would see him on the playground during recess and lunch, and he would just treat me badly. He would tell his friends not to play with me or even to talk to me. I had done nothing, nothing under the sun to him, to cause him to dislike me. He would call me a lot of names, but one in particular seemed to stick: he called me a "nigger." Of course, I had heard that word used in my family but only in joking ways toward one another.

But hearing it from this kid confused me because I had never associated it with hate before. But this time, it was very much connected with how this guy was treating me. Before long, that word took on a new and unique meaning. I didn't have the trust in my stepfather and mother to ask them about it, so I just kept it to myself. Eventually, others children had to stick up for me because I didn't have the will to do it myself. This kid scared me. I wasn't used to being rejected, and it did hurt.

My life would later take another blow. My new best friend was our landlord's youngest and only daughter. Pat and I had become buddies. She was kind of a tomboy but very cute. Pat was no doubt the initiator of our relationship; I was much slower socially than she was. This girl was also a risk taker, the ice-breaker, and my friend.

Pat had three older brothers, and the members of their family were Jehovah's Witnesses. They were all very nice. They had always cordially opened their door for me and my family. So I was over there a lot because Pat was my only friend in that place. But I remember always wanting to hang out with the brothers some too. They would be messing around in their rooms or whatever, but they would never totally invite me into their world. I'm sure it was because I was this little runt of a kid, and they didn't want to play cowboys and Indians with a dopey seven year old.

However, one day that all changed. I was out front playing when they walked up. They asked me to go out in the back to the woods to shoot birds with their pellet gun. This gun was black and heavy; it looked like one of the old 45 magnums. I had watched them shoot birds in passing before, and the birds would fall to the ground dead. Well, I couldn't wait to get back there. My juices were flowing, and so was my ego because I was now hanging with the big boys. I was trailing the three of them as they led into the wooded area out back.

The one with the gun began looking for birds, and I was feeling like a hunter before I even knew what a hunter was. This was very exciting! But then the scene changed, and the gun that was used to kill small birds was now turned on me. Certainly I thought they were joking at first and asked them to "stop pointing that gun at me!" I had no doubt that they would. But soon I realized they were not kidding around; they were as serious as a heart attack!

The one with the gun told me to get down on my knees while completely ignoring my pleas. The other two joined in, pressuring me to do it—or else. Then all of them moved closer around me.

They told me if I said anything to anybody, I was going to die. They said their parents would then put my mom and stepdad out on the street—all because of me. By this time I was beginning to cry because my heart was broken. I felt like they had betrayed me, and in fact they *had.* These were big guys that I looked up to, and now they were treating me like dirt, as if I had no value to my life. And then they turned around and made me *feel* like dirt.

One of the guys walked up to me and started unzipping his pants. He then pulled out his penis and grabbed my head. I kept yelling, "Stop! Stop!" But he heard none of that. He forced his penis into my mouth, and I can't begin to tell you how filthy I felt! To this day, I can see that scenery around me and hear those birds chirping. That day is clear to me, still!

In the midst of the scene, I got a sudden thought: *"Get up and run when you can!"* Maybe that was God's voice; I don't know. But it sounded good to me, and I quickly calculated how I was going to do it. When I saw a gap between two of them, I jumped up and ran through the opening. As I fled away, I kept expecting to be shot in the back of the head. But it never happened. I didn't care, as long as I got out of that painful situation.

Houses back then sat on cinder blocks to be up off the ground, and they were high enough to crawl up under there. I ran so fast because I wanted to hide from those boys and everyone else; and I sat up under our housing complex for a long time, crying and thinking about what had just happened to me. I wished I was big enough to kill them, but of course it was only a dream.

Over the coming months I did see them often, even walking past them with our "little secret" tucked away for no one else to know. Yes, I was afraid to tell anyone because I believed I really would be killed and that my mom and stepdad would be kicked out.

This time, I didn't have those gentle arms to wrap around me and the love to cover those feelings of fear and filth. I did not trust my mom and stepdad enough to open up to them, so I just shut down and kept it to myself. It wasn't their fault; it was just so different now, and trust had not been established among us to this point. So it was a very cold period of time for me, inwardly.

Eventually we moved into another house. I did not know the reason, but I just went with the flow. Likewise, I had to transfer into a new school as well. This time I was enrolled at Park Avenue Elementary. It was a somewhat bigger school, and I came to like it pretty quickly.

My teacher was very nice to me, although I've forgotten her name. I soon made new friends; and to this day when I remember them, I wish I had the opportunity to see them just one more time. I remember specifically George, who became the big brother I didn't have. Scott, Mark, Cynthia, Mary, Aaron, and a few others—we were made up of blacks and whites who got along well.

It was at this school that I discovered I had a natural gift: the ability to draw. I realized how much I enjoyed art and often drew pictures for my teacher to hang on our walls. I also entered a contest involving a different kind of art, the construction of dinosaurs out of clay and strips of newspaper or something, and I won.

My friend George took a liking to me and kind of took me under his wings. George was a black kid that seemed far older than he was, and nobody crossed Big George the wrong way. He was very gentle—until you bothered him. So I was glad he liked me and sought my company. I also remember Mary, one of the prettiest girls I had ever seen. She was white with brunette hair. Her smile lit up the room, and her dimples were awesome.

George figured out that I liked her because every time I was in her company, I acted goofy. Mary also liked me. George talked me into letting her know how I felt, and that's how I found out that she felt the same way. Meanwhile, George and Cynthia, who was a pretty black girl, liked each other too. So the four of us played together for some time.

Before long, a certain white boy took notice. He was one of the bullies in the school and made it known how he felt about blacks.

Seeing me with Mary made it worse, and he started calling me "nigger" every time he saw me. He knew I was scared of him because I would never look at him in the eye.

As time passed, he would take it up another notch and would bump into me occasionally to see what I would do. I wouldn't dare act out angrily because I was flat out afraid of what might happen. I barely even got spankings from my grandma, and I definitely didn't want a beating from this guy, who had made me an enemy because of my skin color.

But one day all that would change. We were outside for recess when the guy and his friend came by. Apparently he had decided to test me again. I still wouldn't react, except to show my fear. I kept telling him that I didn't want to fight him, but he wouldn't take no for an answer.

By this time, George walked up to see what was happening and realized I was the one being hassled. George had obviously gotten sick of hearing about this person bullying me. He told me loud enough for everyone to hear that he would beat up this guy himself, but he wanted *me* to fight him instead. George insisted that I stand up for myself and fight, and he wasn't going to let anyone else jump in. I finally got up enough nerve to hold up my arms and make two fists, despite my shaking and sweaty palms. I let out a loud shout and ran toward the guy.

I found myself swinging with my eyes closed, hitting mostly air; but I was able to land a few here and there. The fight was eventually broken up by some male adults, and I think we both got suspended. I didn't know how to fight, but I think all that yelling convinced the guy that I was at least crazy, possibly dangerous. Whatever it was, he never bothered me again.

Subtly, George's confidence built my confidence, and from my first fight I gained a little respect. That made Mary like me all the more.

A bunch of us lived near each other and often walked together to and from school. We used to pass an old house that reminded me of the one the Munsters lived in—the family in the TV show from the '60s and '70s, featuring Herman the Munster. The kids used to say that a creepy witch lived in that house all alone with a lot of cats. And true enough, an old lady *did* live there alone with a hoard of cats. She habitually wore dark gray dresses that covered her feet, and her hair was silver and gray.

The guys would sneak up to her house, knock a bunch of times, and then run away. It would make her furious. The prank looked like fun, so I was easily talked into joining them. We used to do this every day for amusement. We felt a touch of fear mixed in, so we played with the chance of being scared out of our skin. But one day it would turn out to be a grave mistake.

That afternoon, like clockwork, we crept up to the house slowly. The closer we got, the more scared we became. But this time the lady was prepared for us. She waited until we got just a few feet away and then jerked open her door and yelled at us with high pitched screams. We were frightened to the core! All of us turned around and ran as fast as we could. I'm surprised we didn't leave our shadows on the ground. The sidewalk led through her front picket fence, a rickety barrier that seemed destined to fall over at any point.

The lady's house sat on the corner near the street light. Instead of turning left or right on the sidewalk as the rest of us did, my friend Aaron ran out directly in front of the oncoming traffic. A car slammed into his young body, knocking him high into the air. Aaron fell hard to the ground and died instantly.

The event broke our hearts, especially to see his parents sobbing after arriving on the scene and finding their child dead. I believe we all suffered tremendous guilt from that, notably in having to confess that it was our fault, not the lady's fault in any way. After that, we believed that she really was a witch! And you can bet that was the last time we ever did anything like that again.

Not too long after that, my mother and stepfather decided to move to Pine Bluff where my grandmother lived. I would enroll at First Ward Elementary, which was also a good school. This would be my third school and third home within two years.

Once settled, we lived in an apartment complex about four or five blocks from my grandmother's house. It was good to be back home around her. My Uncle Floyd and Aunt Faye as well as my cousin "Maine" lived in back of us, and my big cousin Evelyn resided in the same complex. So it was great being back around my family.

I used to hang out with Evelyn sometimes when she would babysit me. She was always fun to be with because she treated me like a son and gave me pretty much whatever I wanted. She was there along with my cousin Betty Mae.

Sometimes Evelyn would take me to clubs—basically pool halls and night clubs—where she would meet up with friends. Evelyn would tell people that I was her son and have them give me two or three dollars. I was cool with that! But she always kept me safe.

My mother and stepfather would still fight at times, especially when she would go out to clubs with Aunt Faye. The two of them often dressed alike and always carried switchblade knives to protect themselves. I remember my mother had a pearl-handled one, and the blade itself extended about seven to eight inches. And they were not afraid to use them.

One particular night my mother, her brother Floyd, and some friends went out to a club. When they left the place early that morning, around 4:00 or so, they came to a railroad track. Looking both ways, they believed it seemed clear for them to cross. Somehow it didn't pan out that way, and their car got stuck on the track. They glanced up the track into the light of an oncoming train, but they could not heed the warning of the train's whistle in time. Suddenly the train slammed into them, and they were hurled up into the air.

Amazingly, no one in the car was seriously hurt except my mom. She was thrown through the windshield and suffered pieces of glass in her forehead. I remember vividly the night that it happened. I was in bed, sound asleep. My stepfather, Charles, woke me up and told me my mother had been in a bad car accident. I can remember sitting up in bed, stunned by what I was hearing. I didn't know what it meant—if she was dead or not. All I understood was that it was a very scary time, one of the few instances when I actually felt sad for her. It seemed like I'd only feel moved that way when I perceived that her life was threatened either by Big Charles or, in this case, the train accident. Eventually, though, my mother healed up nicely.

Meanwhile, at that time my Aunt Ruthie and her family moved to California, a place I knew absolutely nothing about. It could have been located in outer space for all I could tell. I was only familiar with my home state of Arkansas. That's how sheltered I had been by having grown up without a TV.

Momma and Big Charles had begun to talk about moving out to that place called California. She had even started to prep me mentally for the move by telling me occasionally that we were moving soon. I requested to stay with my grandmother and new grandfather, C.B. (Charlie B. Dunn), a man I had grown to love. But Mom wasn't changing her mind. I thought that my sisters would be able to come with us, but they were told they would stay with Momma Rena. I didn't like that news, but that was the decision made.

Momma Mag and grandfather C.B.

Fortunately, this time wasn't as traumatic for me as the first time I left, though it was still tough to leave my grandma. I had to make my rounds of "goodbyes" again, a very hard task to do. My friends Victor and Ricky wanted to know the next time I would come back, but all I could tell them was that I didn't know.

Chapter Three

Big Charles went out to Los Angeles, California before us to find work. After he accomplished that, he called us to join him there. So my mom and I set out on a Greyhound bus, a three-day and two-night ride.

The trip was exciting, and my senses were on high alert except when abrupt memories of my grandmother would pop into my mind. I asked my mother if I could sit up front by the bus driver, and she said it was fine. I must have talked his ears off because, after awhile, my mother made me find another seat. But the driver seemed to enjoy my company. He entertained me with his clean humor and storytelling for a while.

In all my eight years on planet earth, I never had any inkling how big the world was. As we passed through city after city, county after county, and mountain after prairie, I saw things I had never imagined before. Those open spaces in the Arizona desert seemed like they would never end.

New Mexico's haunting landscape was quite an experience for me. Normally, I would ask my mother to buy me something to eat at every stop; but some guy along the way told me that in New Mexico dead dogs were picked up off the streets and used to mix in with ground beef for hamburgers. And true enough, dogs *were* lying dead across the roads, so I believed him. I could not eat anything in New Mexico.

The scenery soon began to change, including the roads. The number of cars seemed to gradually mount up, and roads became freeways. Pine and palm trees towered everywhere, and I suddenly realized that we had finally made it to California.

I was simply awe struck by everything. I had never imagined so many people concentrated in one area. And it got even more congested as we began our ride into downtown Los Angeles. I simply couldn't believe it! I felt like I was indeed on another planet.

At last, when we got to the Greyhound bus station, Big Charles and his brother, Uncle Alvin, and his wife, Aunt Alberta, were there waiting for us. I had not known them before. But the first thing Uncle Alvin said to me was, "Big Nephew!" That made me feel good.

The drive through the vast number of boulevards from downtown L.A. to Watts took about an hour or so. Street after street was crammed with people. I noticed kids playing everywhere—in playgrounds, schoolyards, even on broken-down cars. I could not stop staring out the window as we passed from place to place.

I remember we were driving along one particular street, and in the distance I saw a bunch of brick apartments that reminded me of the projects in Hot Springs, Arkansas. It turned out these buildings were where Uncle James and Aunt Ruthie Maye lived. When we pulled up closer, I saw that my cousins Jean and Patricia ("Tricia"), Anthony and Junior as well as others were out front playing. I also spotted my Uncle Carl—Big Charles' baby brother—who was a year older than I was. We would get along well.

Aunt Ruthie Maye and everybody lived in the Imperial Courts Housing Projects, more familiarly known as "The PJs" (ProJects). Everything seemed new to my senses. In fact, when I stopped to consider, my life seemed to be constantly changing. In a two-year period of time, I had been forced to leave the only person whose love I had ever known, my grandmother "Mag"; moved into three different houses; and nearly lost my mother in a train accident. And on top of that, I had been molested several times as well.

Against my will, I was forced to call my mother "Momma" and Big Charles "Daddy." It was Charles who demanded this of me. All bonding was cut off instantly. I had basically gone through the equivalent of a male rape situation by my landlord's sons and had seen my good friend Aaron get hit by a car and die. And now I was experiencing my fourth move; but *this* one was so huge and disorienting that I could not have conceived of such a thing before. Moving to California was a total culture shock.

That first day I met one of Uncle Carl's friends whose name was Kevin Allen. He was so cool to me, and he had a serious afro. One of the first things Kevin told me was not to wear the color red in the projects. Oddly, his warning sounded like a life or death thing, so I took him at his word and decided to leave that color alone. I would soon learn that it was *definitely* a life or death thing.

That same week, just a couple of days later, we were outside in the front playing when we noticed two guys arguing in the street. They were going at it in broad daylight and using all kinds of foul language; I just couldn't believe it. Eventually one of the guys pulled out a gun, pointed at the other's chest, and fired a shot into him. Boom!! I stood there stunned! It just wasn't possible! But the other kids didn't seem too fazed by it. The police finally got there after a long time, and then the coroner arrived. An outline of the body was made, and life went on.

Also, during that same week, my new friend Kevin invited me to what he called "Bible club." *"What is a Bible club?"* I wondered. I was very hesitant because I was new, for one; and I didn't know anybody. But Kevin was persistent and would not let up. He mentioned that "They give out apples and oranges or Oreos and milk every time you go!" That's all he had to say in the first place. I hurried to ask my mother if it was all right, and Uncle Carl vouched for me because he himself had attended clubs too. I got the go ahead, and off I went.

That first day I heard the story about Jesus and His dying on the cross for all of us to give us eternal life. The speaker said if any one of us were the only person on earth, Christ still would have died in our place. That day the message made so much sense to me; and when the Bible portion of club was over, they invited any one of us to accept Jesus as our personal Lord and Savior into our hearts. That day Jesus became a hero to me. I confessed my sins—whatever that meant to me at the time—and asked Christ into my life. Everybody was more than excited for me, at least the adults in the place. Fred Stoesz was my first Bible club teacher and the one to lead me to Jesus Christ.

Over the next four years, I would faithfully attend Bible club each week. It was a time to escape from the pressures of school and home and to be around people who took a personal interest in my life—not in mine alone but in the lives of all the kids in the Imperial

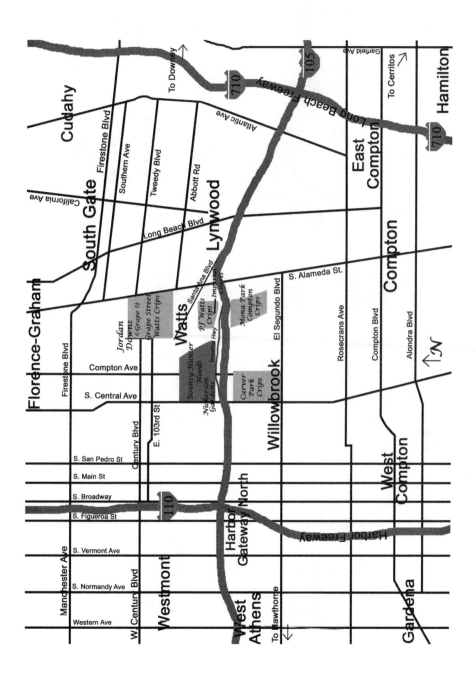

Courts Housing Projects where World Impact began its ministry back in the '60s.

I'm the one with the hat in the lower left corner.

     I looked forward to club because it was fun and generally safe. This was a time when whites faced danger in Watts. The famous Watts riots were just eight or nine years removed, and racial tension was still high. But Keith Phillips, president and founder of World Impact, felt compelled to go inside of Watts—even while the fires were still raging—and reach out to the people in that community, in spite of the strong possibility of his own imminent death. Think of it: a *white guy,* who chose to obey Christ by bringing his love to Watts! By the time I came around, World Impact was up and running and had been doing so for about eight years. At this point Dr. Phillips and those who came with him to help minister to the kids and families had built up the necessary trust with those in our neighborhood. The white staff members of World Impact were the only whites I had ever seen near the projects, unless they were members of a SWAT team or the police.

     The Crips gang had started in 1969, as I understand it. And the Bloods formed in 1965. Even still, God protected the missionaries by demonstrating His faithfulness through them. They were not seen as phony or manipulative but as people who really cared. For this reason, the kids were also respected during the times that Bible club was going on. I used to see those hardened gang bangers speaking to the white missionaries and with respect, at times even hiding their marijuana around them. That was cool!

Yet I remember one particular day, we were out on the gym field sitting in a circle and listening to a Bible lesson. All of a sudden, shots fired out. We couldn't tell what direction the bullets were coming from; but pretty soon, it was over. But never once were we in danger—or at least so it seemed.

When people began to notice that I was the new kid on the block, some liked me; but others weren't so friendly. I tried to get along with everyone because that's the world I had come from, stemming from the values instilled in my grandmother's home. Outside of a few people in the previous two years or so, I had not experienced conflict; and I did not have a hostile bone in my body.

So when people would show hostility toward me, I would be amazed and sometimes even devastated because I felt I didn't deserve it. Increasingly, I had questions that went unanswered such as "Why don't they like me?" and "What did I do wrong?" Those answers would not come any time soon.

At this point kids at school began to tease me about my stuttering condition. I became the center of many jokes. Before this time, my speech impediment had not been much of an issue; but in this unfamiliar environment, it was beginning to take on a whole new aspect.

A certain guy named Johnny asked me one day why I "talked funny." He said I sounded like a typewriter or something and made everybody laugh. Then he kept going until others joined in. It felt like they were inventing new jokes just for me. At that point somebody in the group called me a "f------ stuttering box." That name stuck. From then on, they would call me "stutter-box" when they felt like hurting me, and I was beginning to feel like dirt.

Soon the jokes were not enough, and they began belittling me even more. I had such a quiet nature, very shy and overly nice. I had good manners, addressing adults as "Ma'am" and "Sir" and responding with phrases like "No thank you." My grandmother had instilled good values in me; and now they were despised and ridiculed. I was beginning to feel more different than ever, and a sense of shame was starting to set in. *"Why? What did I do to these people that makes them treat me like this?"* I wondered.

One day at school, a certain girl started teasing me because of my speech impediment. Not only was she pretty, but she had the power of her brothers behind her; and they just happened to be some PJ Watts Crips, well respected in our projects. I didn't know that at the time. In all sincerity, I asked her to stop, but she would not. As the days went by, she continued to make fun of me and humiliate me. Judging that she wasn't much of a threat because she was just a girl, I caught myself trying to be tough with her. I pushed her out of my face one day, so she threatened to get her brother to kick my butt.

The male pride wouldn't let me take that from a girl, so I called her bluff and told her to go ahead and tell. I thought she was just making an idle threat. I will never forget it: she came back with her brother, and I about wet my pants when I saw who it was. Grown men respected this guy.

Right away she pointed me out in the lunch line, and he came charging over. For a moment I tried to pretend I didn't see them; but I finally took off, shooting around other kids and lunch tables. This guy was a raw athlete and put a move on me—and I froze. He grabbed me by the shirt and asked me who did I think I was. I basically begged him to let me go, but he wasn't hearing it.

He began to beat me in front of everybody, totally humiliating me. Finally, my cousin, who was not a gang banger but still had the respect, persuaded him to let me go; and he did. I walked away from it feeling really cheap, almost like I had been raped. I might as well have been because I had done nothing to hold my ground. My lip was pouring out blood.

After that, the girl's brother became my worst nightmare. He got his homeboys involved in terrorizing me from then on. They hated me with a passion, it seemed, and without mercy. And for what? They did it simply because I was perceived to be weak and spineless. The fact that they hated me hurt more than the actual physical abuse. Their abuse was telling me that something was wrong with me even though I had done nothing to deserve it.

That girl's teasing me was the beginning of another chapter in my life because it opened up much more abuse and fear for me. Every time these main guys would see me, they would purposely find something wrong. If I even appeared to look at them for more than a second, that would be enough reason to hassle or attack me.

I was caught away from home one day when two of these guys spotted me. They asked if I had any money on me because they wanted to buy something to eat. I told them that I didn't have any, but they called me over to check me anyway. Immediately they pulled out my pockets and inspected my socks like I belonged to them. They found fifty cents that I'd tried to hide, and it enraged them. So one of them swung on me and hit me in the mouth, splitting my lip. They told me I'd better not lie to them anymore and that I'd be wise to have something for them every time they would see me. Then they sent me on my way, crying. I felt totally violated. But I couldn't defend myself even if I tried.

A series of incidents like this would happen; and each time I would just hide it away in my heart, not telling anyone about it. The gang presence was heavy and pervasive around my neighborhood, and many of them were flat-out ruthless. So I wasn't about to involve my mother in it; I didn't trust my stepfather enough to open up to him about it either.

We lived in a Crips hood; and the gang in a particular area controlled that territory, what you wore, and just about how you lived your life. Blue was the dominate color worn by the Crips as red was for the Bloods. The founders of the Crips gang were Stanley "Big Tookie" Williams and Raymond Washington back around 1969 or so. They were basically like little gods in south central Los Angeles. Everybody revered them and seemed to want to associate with them and others.

I first learned of this when I was about ten years old. My friend Kevin got my attention one day when Big Tookie (as he was called) came into the PJs. If I remember correctly, he was wearing some overalls, some black biscuit shoes, a blue bandana hanging out of his pocket, a huge afro, and was walking with a couple of pit bulls. He looked evil—but cool.

Kevin whispered, "You know who that is? He started the Crips! That's Big Tookie! He's an O'G!" (Original Gangster). I wasn't caught up in it because I didn't glorify violence at the time. Even still, Kevin would tell me all about the Crips and what gang was what. But I didn't care about that stuff.

Growing up alone was very challenging because that made me

the only child in the home. All I had to do was watch TV and draw. I had come to realize that I could draw cartoons without tracing, so I would collect comic books like Superman, Batman and Robin, Thor, the Incredible Hulk, and others. I would sit around drawing these characters, and that helped to occupy some of my time since there was no more bonding in my life. Sometimes I got to spend a night over at Aunt Ruthie Maye and Uncle James' house or Uncle Carl and Big Momma's (Big Charles' mom) but not too often.

But someone was about to walk into my life who would add much fun to it, and that was Edward Robinson. The gym in our projects would occasionally organize field trips to places like the Pike, Knott's Berry Farm, Disneyland, and Magic Mountain. A trip was planned at this particular time for Magic Mountain. Kids from the PJs often looked forward to these kinds of adventures, but this time I was facing the possibility of not being able to go because my mother didn't have any money. Edward had just moved in the PJs along with his grandmother, Mrs. Arnold, and he had signed up to go.

I was sitting out in the yard when he came walking by, getting ready to go and pay his money for the outing. He saw me out there looking like a little lost puppy and asked what was wrong. I told him we couldn't afford the money for the trip; so Edward immediately offered to give me some of his extra money, and that kindness enabled me to go.

Oddly enough, Edward had previously tried to steal my sweat suit off our clothes line, but my stepfather had glanced out the upstairs bathroom window and caught him. He said that he took off running. But *the way* he said it had me laughing so hard that my stomach ached when he was done. From that day on, we became one another's friend. We even sealed it by cutting the skin on the back of our hands and bonding our blood together the way we saw in a cowboy and Indian movie. That bond would last a lifetime, even to this day.

The more we got to know each other, the more we discovered things in common. We were the only children in our homes. We did not know our real father. Our first names began with the letter "E." We were the same age, born the same month. Both of our grandmothers were key influences in our lives. These common factors led us to "adopt" each other as brothers.

Edward too was beginning to be intimidated by these same

bullies, especially after they saw us together. He found himself being chased home a lot; and because we lived about a hundred or so feet from one another, we often played together in front of our homes.

After awhile, it ceased to be a shock to see one of us running home scared after having been chased down. One thing about Edward, though, he always found a way to see the humor in it—especially about himself. He would say things like "Smokey grabbed me by the back of the shirt and wouldn't let me go. I'm thinking that I'm gone, but then I realized I was running in the same spot. Then I felt the mighty hand of Smokey in the back of the neck." Then we would bust out laughing.

Edward made my suffering easier and inspired me to laugh. I can truly say that in many ways he helped me survive. Nothing seemed to break his ability to make people laugh, and maybe that was how he learned to survive, not having anyone to physically protect him. I don't know.

Despite the trauma I was going through, I was a good student in school. I was always one of the best "artists" in the classrooms and continually enjoyed drawing during every chance we got. I did well in reading and writing; and when I'd learn something new—usually by repetition—it would stick. But just listening to the teacher lecturing in front of the class was frustrating because I had tons of questions inside that I was too afraid to ask in front of all the kids. I had learned *that* lesson my first year in the Los Angeles Unified School District.

Previously, I had come from a place where it was okay to ask questions and not get laughed at to the degree I had come to know in Watts. These people laughed at me for their own pleasure, so I kept all the questions inside. I used to love reading out loud, but that too had died.

Still, one day my teacher decided to demonstrate her belief in me. Knowing I was afraid of reading out loud, she asked me in front of everyone if I would like to read for the class. She knew I was a good reader, having heard me read to her privately many times. I used to love breaking down syllables and sounding out the words. She knew how self-motivated I was to learn how to read. But when she asked me that in front of my classmates, I felt betrayed. All eyes were on me, waiting for my response.

For once, the emotions began to boil. I felt that she was trying to get everybody to laugh at the way I talked, so I started crying. Then anger set in, and I started pushing and kicking tables around, even throwing a couple chairs. It was as if she gave everybody permission to mock me without restraint.

I was taken out of the classroom eventually and had to go see my speech therapist, Mrs. Washington, if I recall her name correctly. She understood the mind of a stutterer and the social fears we often encounter, things that non-stutterers take for granted. So she was able to explain what she thought I was going through. I was allowed back into the classroom. My teacher knew that I was a sensitive and well-mannered child.

Nevertheless, my stuttering was spiraling more and more out of control; and my dignity was descending down next to nothing. By this point, I was quickly dying inside. As time went on, I began to feel more and more inadequate; and my once decent grades were starting to show the effects of all the upheaval in my young life.

I felt disconnected and unsure about everything. My uncle Carl would attempt talking me into trying out for little league teams at the gym in our projects. It was kind of like the "Ghetto's YMCA," but it brought so much value to the kids in the community. I remember people like Coach Dave, who brought baseball to us; my cousin whom we called "sister" who initiated cheer leading; and so many others who introduced various activities to our projects. Yet I lacked the confidence to go out for anything.

At Grape Street Elementary, we had many kids from the surrounding areas, both black and Hispanic; and this factor opened up the opportunity to meet kids from other areas of Watts. Some became my good friends, like Albert J., Chris H., Lawrence G., and others. We would race a lot of times during recess, and I was usually the winner or at least in the top two or three every time. People learned I was fast—especially when I was chased home by bullies.

I knew a particular girl named Florence, who was in the sixth grade. She and her family lived close to the PJs. When she started racing us, there was no contest—we ate her dust. Years later I had strong reason to believe that, after hearing her story on ESPN, the late Florence Griffith Joyner (aka "Flo Jo") might have been that girl who used to beat all the boys in racing every time. I was a little younger than she was. I remember all the kids used to go by her place (or it might have been the one next door) to buy candy at the "candy house."

Ultimately it was those races that persuaded my uncle to talk me into trying out for sports. But I was too ashamed that I might fail or blow it for everybody else. Finally, I did try out for football. During the try-outs, coach would have us doing sprints; and as usual, I was one of the fastest—always among the top two or three.

During that season, on the first or second day of practice we had to run around the whole gym field several times. After that last lap, we started to come in; but the coach told me to run an extra lap. "Why?" I asked. He said, "Just do it." As I got around the first turn, I started to cry. I didn't understand why he was making me run an extra lap and not everybody else. Once again, I felt this adult was trying to get everybody to laugh at me. All I could think about was the guys heckling me when the day was over. So instead, coming around the last turn, I kept running and never came back. That was the last and only time I ever tried sports as a child. I learned later that the coach saw signs of potential—as well as low self-esteem—and that I took discipline too personally. He thought he could get me to trust him. But I never gave myself the chance.

Whenever I got lonely or had time alone in my room to think about my hurt inside, I'd remember my grandmother holding me in her lap and rubbing my back. The unconditional love that I felt from her was unmatched because nobody ever loved me like she did. I wasn't getting hugs at home, so I would think about hers and start to cry.

The only grandmother-figure I had now was "Big Momma," Charles' mom. I don't know if it was because she had too many grand-children to give me those hugs or if it was that she and my mother clashed at times because they both had strong wills. Whatever the case, I didn't feel the same love from her that the other grandkids had.

I didn't know Big Momma's heart or her motives. But one day she called all the kids together to give us some money. She gave me less than all the others. I wondered why, but I never challenged her on it. I kept the matter and the pain in my heart. And a few other times something along those lines would happen as well.

Now and then my mother and stepdad would have arguments over Big Momma. Of course he would be trying to protect his mother's innocence, and my mom would be arguing over something she said or did—including how she treated me differently.

One particularly intense fight they had shook me very much.

I was in my bedroom reading my comic books and drawing when my stepfather got home. He was late coming from work, and it was pay-day that day. I had my door closed, as I usually did, when I heard them arguing over his paycheck. I was trying to block it out because of how it used to scare me, but I couldn't help but hear when they were basically right outside my door. Apparently, he had blown his paycheck and only given my mother a fifty dollar bill. That infuriated her, obviously, because it was not enough to cover expenses. In a rage, she took the fifty dollar bill and ripped it to shreds in front of him.

By that time, I was standing in the doorway of the room, begging them to stop yelling and cursing each other out. Of course that ticked him off even more, and he started threatening to knock her out. I couldn't actually understand why she tore up the money, but I didn't grasp the whole picture. Still, he should have known that threats had no effect on my mom; they only served as gas on the fire and inflamed her more. He tried to leave, but she kept stepping in front of him and would not let up. At that point I was pleading with her to stop and let him go about his business. But they both told me to stay out of it and to go back in my room.

My stepfather, who was a security guard at the time, kept guns in the house. He finally got tired of her "bothering" him, so he grabbed his .38 special and put it to my mom's head. He said he was going to kill her if she didn't leave him the "blank" alone. Instead of backing off and getting out of his way, she turned around, ran downstairs, and got the biggest butcher knife in the kitchen. She rushed back upstairs and walked directly in his face, then put the tip of the knife to his stomach and said, "We'll both die tonight!"

I about had a seizure or heart attack or something! I thought she was crazy. By this time, I was scared out of my mind, and I started screaming at the top of my lungs for them to stop it. In a moment of utter terror, I thought they were about to kill each other and I would have been left to explain something that I, just a kid, could not. So I went into a panic mode and just ran. I tore out of the house, not sure if I left the door wide open or not, and ran across the street to Aunt Ruthie Maye's. When I got there, I started banging on the door repeatedly until someone came to answer it. Out of breath, I told her what they were about to do and ducked inside. I truly believed that Big Charles was going to kill her because he told me that back in Hot Springs,

Arkansas.

I spent a night over at my Aunt Ruthie Maye and Uncle James' until the next day. After things had cooled down, I returned home. But I continued to have nightmares and daytime reveries of him killing her or beating her. For some reason, I would always be in my bedroom in those imaginary scenes, listening to them argue and fight. I could hear the blows he would use to hurt her, and it seemed like he would throw her up against the outside walls where the thrust of her body would cave in the siding and leave the outline of her body print. I know that was driven by the inward fear of someday witnessing her death by his hand, and those fears generated the nightmares or whatever they were. This began during the year I was taken from my grandmother and lasted up until the time I began to rebel.

I felt like my life was in a box or trap that kept me from being who I was intended to be. Honestly, I had no dreams, no vision, no hope. Although I was going to Bible club once a week and learning about the 10 Commandments, Joshua and the battle of Jericho, and other stories, it was more like a pastime. While I was at the club, I tasted real happiness for those few hours a week, and then I went right back to reality.

Something was boiling inside me, and I didn't know what it was. School was beginning to lose its appeal, and life had become dry and meaningless. There seemed to be no purpose to guide me, and I began to secretly ask questions within my own world. I had nothing to look forward to. The only time I really had any fun was at Bible club; when playing with my best friend Edward, who kept me laughing; or around Aunt Ruthie. But even they weren't enough to turn down this seething inside.

I would finally hit my wall when I was eleven. As I described in these opening pages, I had become everybody's joke on the playground. My so-called "friends" had humiliated me in front of my girlfriend Jill during recess, mocking my speech impediment and making me feel stupid. If I didn't know how I felt before that day, they put an end to it. They made me feel like dirt in front of the prettiest girl in school, and I felt powerless to do anything about it except to pretend the jokes were funny and didn't faze me. But they did. I had to lie and say I had to use the restroom so that I could cry without anybody seeing me.

I had always felt dirty if I said a curse word or used any harsh language against anybody. Such actions would eat at my conscience. But on this particular day, I asked God to explain why He had made me the way He did and to help me understand why He made it even worse by causing my mother to stutter as well. For whatever reason, I stood there waiting for God to audibly answer me. But He did not. Still feeling a measure of respect for God, I decided to take the anger out on myself instead. I started cursing the very ground I walked on and the tongue that caused me so much shame.

I took my two middle fingers and began stabbing my chest, saying "'blank' me" over and over again as the tears poured from my eyes. That day I despised myself and the gentle Maurice that everybody had known. To be honest, God was the real object of my anger. I felt like He didn't care enough to stop people from treating me the way they did. I felt like He was all love and kindness but was without a spine—like me. I was just too soft to blatantly accuse Him openly.

After awhile, I dried my tear soaked face with my hands and shirt and concluded that God wasn't for me. I guess you could say I became an agnostic, not caring one way or another if He truly existed. I was tired of feeling so weak.

Then my heart turned to the more obvious power of the Crips. They seemed to have strength that took care of business quickly, and many kids like those who bullied me seemed to worship the O'Gs (Original Gangsters). These were basically the elite gang bangers, those who had the voices and the means to make people pay for crossing them.

Chapter Four

After that day, I was determined to find a way to stop feeling like a punk. I thanked Christ for what He did on the cross; but as far as trusting Him to protect me, that was over. I remember finding Edward soon after that and telling him I was tired of running from Smokey and Mark and all the others. I insisted we had to stop it. He agreed.

We were eleven at the time. A movie had come out called "The Boulevard Knights," and it centered on a Hispanic gang. The two main characters were a guy named Raymond, who was once one of the O'G members of the Knights, and his younger brother Chuco, who made the movie and was destined to become a greater legend than even his brother, who was trying to persuade him to stop gang banging.

Everything Chuco did—from ironing his clothing for an hour on one single shirt to the unique way he walked—seemed to captivate my imagination. The guy was fearless and was always ready to put a bullet in somebody. The movie ended with Chuco leading his homeboys in retaliation against a rival gang, and in the process he was killed. His death seemed to bring his legend to an even greater level, at least in my mind. He went out just as fearlessly as he lived, and that impressed me. Chuco had power, and I found myself disappointed at Raymond for trying to take that power away, no matter how right he might have been.

That day I got my answer—sitting in that movie theater in downtown Los Angeles. It was as if I had sold my soul to Satan even though that was the furthest thing from my mind. But in essence I *had* because I was released from what had been boiling inside me for some time, and I was now committed to a life of rebellion. And Edward was ready—though possibly to a lesser degree—to do the same.

Our first step was to create our own gang. We came up with V.G.V., a take-off from the movie in which Chuco's gang was called the same. His meant Varrio Grande Vistas, but Edward and I called ours *Varrio* (that is, neighborhood or district) *Grape Vine.*

The gang that appealed to us was the Grape Street Watts Crips, or WVG St. (Watts Varrio Grape Street). Grape was probably the most powerful of all the different Crips gangs in Los Angeles, and their territory was primarily centered in nearby Jordan Downs. We chose to follow them because the *PJ* Crips—in our own neighborhood—were the ones who treated us badly.

My welfare check came once a month, and I started asking my mom to let me shop for myself now. She finally gave in and one day handed me about fifty dollars to spend. Edward got some money from his grandmother as well, and we both jumped on the RTD street bus and went to a place called Greenspans in South Gate, a place just right outside Watts.

My first gang clothes were some black Levi khaki pants and a black khaki shirt, a white polo t-shirt, a cream colored golf hat, I believe, and a blue bandana. Edward bought something similar. We got back home and ironed our t-shirts and khaki outfit, just like Chuco did in the movie. We thought we were the coolest things since ice.

As the days went by, all we could talk about was Chuco, VGV, and what we wanted to be like. I remember we were outside in front of our apartment one day when some Grape Street Crips came into the PJs. This was during the time that Grape and PJ got along, going to the same schools, with only about five miles or so separating the housing projects that they ruled, the Imperial Courts (PJs) and the Jordan Downs (JDs).

We were outside fooling around when four of the O'Gs from Grape pulled into the parking lot right by my apartment. It was Bone, Gemini Twin, Bruce, and Cecil. I kid you not: their presence commanded much attention. They were like walking gods to us.

They were among the elite Crips, the standard setters. Just the mere sight of them struck fear in people because everyone knew what kind of power these guys held. Edward and I had to get closer to them as if to study their style and gangster mannerisms. It's amazing to think about actually seeing them; it was probably the equivalent of spotting Michael Jordan or some other legendary figure or celebrity strolling into your neighborhood.

When they left, Edward and I were excitedly trying to mimic their walk. This was a big day for us. It hyped us up to recruit like-minded guys who were tired of living in fear and running from people who wanted to control us. Our first recruit was our buddy Sean. Sean's cousin was a Bounty Hunter from the Nickerson Gardens Housing Projects. The Bounty Hunters were Bloods, and it was probably the fiercest Blood gang in L.A. and the biggest rival to the PJs and Grape.

But Sean lived in an all Crips neighborhood. In L.A. you typically gang banged from the "hood" (neighborhood) where you lived. So Sean became a Crip with us. Oddly, Sean had a mom and a dad who loved him very much as well as two sisters and a younger brother. His parents were married and committed to their kids, so I couldn't understand why he wanted to bang, but who were we to stop him?

Edward and I managed to recruit ten to fifteen other kids to be a part of VGV. Soon we decided to change the name of our gang, not knowing how Grape Street Watts would react if they found out about us. So we changed it to WVL (Watts Varro Locos). Soon we were up to about thirty people. Edward and I "courted" most of them in. People now say "put on," but back then we called it "court in"—that is, to initiate someone into a gang.

We had heard about how it was done. You had to fight against whoever was on the scene at the moment, for a certain amount of time—nonstop. No matter how many it involved. Edward and I courted each other in by hitting each other in the chest while standing toe to toe. So that gave us the pleasure of beating up others—with their permission, at that!

Naturally, the change in our behavior began to show at home. Every time we were told to do something, we would smack our lips or talk back to the adults, which, in my case, was my mother and stepfather, Big Charles. Edward had a little bit more freedom than I did, and that made it harder for me to break away from authority.

We still stayed close to home because, though we were in our own gang now, we had not yet been discovered or tested. No one was sure how we would react if we were confronted, so we were still closet

Crips—or wannabes.

Sean, Edward, and I lived in the front rows along the street, Gorman Avenue. My building was separated from theirs by an aisle (sidewalk). So we played out front a lot, scared to be caught away from home.

Every night when the street lights would come on, Big Charles would stick his head out the upstairs window and tell me to come in. Of course, Edward and Sean would make a joke about it because they got to stay out a little longer than I did. I began to hate when Big Charles would call me to come inside. Soon I started hesitating, which made him angry. So he'd start aggressively shouting for me and sometimes cussing as he called. It used to humiliate me in front of Sean's sister Kim and their cousin Lisa, girls I respected and liked very much.

After awhile, I began to resist Big Charles' authority as well as my mother's. He would yell out the window, "Time to come in the house" or "Don't you leave the yard"; and as soon as he turned his head, I would do the exact opposite. Sometimes he would come outside with his thick leather security guard belt with all the holes—the one I had always dreaded—and force me inside. I felt totally embarrassed.

Still, the next day I would turn around and do the same thing. One afternoon this common situation occurred, but this time I decided I wasn't going to acknowledge him. I thought back to times when I'd go outside while he was working on the car and just innocently watch him tinker. He would realize I was standing there, glance up, and tell me to take my a-- somewhere else to play. It was during those moments that I felt he didn't care about me. I was only trying to give our relationship a chance, but he made me feel rejected.

Even more, I thought about the time I was chased home from school in tears. I had run into the house crying and obviously frightened. He asked me why I was crying. I muttered out something; and instead of encouraging and comforting me, he told me to stop bawling like a little sissy. He said, "If you don't go back out there and fight like a man, I'm gonna give you something to cry for." I chose to stay inside, and I got a whipping.

Such memories fueled my hatred for him. That day he came out to get me and grabbed me by the shirt. I jerked away but finally went in with him. He told me to go up to my room and wait for him.

I sat there on my bed, thinking about how I was going to react to him when he came in. A part of me was scared, but I resisted it. I decided that if he whipped me, I wasn't going to cry. And sure enough, Big Charles came upstairs with his belt, questioning why I didn't listen to him and why I put on a show in front of my friends. I tried to explain, but he wasn't hearing it.

He told me to lie on my stomach on the bed, but I chose not to. He then started hitting me across my bottom, and my moving caused him to slam me on my back as well. But I never shed a single tear. I refused. I don't know what was going through his mind at the time, but I guess it was the first defense of my will not to be broken anymore. That was the first of many times that I would rebel because he had taught me to despise authority. It was all authority and no relationship.

Chapter Five

By the time I was in the sixth grade, I had died inside to the person I had been before. Grandma's sweet little boy had changed. I had learned since moving to L.A. that it did not pay to be nice. In the streets there was no reward for being kind to others.

Edward had already started junior high a year ahead of me even though we were the same age, born in the same year. I was held back a grade when I left Arkansas and moved to L.A. because my birthday occurred after the cut-off date when the school year had started, as I understand it.

When I was about twelve, the Twins from Grape and their grandmother, Ms. Helen, had moved across the street from the Imperial Courts, the PJs. Along with her was one of the Gemini Twins; their younger brother, Marv, whom we called "Monk"; and their baby brother, Randall.

Ms. Helen was a very nice lady, a person I would come to love and respect. I knew Monk and Randall from Grape Street Elementary, and the twins had graduated the year I had started going there. They had risen to such heights in the Crips that they had become members of the elite. The image that stood in my mind was when the Baby Twin (Eric) came in the PJs with Bone, Cecil, and Bruce. Edward and I were both influenced by their very presence.

So when they moved across the street from the PJs, right down the street from me and Edward, we were simply blown away. I knew I had to find a way to enter into their lives somehow. And that day would almost fall into my lap.

By this time I had started junior high at Edwin Markham Jr. High, a highly recognized gang-infested school. It was probably tougher than most high schools and was definitely as well known. The two predominate gangs there were the Grape Street Watts Crips, mostly from the Jordan Downs, and the Bounty Hunters from the Nickerson Gardens who pretty much set the standard for Blood gangs. They wore their dominate red, symbolizing the "Bloods." The Crips wore their dominant blue, symbolizing the "Crips."

Going to Markham gave me glimpses of the magnitude of the gang banging world. There were Crips from Grape, PJ, Nut Hood, and Compton Avenue. There were Bloods from the Bounty Hunters, Hacienda Village Boys (HVB), and Circle City.

I had always heard about how they used to fight up there every Friday and how some of the L.A.P.D. would get out of the car to watch the Crips and Bloods go at it—until they brought out guns. It wasn't uncommon for two to three hundred gang bangers to be out there on the tracks, looking to throw blows at each other every Friday. Kids who were not gang bangers used to skip sixth period (hour) just to leave the school early before they started banging (that is, fighting, etc.).

On the one hand, I was afraid of going to school there; but on the other hand, I was excited because I knew that a lot of people from the Jordan Downs and the New Homes were there who represented Grape Street Watts—and I wanted to be a part of that bigger picture. I knew that Edward and I and our Watts Baby Locos would not be recognized by Grape if I didn't put myself in a position to be known.

That's where Monk Marv came in; he was the Gemini Twins' brother, who was also a well-respected Grape. Monk was sitting on his porch one day when I was walking by his house. I had seen him at school a few years earlier when he went to Grape Street Elementary.

You have to understand: kids in those days and in that environment were well beyond their years. In terms of the street game, Monk was already like an adult, and he was only in the ninth grade when I was in the seventh.

I certainly didn't know what to say to him, but he could tell I wanted to say something. So he struck up the conversation. "What up, Lil' Cuzz?" Just having him acknowledge me was a window into the person. He set me at ease and allowed me to freely open up. Quickly

I got to the point. "What's it like to be in Grape, Marvin?" (He later told me to call him "Monk.") He quickly explained all about Grape and about those of the highest level, including his older brothers, the Gemini Twins. We called the elite "O'Gs." He painted a vivid picture of Grape that showed it was the standard by which Crips should be measured; they were truly the big boys on the block.

Monk said that the O'G Grapes were big time gangsters, and all others were put on notice not to cross a Grape wrong, thinking they could get away with it. He made it clear that if I were from Grape, I would have backup whenever I needed it and people would respect me because I represented Grape. But I was too afraid of getting beaten up by these grown men for two minutes or so during the initiation, so I put it off.

Monk Marv

Monk was patient with me and did not pressure me to commit to being initiated. Obviously he had taken a liking to me and probably figured he'd keep telling me stories and teaching me the game; that in and of itself would persuade me finally to do it. In truth, I was just blown away by the fact that this guy with first hand access to the highest levels of Grape and the Crips in general would care enough to give me his time.

Monk and I became good friends; actually, he was more like a big brother to me. Everything he would teach me, I would go back and teach Edward and the rest of the Watts Baby Locos. I would explain how to stand like a Crip, to walk like one, and would share all the different street slang I'd pick up from Monk Marv.

I loved going into his room and especially in his twin brothers' room. It was like walking into a gang bangers' shrine. I would have sat in there for days if they would have let me. I saw writing everywhere and pictures of all the baddest Crips in Grape as well as images of different Crips from Hoover Crips, East Coast Crips, and those from various prisons like Folsom, San Quentin, and others.

The more I became exposed to the Crips, especially Grape, the more I wanted my independence from all forms of authority—above all from the iron rule of my stepfather. I was changing quickly. Not only was I entering into the adolescence period of my life, with all the hormonal changes, but my very innocence was long gone.

Big Charles was finding it more and more difficult to control me in all areas. He'd tell me what to do, and I'd do the complete opposite. Every command from him was like someone putting a pillow over my face, trying to suffocate me. I could not allow it.

Around age thirteen or so, things took another turn in our home. My mother and stepfather were at an all time low in their relationship. Joy was absent from the home; they had no peace and no forgiveness from what I could tell. This environment gave me greater justification to run my own life.

There was a lot of drinking, cursing, and constant irritations that seemed to just pile up. My mother had been working at a hospital in Lynwood, but she had quit her job for whatever reason.

Her drinking seemed to be getting worse, but who was I to tell her to slow down or stop? I was too busy trying to earn respect and acceptance on the streets. Meanwhile, she and Big Charles always seemed to argue and fight—and when I say fight, I mean *fight*. I would just leave.

One day Edward and our homeboy named Carl (not my uncle) had snatched a lady's purse because it was close to check day. We called it "county day" because it was the day that women got their welfare checks. I wasn't a part of the theft, though I wished I had been. And of course, I wanted in on the goods—cash, change, or even food stamps. I didn't care.

I ran into the guys after the fact, but the lady saw me with them later on because she had been looking around the projects for them. She came charging up to us, demanding that we give back her purse. I told her that I didn't grab her purse, and Edward and Carl joined in the chorus. She finally left, threatening our livelihoods. Later Big Charles sent my cousin to find me. I didn't know what he wanted me for, but I went anyway. I found him at my Aunt Ruthie Maye's house together with my mother and other family members who just happened to be there.

When I got there, he started accusing me of taking the lady's purse. I explained that I didn't have anything to do with it, but I wasn't going to tell on my homeboys. I just had to suffer the consequences. Instead of listening to me, he continued to accuse me, choosing to believe the lady who I didn't realize knew him. Apparently, she had run into Big Charles and told him that I helped snatch her purse. I was furious. He told me to go home and wait in my room until he got there. About fifteen minutes later he came up to my room with the belt.

I had already decided I would not shed a tear and that I was going to stand up to him. He tried to whip me across my bottom, but I would catch the belt and hold it. Being a man, he must've thought, *"Who is this snotty-nosed kid trying to buck up to me?"* In frustration he dropped the belt and proceeded to push me onto the bed. He then jumped on top of me and started choking me, so I started choking him right back—or at least trying to. He was a big man. I didn't know what the outcome would be; but all the disappointments, the hurt, and sometimes humiliating feelings began to pour out of me.

I started screaming to him "You ain't none of my daddy! I hate you! F--- you, nigga! If you ever put your hands on me again, I'll kill you!" That was the first time I had expressed my rage toward him in that way.

He was evidently shocked by the things I was shouting because the energy just seemed to leave him. Looking back, I believe it was at that moment when he realized how much he had hurt me because he got off and slowly walked out of my room. I kind of felt sorry for him, but I rejected those rising emotions; I denied their existence and closed the door on them, if you will.

Big Charles not only had my mother angry with him for various reasons, but he had me furious as well. He began to stay away from home more and more, and rumors of his having an affair began to pop to the surface. The arguments and fights from that issue soon led to his abandoning the home altogether. It was tough on my mom because it left her to contend with an iron will of a son to raise alone.

Eventually the rumors of Big Charles' affair were confirmed after we found out he had moved in with the alleged "other woman." The two of them would later get married, destroying any possible notion of reconciliation between him and my mother.

Still, the destruction of their relationship to me meant fewer obstacles to deal with. I was glad he left us because my quest to run my own life at the ripe old age of thirteen became more of a reality.

Before my thirteenth birthday, I had finally agreed to be initiated into Grape. I had gotten to know Spider and Lefty from Grape, two O'G Grape Streets who happened to be Hispanic. They were in their early thirties, I believe, at the time. I used to stop by their house every day after school to get connected with those who had founded Grape—the Hispanics.

Spider was the elder of the two brothers as well as the wiser, it seemed. But Lefty reminded me of Chuco in the movie. The two of them eventually finished what Monk Marv had begun, trying to persuade me to join Grape. So one day after school I stopped by their house and announced that I was ready.

They called up Loki and another homeboy, both blacks, and another Hispanic Grape Street; and for thirty seconds I had to fight three of them while Spider and Lefty watched and kept track of time.

When Lefty said "Go!" fists were flying from every direction, and blows seemed to land repeatedly. I felt overwhelmed, but a fire lit inside me; and I started swinging back at whatever was in front of me. This event took place in back of a church, which caused me some guilt.

Spider and Lefty kept yelling "Swing back, Eric! Swing! Swing!" I refused to give up, and I kept swinging at air and all. At the end of the thirty seconds, I had a swollen lip; and blood was running out. Different parts of my face, arms, chest, and back were throbbing in pain. I felt like I was in a daze, but the joy I felt from not giving up outweighed it all.

The fact that I stuck it out demonstrated the seriousness of my intentions. That won their respect, and they embraced me as they celebrated my becoming a member of the Mighty Grape gang. I was given the nickname "Cricket" because of my speech impediment. They called me "Little Cricket" or "Lil' Cricket" because there was already an O'G Cricket from Grape.

When I left them that day, I felt invincible—as if I had just come from among gods and had won their favor. The one aspect that appealed to me most was that I was now connected to a power and had the backing of that power. Being officially accepted by Grape meant that I couldn't be made a victim anymore. And Grape became more and more my purpose for living.

I couldn't wait to get home to tell Edward and then Monk, who I believed would be proud of me. And he was. But I didn't want to enjoy this new way of life without my best friend Edward. He wasn't ready to be officially recognized by Grape yet, mainly because he didn't want to go through the pain that I had finally come to accept. But eventually, he too was initiated.

At that point, Edward took on the name "Chepo." Now that both of us were members of Grape Street Watts, we took Watts Baby Locos to another level. We ended up "courting" in at least fifty people to the Baby Locos, including Voscoe, Spango, and a guy named Edgar from the Jordan Downs, the heart of Grape.

This newfound confidence seemed to compel us to be more open and known among the PJs. Despite our growing number of members in Watts Baby Locos, we were still untested and could be considered a bunch of cowards. We talked a good game, but would we back it up when the PJs caught on and then confronted us? That remained to be seen.

Chapter Six

Well, that day eventually came. We had been writing Watts Baby Locos (W.B.L.) all over the walls on our particular side of the projects. The Imperial Courts was divided up in sections by the people who lived in them. We had the "Bull Side," the "Funny Side," the "Peel Head Side," and the "Island Side." Each had a story behind it. Our particular area was called the "Island Side" because it was the smallest section in more than a seven hundred apartment federal housing complex.

The PJ Crips began to see writings about Grape Street Watts and W.B.L. all over the Island Side walls. Grape was well known by every gang in Los Angeles, but who were these Watts Baby Locos? Edward and I decided to make W.B.L. a clique within Grape—something like a baby Grape Street clique made up of younger Grape Streets.

I'll never forget what happened on Labor Day. Edward, Dale, Sean, and I were preparing to go see a movie downtown. Dale had not told his mom about it and wanted Edward and me to ask for him. So we went down to his house, on the opposite end of the Island Side, and asked his mom. After we got her consent, we were going back down to our side to get Sean when Smokey and Ant came riding by on bikes. Smokey was one of the main guys who had terrorized us for years. Smokey and Sparky, his ace homeboy, had chased me home many times and had cornered me and taken my belongings. They had split my lip repeatedly because I was different and too soft, I guess. Around those two, I might as well be dead, I felt. They felt nothing for me.

When we spotted them coming our way, we were all of one

mind: we decided to run for it! But after about ten yards, I thought, *"If we don't stop running now, we'll never stop."* Suddenly, I realized I should be the one to stop and set an example for the Baby Locos. At once I put the brakes on, turned around, and waited for them to come to me. They always seemed to love the fact that we were afraid of them, and that fear seemed to reinforce their thirst for more power over us. But when I stopped, I wonder if they thought, *"What is this scary butt nigga doing?"*

In my heart I knew there was no turning back; I understood that fear had become an enemy that needed conquering before I could defeat those who had made me afraid in the first place. Earlier that day I had found a box cutter in my house—one of my stepfather's utility knives. Thankfully, I had put it in my pocket that morning.

The two of them got about ten feet from me, and I spouted, "If you come up on me, I'm going to cut your heart out!" They figured I was talking noise and would not back up what I said, so they moved toward me again. I pulled out the box cutter so they could see it. Then they stopped.

Racing through my mind were all the times they had humiliated me and treated me like their Monday morning trash. I thought about the time Smokey put his hand into my pockets and took out whatever he decided, daring me to stand up for myself.

They must have seen the bitterness in my face and kept their distance. Maybe on another day, I would have caved in to the challenge, but that day I was prepared in my heart to indeed cut their hearts out. I didn't do a lot of speaking because of my stuttering situation but just listened as they talked trash. For the first time, I saw doubt in their eyes; and I knew that fear was now in their hearts instead of mine.

They finally left because I wasn't going to turn my back on them and hope to tell about it. As I watched them pull out of the parking lot, I couldn't believe what had just happened! It was like being kissed by your first childhood girlfriend. I was on cloud nine and couldn't wait to find Edward and the guys to tell them.

When I found them, they were amazed that I was okay and undisturbed. Usually one of us would return with blood running out the corner of our mouth or our face stained with tears. But I told them everything. It was truly a good day.

That run-in with those two PJs became an example for the rest of my fellow Baby Locos, and it seemed to embolden us. We started coming out of the shadows more and more by writing our Grape Street Watts name all over different walls on our side.

Before long, more PJs began to hear about this unknown gang that was growing up right under their noses. They knew about Grape, but they had no idea about W.B.L. But needless to say, their curiosity caused them to find out.

Our Island Side was no doubt the least of all of the sections of the projects, and no one wanted to hang out over there. But now PJ Crips were coming over more often, trying to see what was going on and who was writing Grape and W.B.L. in their hood.

The PJs also had cliques within PJ Watts, and it was the Funny Side and the Peel Head Side that had terrorized us the most. They were leading the charge to try to squash us before we really got off the ground. As they began to find out who the Baby Locos were, they took every opportunity to try to intimidate us. Most *were* intimidated—including me; but as I mentioned, I was committed to not letting people make me into a victim ever again.

Even though I was now a real member of Grape, still 99% of them didn't know who I was. We're talking probably fifteen hundred or more Grape Street Crips, including grown men whose respect I had to earn as time went on. Unlike many wannabe Crips who think you can just jump on the bandwagon and be accepted by the tip-top O'Gs immediately, Monk Marv had already taught me that it didn't work that way. Everyone had to pay his dues, so to speak.

Not knowing how all this was going to play out, I did have some fear that if I ever needed Grape, would they be there to back me up or not—since I was not established? I figured I needed to be careful not to go around starting fights with people, just so I could find out.

At Edwin Markham Jr. High School I got to know other people from the surrounding area. The students came from three different housing projects: The Imperial Courts (PJ Watts Crips), the Nickerson Gardens (Bounty Hunter Bloods), and the Jordan Downs (Grape Street Watts Crips), the New Homes housing community (Grape Street Watts Crips), the Hacienda Village (Hacienda Village Boys Bloods), and what is called "The Funk Fives" (Crips)—and from everywhere in between.

This environment allowed me to become acquainted with other

Grape Streets instead of just Monk Marv. I got to know other younger brothers of some of the biggest names in Grape. I'm talking junior high school now: these kids did not act like kids. They were so much faster than I was in the street game and far tougher. Markham had a wide reputation for being one of the baddest schools in the Los Angeles Unified School District. If you have ever seen the movie "Lean on Me" with actor Morgan Freeman, it was pretty close to that, except it was probably worse because of the high gang rate.

The two biggest and most powerful gangs at Markham were the Bounty Hunters and Grape Street Watts: arch rivals in the fullest sense of the word. One of the things that drove me to get to know these other Grape Streets was so the PJ Watts Crips would see me in the company of Grape and would think twice about trying to "sweat" (bother) me back in the Imperial Courts.

I was warned by the PJs to stop writing Grape on their walls—or else. But we continued to do it anyway, no matter what. Edward and I started the guys snatching purses on "County Day" to get money. With the cash, we'd go to the Hercules burger joint and buy chili cheese fries or whatever. We were beginning to do more and more criminal things, just to get our name out there.

One of the ways I thought we could accomplish this was to "hit it up" (write) wherever we could. That meant going outside our comfort zone. Very few of us were willing to do that—out of fear. But Edward and I in particular began doing it more and more.

Lynwood was a town immediately east of Watts, and we would walk a couple of miles to a bowling alley where we'd learned that Lynwood's Neighborhood Crips hung out. They had heard of Grape and were pretty much in awe. So we capitalized on that. We got to know some of them quickly, and they came to respect us. We returned the respect and were welcomed in their hood at any time, a situation of which we would frequently take advantage.

I had met a particular guy named Wanky at Markham, who lived in the Jordan Downs Housing Projects. Wanky and I were both in the same grade even though I was a year older. This had to do with my birthday's being in October (past the cut-off date for entering school) and our moving to L.A. from Arkansas. I'd had to repeat the second grade.

Wanky and I became good friends, and he soon began inviting me over to his home. I met his mom, three sisters, and his younger brother, who promptly embraced me as one of their own. They lived in the very heartbeat of Grape, the stomping ground of the O'Gs, the elite. Walking around the Jordan Downs was like being in another world. I can hardly explain the overwhelming awe that I felt there, seeing what many believed were the standard setters.

At the time Wanky had no desire to gang bang or to have anything to do with it. His older brother, Rainbow—who was locked up at the time—was among the elite. But that had no influence on Wanky. I was amazed by his unwillingness to be a part of gang activity; but by virtue of his having an older brother who was well respected among the highest in Grape, he had respect just for being related to him.

Well, I couldn't depend on anything like that. I didn't have that kind of protection and felt I had no choice but to continue with gang involvement. Wanky tried his best to talk me into staying with him every time I went over to his house; but like a powerful magnet, I felt drawn to leave there and put myself in the company of the O'Gs.

Wanky was a good influence on me for a while. He was one of a few that were, including my friend Alex; but I can't say I was that way to him. I respected Wanky's choice not to be a part of gang activity, but secretly I was afraid to give up what I thought would guarantee me from being a victim again. Fortunately, he stuck by me.

Probably one of the things that demonstrated to me how much I was accepted by Wanky's family was the scene after his oldest sister was killed. She had been telling everybody that I was her little cousin, and soon all of them were saying the same thing. And at her funeral and family gathering for mourning, they included me in the mix of it all. I didn't feel worthy to be around them at such a time as that, but for once I really felt like family.

Meanwhile, the Baby Locos weren't moving fast enough; and a certain loyalty issue seemed to be splitting us. Many of them, who went on to be PJ Crips, began to fall away due to fear. They were, in Edward's and my opinion, becoming afraid to stand against the PJs, who were stepping up their pressure on us.

Around this time, on the Bull Side of the PJs, Big Happy, Tiny, Louis-T, Steve, and others were taking note of us. Most of them sided with Grape and even claimed Grape. They wanted us to join them under the Bull Side Crips' banner, since they sympathized with Grape too.

I decided to do it one night and went on their side to look for them. I found Big Happy, Steve, Tiny, Louis-T, Andre, and Wayne. I told them that I wanted to get "courted" in, initiated, as long as Grape was the big dog on the block and that's where their loyalty was. They assured me Grape was number one.

Louis-T and I decided to put 'em up. Louis-T was well known and had been in and out of juvenile halls like Y.A. (Youth Authority) and L.P. (Los Podrinos). He had been known as a scrapper, and he was ripped (muscularly well defined). I was pretty scared to fight him, not knowing how I was going to take it. But I had already gone through one initiation under Spider and Lefty from Grape, so I had an idea of what it would feel like to be pounded with blows from every direction at once.

Big Happy and Tiny kept track of time as we threw up our fists. We sized each other up for about a minute, stepping from side to side, waiting for the other to swing first. Privately, I thought I was going to get knocked out on the first swing; but finally I just thought, *"Forget it!"* and went for what I knew, willing to let whatever would happen, happen. Surprisingly, after the first couple of blows from Lou, I came at him with everything but the kitchen sink. By the time the minutes had expired, I was still standing—and more confident than ever. I walked away with their respect.

Yet even that wasn't good enough! Andre wanted to test me, and I got the best of him. And finally Wayne wanted a piece too, but he quit in the middle of our fight. In short, the Bull Side accepted me, and I was able to make up a hand sign for the Bull. That same night I went back and talked to Edward, and later he went and got initiated in as well.

Since the Watts Baby Locos were split, Edward and I decided to take it to the Jordan Downs. These guys from Markham, who lived in the JDs, were our friends. We introduced the Baby Locos to them, and they took over. Voscoe, Spango, and Edger brought more people in, like Big Black and others. And they took it to multiple levels from there.

The Watts Baby Locos would go on to be absolutely feared, reaching even national magazines like *Newsweek* and *Time*. They basically put Grape in the national spotlight and were running jail houses, I'd learn later. Because they were basically baby Grape Street Crips, their predominate color was purple—a privilege only Grape would have of promoting both purple and blue.

Having turned over the Baby Locos to the Jordan Downs, Edward and I decided to represent only Grape and to do it to the fullest. "Can't stop! Won't stop!" was our motto. We would continue to go to Lynwood to make our presence known, sometimes too much. This new access into Neighborhood Crips' (NHC) hood made us popular with the girls over there. We took pride in "conquering" their girls and enjoying them.

Our names individually, as well as the name of Grape, began to pick up big dust. In particular, house parties became a time to showcase Grape. Neighborhood Crips would be throwing up their "set"— their gang signs—and we'd be throwing up ours. Even though we were among the youngest in the parties perhaps, we were no doubt the attraction, waving our purple or blue rags in the air.

At this time I sensed we were getting more respect in other Crips neighborhoods than we were in Watts, in our own. Grape was revered big time outside of Watts, and we were beginning to build on that. But winning the respect from the O'G Grapes, the elite, would have to be earned through many tests.

One day I was going over to Wanky's house after school and decided to cut through the New Homes, another Grape territory. I wanted to find out if I could see some of the O'Gs. I ran into Ray-Ray, whom we called "Cisco," a guy among the very best that Grape had ever seen, as well as his cousin, Theodore, whom we called "Roscoe." I remembered them from the PJs before they moved away in the early '70s. Cisco was the kind of person that if he stared at you, you would think he was literally about to kill you. He always had a crooked smile but was very intimidating to look at.

My mother had given me money to buy my gym clothes that day and told me to bring back her change. So I had probably five or six dollars left in my pocket. When I approached Ray-Ray and Theodore, I said, "What's up, Cuzz?" Cuzz was the Crips' greeting, and "Blood" was the Bloods' greeting to one another.

Ray-Ray responded with "What up, lil' Cuzz? You got a couple of dollars on you? Me and Roscoe wanna get a quart of 800." I told Ray-Ray I was broke. He said, "You wanna be from Grape, lil' Cuzz? You gotta treat the homeboys right. I know you don't want me to come and search your pockets?"

At that point, my heart nearly jumped out of my chest. I'm thinking, *"If they rush me, there's nothing I can do about it and no one I can get to protect me. Just give him a dollar."* This was my mother's money, and they're forcing me to choose to obey her or them.

So I pulled out a dollar bill, trying my best not to show the others. Roscoe walked over to me. My heart seemed to pick up the tempo. I gave him a dollar. He said, "Come on, lil' Cuzz. I know you got more." I admitted, "I think I might have one more." By the time they finished, they had all of it. Now I had to face my mother and had to think of a wonderful lie to tell her so she wouldn't get crazy on me too.

When I got to Wanky's house, I told him what had happened; and he repeated what he had been telling me, "See, those niggas ain't your friends, and you wanna be from Grape?" He was right, but that just made me all the more determined to quit being a victim. When I told Edward about it, he made it into a joke that kept us laughing for days.

Edward and I couldn't wait for check days to get money from my mom and his grandma to buy clothes. We only wore "gang" clothes by this time. One day we went to Huntington Park on the street bus to a store that sold white polo t-shirts and khakis and golf hats, and we stole a bunch of items by stuffing our pants and in other ways. And we got away with it.

On four or five occasions we did this, believing we would pull it off like each time before. But on one particular occasion, it didn't turn out that way.

Edward cleared the front door and got out scot-free. I was

getting ready to slip out with about three or four hats on my head and arms filled with t-shirts and Pendletons. Just as I was about to push open the door, a huge hand grabbed me from behind. I tried to pretend like I had left my money out in the car and was going to get it. But it didn't work, and I was hand-cuffed.

Edward, like a true friend, came back when he noticed something was wrong and turned himself in so we both could go to jail together. He was all happy about it, but I was scared to death because I knew my mother's lid was going to blow off when she found out about the incident.

All the way to the sheriff's station I was begging and pleading with the officer to let me sweep the police station, to take out their trash, or whatever—if he just wouldn't call my mom. But he wasn't hearing it. Even after we were placed in our old drafty cell room, I kept yelling out to the sergeant to let me slide with this one.

Edward was laughing his head off. "Man, shut up!" he exclaimed. "We going to be some O'Gs, Eric!" The cell was full of gang writing from different gangs, especially F13s (Florencia 13 or Florence 13), a Hispanic gang in Huntington Park. They hated Grape St. and often sided with Bloods. We somehow managed to carve our names and our set into the wall, to leave our mark for all who came after us to see.

Once my mother and Edward's grandmother, Mrs. Arnold, got there, I knew what was going to happen: my mother was going to go wild on me. When the officer came to get us, my mother's eyes seemed to penetrate to my soul for getting in trouble in the first place. I was afraid to walk up to her—not so much for what she would do to me physically but of her embarrassing me in front of Edward, his grandmother, and the officers.

When I got up close to her, before I realized it, she had planted her fist in my chest. The sergeant spoke up quickly, "Ma'am, you can't hit your son like that in here." But my mom blasted him with "I'm the one that f------ and had him. He's my son!" After checking us out, we all left. True to form, Edward made sure there was comic relief for a while. But now we had a record, and we believed it was going to make us more acceptable to those that mattered, Grape.

Chapter Seven

By the time I was in the eighth grade, my name was becoming known by a number of Grape Streets, including those in the Jordan Downs, since I had gotten to know many of the O'Gs' little brothers and cousins, like my friend Wanky.

Wanky, too, was going through his problems with certain peers. Like me, he was faced with the fact that, if you didn't learn to fight back, people would violate you. Wanky didn't go around broadcasting who his big brother was, even though Rainbow was in jail at the time. So some didn't realize who his brother actually was.

After one incident that left Wanky in a corner, I convinced him to fight one guy in particular. After having gone through it with certain individuals in the PJs, I learned that if you stand up for yourself, they would back off. I put Wanky to the test one day. We were in his room hanging out, and he said something I didn't appreciate. So I called him out. I challenged him to go in the rest room with me, turn off the lights, and go for what we knew. We did just that, and I started firing on him. Boom! Boom! He was swinging at me as well. We fought for a couple of minutes until his sisters, Lois and Dee-Dee, and little brother, Dwayne, ran upstairs and yanked open the door.

Lois started laughing and teasing, "Ooh, I'm gonna tell momma y'all fighting." We stopped and went downstairs where Wanky's mom was calling out to us. Hazel lectured us about fighting and how we were friends and shouldn't do that to one another. Shortly after we went back in the room, I told Wanky why I did what I did. He understood, and we made up. He and Edward were my two best friends, guys I would have died for if necessary. I just didn't want him to go through what I was trying to get away from myself.

That incident lit a fire in Wanky, and he became open to the option of joining Grape. I gave him the name "Beaver" because he had a missing front tooth. Wanky began to look for opportunities to hang out with Grape too.

One of the O'Gs that I met was my homeboy Tank (Dale H.). He was one of the most influential Grape Street Crips. For some reason, Tank took a liking to me. I think he got a kick out of my stuttering; but more than that, he respected my desire to be a part of Grape.

Whenever I would go over to the JDs, if Tank saw me, he would ask me to go to the liquor store with him to get a quart of Olde English 800, or to his house, or wherever. He would take me where all the O'Gs hung out, where they were gambling, selling dope, or just kickin' it.

I now had personal access to the very pulse of Grape—where the center of power was. I met people like Bam-Bam, Dar, Crazo, Penjuan, Mice, Butter, Steve-O, Big-Tony, Marckey, and none other than Bone. Many of the homeboys would come and go from what we called "The Big Sidewalk."

If you've ever seen the movie "Menace II Society," in the scene where O-Dog and Caine were hanging out in the projects (the JDs), and in the background were some guys shooting dice on a sidewalk—that's the Big Sidewalk where homies hung out. It was not uncommon for Grape Streets to be packed with guns stashed everywhere—in bushes, in paper bags, under cars, out on the big sidewalk.

Edward didn't hang out in the Jordan Downs as much as I did, but that didn't keep him from being known. He and I, after we cut open our hands and bonded our blood together as kids, started telling people we were brothers because that's the way we acted. So the O'Gs got to know him mostly through me.

My time now became split between Edward and Wanky, so I would walk back and forth between the PJs and the JDs, which was about a two and a half mile distance. On the one hand, I was quickly becoming one of the most hated people in the PJs, if not *the* most hated, because I chose to give my loyalty to Grape and not the PJs where I lived. But on the other hand, I was an outsider of the Jordan Downs Housing Projects (the center of Grape territory) because I didn't live there. The PJs and JDs were a growing rivalry.

I guess some of the PJs who went to Markham Jr. High and saw me hanging around people from the JDs more and more would tell the PJs about it. When I was at home walking around the PJs, I could feel the glares of my enemies piercing through me. But I felt they had pushed me into the arms of Grape by treating me like I was dirt under their feet.

I would hear them sometimes saying, "Look at the fake street! We don't want no Grape Streets in our projects." I'd keep walking, or if I was with Ed, we'd keep walking, not wanting to get into a big brawl with them with no backup there with us.

Being in the eighth grade and still somewhat new to Grape, I still didn't know if I had the backing of the heart of Grape, the elite, the O'Gs, those that counted. So I would usually just let them talk.

But the more I hung out with O'G Tank, the more the O'Gs became familiar with who I was. Being in Tank's company gave me a degree of notoriety and acceptance, but that didn't carry quite enough weight. Sometimes Tank would tell me to snatch some lady's purse around "county day" (welfare check day). Or we would go to the liquor store and walk out with quarts of Olde English 800 (or "8-Ball" as we called it).

The test to me was not in accomplishing those things but in having the heart to face whatever might come out of it. Tank became the big brother that I didn't have, and he made sure I got to watch him closely and how he dealt with situations.

I remember one day Tank and I and a couple of other O'Gs walked across the street to the liquor store to get some 8-ball when Tank said something to a particular lady he knew. Her boyfriend (or husband) took that action out of context; he thought Tank was trying to romanticize his woman, and he told my homeboy to basically back off. Obviously he didn't know Tank, a guy who had been known for breaking people's jaws. I had personally watched him break a few. He kind of looked like a young Mike Tyson—somewhat short, maybe 5'10" or so, and solid as a rock.

Tank asked him in effect, "Why are you all in my business? Am I talking to you? You better check yourself, punk a-- nigga!" The guy kept yapping. Tank told him to step outside and talk that stuff. The guy made a mistake and followed Tank.

As soon as Tank moved outside and the guy was barely a foot out the door behind him, Tank whirled around and "stole" on him: fired one straight to the chin. The guy fell asleep before he hit the ground. The lady at this point was screaming. Tank took the time to wake him up, stood him on his feet, and knocked him out again, relentlessly. We kicked him and stepped on him repeatedly, and Tank spat, "Tell that nigga don't mess with Grape!" And we walked off with our 800 malt liquor into the sunset.

To knock somebody out cold was like being awarded a trophy in a sports contest. It was a badge of honor. People lived to be able to say, "I'm knocking niggas out!" So that became a goal of mine after seeing Tank do it so effortlessly. And the more Tank let me hang around him, the more confident I became.

Still, that confidence would be tested even by Tank himself one day. I had found out that Lil' Ced (Cedrick) and his big brother Ricky, whom we called Rick-Rock, were my cousins by marriage. They were both from Grape and were both O'Gs as well.

Lil' Ced knew the passion I had for Grape and apparently wanted me to prove my loyalty. He had a lot of guns and gave me one to keep for him for a couple of days. It was a chrome, nickel-plated .25 automatic with a black handle. I made the mistake of walking around with it under my shirt, flashing it to certain people here and there—including Tank and my other O'G homeboy, Stephon, whom we called "Bolo."

Stephon asked to see it, so I took it out of my pants to impress them. Tank grabbed me from behind in a bear hug-like hold, and Stephon took the gun out of my hand. They were acting like they were just kidding around with me but were serious at the same time.

I didn't trust Stephon anyway because of how he'd tried to intimidate me on a couple of occasions. But Tank had disappointed me; I felt betrayed by him. I'm telling them to "Raise up, Cuzz! Stop tripping. Tank, why you trippin, man?" By this time I was angry and was expressing it without fear. But I wasn't on a higher enough level to stop them. Tank let me go, and then both of them started to walk away, saying, "We cool, Cuzz, Don't trip! Ced know us."

Now I had to face Cedrick and tell him what had happened. He was disappointed in me for flashing the gun around and getting it taken away. I told Tank the next time I saw him to screw himself for doing me like that. Of course, Tank could have taken me out in a heartbeat; but I think he realized how he'd treated me, his little admirer, and in his own way helped me to trust him again. He and Lil' Ced had worked it out like two O'Gs, as I understand it, and returned the gun.

But through this incident, Tank saw I was willing to stand up for myself, even against him. So I believe that helped to win his respect a little bit more because he then started letting me go places with him and the homeboys, like to other hoods—some friendly, some hostile. If you didn't have heart, that wasn't happening.

Meanwhile, things at home weren't getting too much better without Big Charles around. Financially we began to struggle more. We would go through periods where there was literally no food in the house. That was a time—with my stomach growling, thoughts that no one cared flashing through my mind—when I felt like the world was against me. But I remember my mother going over to her good friend's house, Ms. Daisey, who lived directly behind us, and asking for a plate of food for me. That day she came back with food piled high, and all she took was a bite from it and gave me the rest. My mother wasn't the emotional or nurturing type at all; but during times like that she demonstrated her love for me by her sacrifice, choosing to go hungry just to see me eat. I just kept those moments tucked away in the privacy of my own mind.

I remember another time when my mother had to choose between having a roof over our heads or having electricity. She chose to keep the roof. But she worked it out with our next door neighbors, and they let us run an extension cord between our upstairs windows so we could watch television. I also recall times when all I had to eat was mayonnaise sandwiches or mustard and sugar sandwiches. And if I was really desperate, I'd take a spoon and scrape the ice off the walls of the freezer, just to get a taste in my mouth.

Mom (in later years)

Due to various reasons, my mother began to drink more and more. Her alcohol of choice was beer—Schlitz malt liquor and then Colt 45. Her occasional drinking began to take a more aggressive nature, becoming much more frequent. And my emerging rebellion didn't help to stop any of it either. It seemed that the more I began to gang bang and put my life in danger, the more intensely she would drink.

I was feeling an emotional split on the issue. On the one hand, I was watching my mother's drinking behavior become worse and worse; but I felt to become emotionally involved would pose a threat to my own security. Becoming the hardest Grape I could be was my destiny, and that touchy/feely stuff I felt would get in the way of what I was chasing. So somehow I took on an attitude of denial about it.

In many ways I began to use her drinking against her. I'd wait until she had been drinking a lot to ask her for money, to slip out of the house at night without having to go through explaining myself, for Edward and me to bring girls up in my room, or whatever. Of course, I had been raised by my grandmother to be compassionate toward people and to care; but now I was trying to reject those feelings because they meant doing something about it or giving up my pursuit of power and a name. As long as no one tried to hurt my mom or take advantage of her, I was cool. I just had to get away from family matters.

Chapter Eight

We had a lot of security problems in our school, Markham Jr. High. An on-campus security department had a significant presence, and we had frequent visitations by the L.A.P.D. I was becoming involved in the center of many things, and hostilities were always high. I could be sharing a classroom with Bounty Hunters, HVBs, or CCPs, and a fight could break out at any time.

I was friends with one particular BH who was in the seventh grade. At that time he wasn't gang banging—or at least not in the open. We were cool with each other. But in the eighth grade Norman became Bounty Hunter Norman, and our friendship died at that point. He wasn't the only one. I watched Bounty Hunter Norman, Teavin, Jerome, and others take a turn the year after I got there, and now friendships were buried and gone. Most of us had to make those choices.

One day at recess, Wanky and I and some other Grape Streets were walking around, basically looking for trouble. Bounty Hunter Norman, who used to make me laugh, was now my enemy. He and some of his homeboys saw us and started "slobbing" us, as we called it. In other words, they were taunting us with "What up, Blood? What that BH like?" So we came back with "What that Grape like, niggas? What's up with you Bottle Hustlers Slobs?"

I stepped forward and one of them did as well, and we stood nose to nose; then I fired my fist at him. We were both locking up when the security guards came rushing up to us and yanked us to the security room. One of the security guards was a lady—Mrs. Jones, if I recall correctly. She used to try to talk me out of the dangerous road I was beginning to travel because I think she somewhat cared, but I wasn't hearing it. She looked at me with motherly eyes as if she wanted to beat me. We got detention after school, and it was over.

My name was connected to many things. In the seventh grade, you're called a "seventh grade scrub"; but by the time I was in the eighth grade, I was in the middle of it all at Markham. Solo and all the ninth graders had gone, and I felt more accepted by the next group of ninth grade Grape Streets.

As I said before, Markham had a well-known reputation for being one of the most hostile schools in L.A., even more than most gang-infested high schools. It was not uncommon for someone to get killed there because of the intense rivalry between the Crips and Blood gangs that were so prevalent in the place.

My step-grandmother and I never really bonded with one another, and I didn't know why. But secretly, I didn't think Big Momma liked me personally but merely tolerated me because I was her son's stepson. But on one occasion I got to see her heart.

On that particular day, someone had contacted my mother and told her there had been a shooting at Markham and that I was lying on the gym field dead. News quickly spread, and the rumor was all over the PJs. At once, my mother, my stepdad, Big Momma, Aunt Ruthie, Auntie Annette, and I think my Uncle James, came up to the office to find out if the rumor were true.

The office quickly summoned me from my classroom; I think I was in English class drawing or sleeping or something when I got the call. I was allowed to go to the office. When I walked in and saw everybody and the joy on their faces, I became shocked and wanted to know why they were all there.

When they told me what they'd heard, I basically laughed because it seemed so comical to me. But Big Momma surprised me the most with tears of joy in her face to see me, and she held me close. That touched me, and I really appreciated her for caring for me because I had never believed she did. That frightening rumor turned out to be a blessing for me and Big Momma because from that day on we related much better as grandmother and grandson.

Yet this new relationship would be short lived; Big Momma died not long after that. She was getting ready to go to her doctor's appointment since she hadn't been feeling well. When she went upstairs on the way to use the rest room, she suffered a heart attack. I remember that day vividly. All the grandchildren were taken out of school, including her youngest child, Uncle Carl.

When we got home, she was lying upstairs on my little cousin's bed. I can remember just staring at her and marveling, *"She's gone."* I was glad our relationship ended on such a positive note when it could have ended on a sour one for me.

The same night that Big Momma died, I had to watch my cousins Jean, Patricia, Baby Jr., and Tomeka because the grown-ups went somewhere that night. Big Momma happened to have died in my cousins' room where they slept. All the kids were huddled up in the queen size bed, but I had to sleep in the same bed that Big Momma died in.

Now, I was this tough aspiring gangster Crip, but that night I was scared to death. I don't think I slept at all, and every so often I'd pull the cover off my head to see if a ghost were in the room. Needless to say, nothing happened—except a night of humility in being face-to-face with my fears.

However, life would go on. Big Momma's death wasn't enough to convince me that I needed to slow down. Gradually I was becoming quite well known because of how I spread my name: I was always down to "hit up" (write) "Grape" and my name just about anywhere— on street buses, buildings, sidewalks, cars, parks, you name it, with the exception of churches.

A girl named Sandra from school started having a crush on me, but she lived in the Nickerson Gardens—Bounty Hunter territory. She began flirting with me just about every day over the course of a semester or so. Her younger brother and his friend Brian, whom they called Smokey, had become admirers of mine even though I was a Crip and they lived in Blood territory.

Still, for some reason, I didn't really trust her because she kept trying to talk me into coming to visit her in a place where, if caught, I could be brutally put to death. I tried to talk her into coming to my hood (neighborhood), but she wouldn't.

I found that Sandra worked in the counseling center as a student helper. I soon began to be suspicious, knowing that she had access to students' phone numbers and addresses. After awhile, I began getting calls at home from Bounty Hunters, telling me I was going to die. They'd also send me letters with red circles around my name with a line drawn through it and with all kinds of profanity directed at Grape in general and me in particular. I made the "mistake" of sharing a letter with my mom, who obviously feared for my life. But I myself took it as a build up of my legacy. It made me feel like I was a threat to them and got a laugh out of it with Edward.

The timidity that I had as a child was quickly dwindling with each test. I feared not being accepted by the O'G Grape Streets more than any outsiders because I was in the process of learning the game and how it was played. No easy road existed to becoming a member of the elite. You had to earn the respect and the acceptance if you didn't have an older brother or some relative already in the game.

Meanwhile, an apparent contradiction, I was continuing to go to Bible clubs with World Impact. Edward and I both thought we had begun to drift away. Every so often we would be invited to spend a weekend or night at some Christian campground or in the dorms at a Christian school. Those were always fun—especially being ghetto kids from Watts who rarely ever got out of the Los Angeles city limits.

I remember on one notable occasion we were going out to the Rolling "J" Ranch up north, and on the way there on the Harbor Freeway, or I5, we saw Penny Marshall and Cindy Williams of the "Laverne and Shirley" TV show. We were having fun waving and making faces back and forth at one another for a few moments. It was definitely a highlight.

But one of the things Edward and I became notorious for was going to the Nickerson Gardens to pick up some kids for the Bible club. Antonio and his brother David went to Markham as well, but they were cool. Kim Szalay and Charlie Esters, our Bible club teachers at the time, would load all of us in the back of Kim's camper. They would plead with us not to start anything.

One time the two adults had to get out to go inside Antonio's house to talk with his mother. Meanwhile, Edward, Tyrone, Kevin, Vernon, and I were in the back. Now all of us lived in the PJs, but only Edward and I were actively in a gang. We had brought our blue rags (bandanas) like we always did. Edward got the idea to get out and sneak around the building to see if we could spot any Bloods.

The other guys were tripping out, not knowing whether to be scared or to laugh at our apparent suicidal behavior. Edward and I crept around this particular building, hiding in the dusk of the growing night. We saw a pack of Bounty Hunters hanging out, drinking, and gambling.

All we could see were red rags, red sweatshirts, red shoes. We glanced at each other, waved our blue rags, and yelled "What that Grape like, Cuzz?" They whirled around, scanning in multiple directions. Instantly, we took off back to the truck and jumped in the camper, hearts beating like crazy. But we were pumped!

Fortunately, Kim and Charlie were coming out just after we had leaped in the back. Through a window we told Kim to take off quickly. As we were leaving, all kinds of Bounty Hunters came out of the woodwork—I mean grown men and teens alike with pistols and sawed off shotguns. Luckily, they didn't see us get in the camper, so we were able to leave without notice. But Kim and Charlie weren't too happy with us, to say the least.

By the time I was in the ninth grade, many people knew who I was. I had been a part of a few initiations; and during one in particular, this one guy we were putting in couldn't take the blows, so he tried to run. Since I was fairly quick, I was able to chase him down and clip him from behind.

My O'G homeboy Spike made a joke out of it—about how the scene looked—and used the word "clipper." At the time, I knew nothing about the NBA Clippers' franchise, so the word was foreign to me; it was the first time I'd ever heard it. But I liked the sound of it. The O'G Cricket didn't seem to appreciate my using his name, so I wrote the word "Clipper" on a wall in the Jordan Downs and liked it. From that day on I would be known as Clipper from Grape Street Watts Crips, and it took off from there.

Tank and my other O'G homeboy Jay-Jay, whom we called "Grumpy," took me to Huntington Park with them to buy them some clothes. While we were there, I told Tank it was my birthday; I had just turned fourteen. Tank suggested that, if I would let him, he would get my left ear pierced as a present. I was hesitant because I wasn't sure what my mother would think, but he and Jay-Jay persuaded me to get it done for Grape. I gave in and got my ear pierced. Later that day, Edward and I got a tattoo for our birthdays even though his was twenty-four days before mine. Our homeboy Big Oso from CV3, a Compton Hispanic gang, did it for us. When my mother found out, all she could do was give me a tongue-lashing. So I took it.

Later that year, before the summer, another situation occurred that seemed to strengthen my case in becoming one of the O'Gs from Grape. We were out on the gym field during P.E. when I saw a couple of my O'G homeboys Mice and Baby Bam riding by on bikes, heading toward the Nickerson. That was odd.

A bunch of young Grape Streets ran over to the gate facing Compton Avenue. We asked, "What the Grape like, Cuzz? What's jumpin' off?" They told us they were about to swoop by those Bounty Hunter "slobs" to see what they "C" like. "C" was a way of bypassing the letter "B," as in Blood. I yelled back at them to "C" careful and to watch their backs.

About fifteen minutes later, they came back sprinting in the direction from which they came with their Crip blue on. Baby Bam was shouting, "Bounty Hunters shooting at us, Cuzz!" So I ran off the gym field to get to the east side of the school, knowing that was in the direction of Grape.

I hopped the barbed wire fence and ran across the railroad tracks, hoping to cut them off. BH Whitey was trailing by about a quarter of a mile, shooting at them with a .44 magnum. I spotted my homeboy Bob Ray (aka Jumbo) near the New Homes on the tracks and communicated what was happening and that I wanted to save Mice and Baby Bam by distracting Bounty Hunter Whitey. I found out later that Whitey and Baby Bam had met up and fought each other. Bam had managed to knock the gun out of his hand and somehow escaped death.

Jumbo and I hopped the wall that secured the New Homes and ran through several backyards until we finally saw Whitey. When he noticed us, we started yelling, "What that Grape like, Cuzz?! Come on with it!" Immediately, he started chasing us.

We ran through a yard, leaped over the brick wall, ran across the street into another backyard, and then went on to another. Whitey managed to find us by going around by 103rd Street. We were on

106th St., I believe, when he saw us in an open field. By this time we were really out of breath. He pulled up to where we were within 150 feet or so where we were just a couple feet from an alley. Whitey fired two shots at us. Jumbo said he'd meet me at a particular location, and I said "Cool" or something to that effect.

I tried to jump over the next wooden fence, but I was so out of breath that I didn't have the strength to do it. Whitey fired another shot at me, and the bullet missed my head by about a foot. At that, somehow I was given the strength to climb the fence, scrambling onto the top with one pull. When I was just about over, I glanced up and saw Whitey putting in another clip; so I took off. After landing on my feet, I was staring into the eyes of a big dog who started barking at me as though he meant to tell Whitey where I was. I swore on the spot that if the dog charged at me, I was going to kill him, mercilessly. So I gave him a growl, showing teeth and all—and it worked! The dog shut up, so I left amazed that nothing happened.

When I got to the front of the house, I looked carefully both ways, hoping not to be seen by Bounty Hunter Whitey. I glanced cautiously down both ends of the street, making sure that it was clear to go. Once I was satisfied the way was safe, I ran across the street between two other houses, one of which was abandoned.

I noticed an old car in the driveway and squatted down for a few minutes. I heard a voice say, *"Stay down. Don't leave yet."* But after a few minutes, another voice urged, *"Leave! Leave now! The coast is clear."* It seemed to pressure me into getting out of there as though it was trying to tell me Whitey was gone. But still, the first voice said, *"Not yet!"*

I trusted the second and louder voice and decided to take off. Venturing out into the open nervously, I could look across the street and saw the Watts Towers parallel to the tracks that were running east and west. I turned onto the sidewalk and headed east.

About a hundred feet or so was a salvage yard that had tin along the gate, blocking the view of the other side. I could see the streetlight at the corner, and right across the street was Barney's Park: Grape territory. I figured if I could just get over to Barney's, I'd be safe.

With each step, I felt I was one step closer to safety. But at the same time, with each step I wondered if I'd run into Bounty Hunter Whitey. When I finally got to the corner, bamm!—Whitey pulled up

The Watts Towers

on his bike. I can still see the scene as if it were yesterday.

He was wearing some beige khakis, a red sweatshirt, some white All-Stars (Converse) with red shoe strings, a red bandana hanging out of his back pocket, and a black pullover cap (what we called a "hard beanie"). I had on a black sweatshirt, with the words "Grape St. Watts" in gold Old English letters on the back and "Mr. Clipper" in smaller letters in the front across my heart.

Grape St. Watts

Whitey was known for carrying guns on him all the time and for using them. I had heard about his having killed people. And now I found myself face to face with him. I had not seen him personally, but he recognized my name. He said, "You that Grape St. a-- nigga, Clipper? What the Bounty Hunter like, Blood? You gonna die today, Blood!"

As scared as I was, I had the presence of mind not to show it. I had already learned a critical lesson in such a short time: no matter how scared you are, never show it because you would lose respect, and you would give your enemy an advantage. So I said, "What that Grape like, Cuzz?!" My hands were just below the chest at this point. Whitey continued to spit out his venomous words at me, but for a brief moment I could no longer hear him.

It was almost as if I were in a dream. I seemed to view myself back in Bible club as a child, the camping, the Bible stories, the snacks, the innocent years. Then I saw myself in gang bang situations and how I was not so merciful toward different people. Then I watched my mother standing over my coffin weeping bitterly.

When I snapped out of it, Whitey was still cursing me; and the gun was aiming in the direction of my head. I visualized the hole a .44 magnum would put in the back of a head and knew I wouldn't have a chance to say goodbye to my mother. I asked God to save me and promised I would be His if He did.

I saw Whitey getting ready to squeeze the trigger, so I threw my forearms over my head and prepared to die. Actually, I was more afraid of the impact of the bullet's entry than I was about death itself. Suddenly I realized I didn't hear the gun go off, and I wasn't shot after all. So I rose up to see what was happening.

Whitey was looking disappointed and then rushed toward me before I was fully standing straight up. He started hitting me with the back of his gun. It felt like I had been hammered with a skillet. Then I started trying to get him off by swinging up at him, scraping my knuckle on his teeth.

In the midst of the brawl, I managed to catch a glimpse of a bus of high school students that had come to a stop at the light. Girls were screaming on the bus, probably scared at what they thought they might see. One girl in particular caught my eye as if she were very sad for me. The bus driver pulled off when the light turned green.

O'G Alpo from the PJs drove up in his '63 Chevy, honking his horn, and managed to scare Whitey off. He kept going and didn't stop, but at least he got Whitey out of there. I staggered over to the office at Barney's; and two of my homegirls, Cheryl Daye and Carman, attended to me.

Cheryl told me I was bleeding on my back, and they realized the back of my head was split open. I was surprised because I thought the moisture was just sweat. My back and shoulders were covered in blood as well. Carman and Cheryl cut my hair from around the wound and placed a bandage of some sort on it.

Soon word got back to Grape, and before long Barney's was flooded with Grape Streets. My homeboy E-Quake, Cheryl's big brother—who was probably one of the most feared Crips ever—was packing a 357 Magnum. He was ticked that a "slob" would come in our hood and do something to one of the homeboys, referring to me. Wow!

Eddie Boy and Crazo put me in Eddie's car and drove me home to the PJs. The homeys told me those slobs were "going to pay." And in fact, I found out later, they went over to the Nickerson Gardens and sought revenge for me, causing much damage. I felt that even though my life could have ended by this event, my Grape Street homeboys showed true love for me by getting revenge. I forgot about God, and my commitment to Grape went to new heights because I realized I was finally accepted by the O'Gs, the elite of Grape.

My mother and cousin Evelyn took me to the clinic where I received eleven stitches. Over the next couple of days, I was getting visits from all kinds of people, especially from Grape. Looking back, I believe the thing that drew them was that I put my life on the line to save my homeboys Mice and Baby Bam, two of Grape's highest.

When I finally went back to school, I had bandages around my head; and I kept a hard beanie over it. My science teacher, Mr. White—who didn't seem to like me—didn't want me wearing my hat in class. He asked me to take it off, but I told him I didn't want to because of my bandages. He wasn't hearing it. I didn't like him either and thought he was prejudiced against blacks, so I told him, "NO!" We got into an argument; he sent me to the principal's office where I would win approval in light of my situation. But what grabbed me was the support of my fellow classmates. They rallied behind me, and I appreciated that.

The funny thing about it all, someone had spread the rumor that I was killed by Whitey. So people were shocked who didn't know the truth, especially my friend Brian, who was called "Smokey." He was a member of the Lot Boys (named for the parking lot where they sold drugs), who were from the Nickerson Gardens; but they were primarily about making money through illegal drugs.

When Smokey saw me heading to my next class, he ran up and gave me a huge hug. He was excited to see me alive and moved to tears. Smokey had proven himself my friend, not allowing the gang stuff to separate our friendship, and I trusted him. He later pulled out a thick roll of fifties and hundreds and peeled off two fifties. He urged me to buy some more bandages or whatever and, if I needed more, to let him know. He was a year under me, an eighth grader. I would later put my life on the line for him too, and I would have protected him to the fullest.

This encounter with Whitey shocked many Crips because I had lived through it; everyone was aware of his reputation for shooting people. At that point, Whitey became a marked man. I saw him once after that, but he didn't see me. He was packing at the time, and I wasn't. If I would've had a ghat (gun) on me in that moment, I would have taken him out without hesitation. But that incident brought me a little fame.

Chapter Nine

Life went on, and I continued to gang bang, representing Grape with my whole heart. Death always seemed to be imminent even though we never felt that it could happen to us personally. In fact, that situation kind of made me feel invincible. But unfortunately, that wasn't the case for all.

I managed to pass through junior high when I shouldn't have, failing almost every semester, including homeroom. This occurred not because I couldn't pass the classes but because I didn't care. I had closed my heart to learning in the sixth grade, believing that I would never amount to anything anyway; so I had said, "Screw it!" I believe I was passed from grade to grade just to get me out of Markham as soon as possible. But that summer, between the ninth grade and the start of high school, I spent some time at Markham during summer school—which turned out to be a waste of time.

A certain Bounty Hunter and I got into a fight, and I was body slamming him, trying to break his back, until we were stopped. Trouble was always on the horizon, so learning was never my goal, even in summer school. My homeboy Nite-Owl would come to visit that summer, and he and I became better friends.

Still, tragedy would happen during those months. I wasn't at school on that particular day, but I was told that Nite-Owl and Bounty Hunter Loaf got into a fight, and Nite-Owl ended up on top of him. He pulled out his buck knife and was getting ready to stab Loaf, but Loaf managed to grab Nite-Owl's hand. Abruptly, Nite Owl lost grip of the knife and dropped it; Loaf got hold of the knife and then pushed it up into the chest of my homeboy Nite-Owl and killed him. When I found out about it later that day, I was simply stunned because I had just seen my homeboy the day before. Unquestionably that stirred up the hate in me even more for all Bloods.

Back in the PJs, the climate was not any better either. Needless to say, I wasn't the most liked in the Imperial Courts. My young homeboy Sean, who was one of the original members of the Watts Baby Locos, had several cousins who also claimed Baby Loco; but after we broke up in the PJs, his cousins started banging with the 117th St. Watts Crips, which was on the border of Compton and Watts.

Actually, 117th St. Watts was better known as 7 St. Watts. Sean's cousin Popa had come over to visit me. As it happened, 7 St. and the PJs had had a falling out; so, even though they were Crips too, they were banned from the PJs. I told him to come anyway.

After his visit, I went to walk him through the PJs over to Imperial Highway so he could go home safely. But he was spotted by one of the PJs. We heard somebody call out, "What that 7 St. nigga doing in my projects? Clipper, why are you bringing niggas over here in our hood? You go mess around and get barred too." I replied, "Nigga, I been living over here just as long as the next nigga. You can't run me out!"

The guy came toward me as if he wanted to fight, so I grabbed Lil' Popa and encouraged him to run to my house. I ran with him about ten yards, making sure Lil' Popa was clear; then I stopped, turned around, and went back. The guy must have thought I was crazy, but I wanted him to think that; and I was planning to back it up.

I strode up to him and demanded that he "Come on with it!" He swung on me, and the next thing I knew we were locking horns. Finally, I had backed him up into my mother's friend's apartment screen door, socking him in the face and chest. I was clearly overwhelming him. He was one of those who used to chase me home as a kid, so I was thinking about that too.

My mother came running around the building and jumped in between us equally. Because she pushed us both apart, he told her not to put her M.F. hands on him. At that point, I reached over and grabbed his shirt, yanking him toward me. I drove him into the brick wall and then into the grass while a sprinkler was going off. He was all bloodied up, but I wasn't.

88

My mother ordered me to let him up, so I did. We were both soaking wet, with grass stains all over us. But I chalked it up as a victory for me because this guy was another one of those who had abused me; I had to convince him those days were over. He got up cursing me out as well as Grape and muttering that I was going to get mine. I kept asking, "What that Grape like, Cuzz?!" just to rub it in.

I understood the underdog role well, and this had become my attitude: if you're with me, I'm not leaving you; I will back you up until the end. And people were beginning to take notice of that.

One bright spot in my life came when I met a certain young lady back at Markham. She was a student helper in the library. We were taking one of those standardized tests or something in the library room where she worked. Her name was DeLois Austin, but her family called her Jeanette. She was very beautiful and modest, and for the first time I noticed how different she appeared.

I found myself going into the library more and more often, pretending I was interested in reading but knowing I had absolutely no desire to go in there for that purpose. Rather, I just wanted to look at her, hoping that she would finally notice me. And near the end of our final year at Markham, she did.

Jeanette and her friend would look over at me and grin; finally, I got the nerve to go and find out what they were smiling about. Her friend told me that Jeanette thought I was cute. I asked her if I could have her number so I could call her over the summer, and she said yes.

During the summer, I did call; and we had a good conversation. I found that she was very down-to-earth and talkative. She won my respect quickly—unlike most girls that I had no respect for or trust in. In contrast, Jeanette, whom I would come to call Lois, was very calming to me. I was able to relax when I talked with her.

We continued to talk during the course of the summer, and I finally asked her to be my girl. She was glad to be. Next I needed to meet her family: her parents, Mr. and Mrs. Austin; her sister, Crystal, whom I knew from Markham; and her little brother, William. Her family embraced me by phone, basically—until I got to meet them in person.

They knew I was in the Crips, but I made every effort to be respectful. I went to visit her one day; and beforehand, she warned me to be careful not to wear too much blue. She lived off of Crenshaw and Western, I believe, in the Crenshaw Mafia hood, which was Blood territory.

Her family treated me very well, which I certainly appreciated. One particular evening I visited her, and we were playing a game when the news made a breaking report. Michael Jackson had just been taken to the hospital; it was the day he was shooting his Pepsi commercial when his hair caught on fire.

Before long, we made arrangements for Lois to catch the bus out to Watts to visit me and meet my mother. I met her at the bus stop in the Jordan Downs because I wanted to be seen with her. My homeboy Tank thought I was scared of girls since he had never seen me with one. Due to my stuttering condition, I wasn't as aggressive in crowds; so I had to compensate in other ways. But many girls were attracted by my stuttering; they thought it was cute.

My mother loved her from the beginning and came to treat her like a daughter. Lois didn't like my gang banging, but I think she got a feel of how disliked I was in the PJs. Walking with her through the projects drew eyes for a couple of reasons, I believe: one, because I had become a hated man, and two, because she wasn't from there, and she was very beautiful.

On another occasion, she and her sister Crystal came over. My homeboys O'G Big Tony, Andre (aka Tap), and Wanky had also stopped by. Both Wanky and Big Tony were kind of competing for Crystal, who was also a very pretty young lady.

We were all in my living room talking, when we heard somebody calling out, "Clipper, bring those Grape Street niggas outside. We told you not to be bringing them Fake Streets in our hood. Come and get some of that PJ Watts, Cuzz!" By now, Lois and Crystal, who were totally isolated from anything like that, were frankly afraid.

My homeboys and I heard the challenge and took it. Lois was almost begging me not to go outside, but I had too much pride to refuse. Wanky took the lead by telling us that those PJs weren't going to run anything and that Grape wasn't going to be disrespected like that. By this time, Wanky had become a force to be dealt with. O'G homeboys like Ced-Mc and others were paying Wanky to knock people out cold at fifty dollars a wop. He had become fearless and feared. We were all in agreement about our next move, no matter what. I told Lois and Crystal to stay inside.

The four of us strode outside to a crowd of about thirty people, including a few women and kids. Maniac led the group, yapping about how my homeboys weren't allowed in the PJs. I told them these were my guests and it wasn't any of their business who I had in my house. This was Grape, Cuzz! All day long.

With no delay, we pulled off our shirts; and they chose the ones they wanted to match up with. We were getting ready to start throwing 'em. But my mother came outside with my girl and Crystal, and Mom went ballistic. She ordered everybody to get out of her yard, using some choice words to make her point. Thankfully, the PJs respected her enough to do what she said though they continued to mumble threats as they walked away.

I didn't find out until later that my mother had her .357 Magnum tucked away under her shirt behind her pants, and I have no doubt that she would have used it if the situation came to that. My mother had always been one of the toughest people I've ever known in terms of not showing fear of anyone. I've never seen her flinch in my life.

She had grown up during the turbulent '60s, being in the company of the Black Stone Rangers and the Black Panthers. She could be as kindhearted as could be, and sometimes family members and so-called friends would take advantage of that. But she could also be as tough as nails if she had to be. It was not only my mother, but toughness ran through my family.

A Watts Summer Jazz Festival was held that year, and musicians from everywhere came to share their talent. People from all around arrived to enjoy the week-long event. Families barbecued, picnicked, or ate from the various vendors that were stationed all around.

But also Crips from what seemed like every hood imaginable were there as well—Main St. Crips, Hoover Crips, Raymond Ave. Crips, Compton Ave. Crips, 8.9 (89th) St. East Coast Crips, including 7.6 East Coast Crips, Fudge Town Crips, PJ Crips, and of course, Grape St. Watts Crips. We were looking at maybe three to four thousand people, easily. Grape alone had maybe five hundred up there.

"Sinister Crips"

Everybody else was present just with family and friends. We got along for the most part. But one of the problems Crips always seemed to struggle with was ego: everybody wanted to be the biggest dog on the block, and often we'd find Crips fighting Crips.

Each person was representing his "set" (gang) to the fullest. Blue rags were hanging from everyone's pocket, including Grape who wore blue or purple. Everybody was throwing up the hand signs representing his particular Crip gang or was yelling it out. But these 8.9 Crips who did not like Grape kept trying to throw up their set around Grape—to irritate us, I guess.

No question, we had to squash that quickly: not by fighting but just by imposing our will with sheer power of numbers and face-to-face confrontation. But later on in the week, they started it up again. We were just relaxing on the grass, smoking weed, eating, and enjoying the music. My homeboy, who was facing death row last I heard some years ago for a separate crime, pulled out his pistol and fired into 8.9's crowd. The problem was that a little girl was walking in between us, and she caught the bullet. All my homeboy said was, "She shouldn't have been in the way," and he grabbed the 800 and started drinking it.

The deeper I got involved in gang activity, the closer I came in contact with death it seemed. I remember Edward and I were kicking it in the PJs near a playground two rows behind our apartments. We were on the grass near the street, smoking weed or something, when a car packed with about four or five Hispanics from 18 St. (XVIII St. as they promoted it) drove up to us quickly—before we even realized it.

We heard a loud screeching sound, glanced up, and saw they were right in front of us with shotguns and whatever else, pointing straight at us. There was not one thing we could do if we would have tried something. One of them looked at us closely and said, "That's not them, Homes! Let's go."

Apparently, somebody had sold them some bunk sherm (a type of cigarette dipped in PCP), and it ticked them off. They were coming back with a vengeance and were planning to make a scene. We were fortunate that one of them realized that neither of us was involved, or we would have been as dead as a doorknob. Or, they could have just taken out their anger on us.

One thing you learn in the streets of L.A. is that, especially in gangs, loyalty means everything. I took that very seriously, and I grew to despise fakeness. If a guy was going to claim a set, he should do so in a crowd and out of it as well. He should never claim something if he wasn't willing to back it up with even his very life, if necessary.

I was never more tested than in the PJs. Sometimes they would corner me if I was by myself, hoping I would stick my tail between my legs and run. But those days were long gone. One thing they had to come to grips with: I didn't act one way around my Grape St. homeboys and another when I was alone.

A couple of PJs were out of their hood one day, and I was with some of my homeboys. This was during a time when tensions were pretty high. They were clearly out of their element as well as out-numbered, but I made a special point to speak to them. To their surprise I said, "What up, Cuzz? What y'all up to?" I never came at them with "What that Grape like, niggas?" trying to provoke a fight, and I think it made an impact on them because tensions between the two of them and me subsided significantly after that. I wanted them to see that even though I had the numbers and the power to crush them, I didn't want to treat them as they had treated me over the years.

In my freshman year at David Star Jordan High School, I continued to show no interest in school. I figured—how can a dead man have hope to be anything? I was dead inside to the outside world and to anything that academics or sports could offer me. I basically went to school to please my mother, who had hoped I would graduate from junior high, doing the prom thing and all. No, that wasn't for me.

I had an English teacher whose name, I believe, was Ms. Lyons. She was very nice to all of us students, especially to troubled kids like me. I don't know if she was Jewish or Italian or what, but something about her gave her an ethnic look. Yet something more set her apart from all the other teachers: she was a Christian who was full of love.

Ms. Lyons would say things to me such as, "Eric, you shouldn't be involved in gangs. God has many plans for your life, and He wants to bring Himself glory through your life. He knows what you're going through, and He loves you very much. I'm praying for your life, Eric."

She made me slightly uncomfortable around her because I knew she was going to find some way to tell me how much Jesus loved me. I was invited to her Bible study one night; and strangely, I decided to go. Still, my underlying motive was that a male classmate mentioned that they go out to dinner, to the beach, and other fun things. So I went just to get away.

I found out that my teacher lived down the street from the Jordan Downs, across the street from my friend Lee Phillips, who used to go to Bible club with me. I was shocked that this single lady lived in such a hostile environment alone. I made sure I never told any of my homeboys.

At one point, Ms. Lyons gave me a Bible designed for teens with my name engraved on it. I have kept that Bible to this day. I never gave her the respect that she so deserved, and I wish I had the opportunity to thank her today. Ms. Lyons, if you're out there, thank you for caring for me and trusting God over my life even when I couldn't myself.

Unfortunately, all she did and said could not change me at the time. After several visits to her Bible study, a trip to the beach for food and fun, and a barbecue out to a black family's home for an evening, I quit going. This black family was very wealthy and lived out in Baldwin Hills or somewhere in a rich neighborhood. The man was a doctor, and his wife was a judge, I believe, like the Cosby family on TV. But they were a very loving family who cared for their black people who were less fortunate financially and without Christ. They had two daughters who were very polite, with good manners.

I went back to doing my usual thing. I was too sold out to Grape to give my life over to Christianity. Again, just like back in elementary school, I believed God was all love and forgiveness but was without the backbone to protect me. So that phase passed. In fact, I was too guilty to continue in Ms. Lyons's class. She never made me feel that way, but her godly life exposed my sinful heart.

Chapter Ten

Meanwhile, things would hit the fan; trouble would come about later that year. My homeboy Mice's nephew Bubble, who was also a good friend of mine, was out kicking it on the big sidewalk one evening when a car pulled up.

I wasn't around there at the time; but from what I understood, a guy got out of the car and came over to Bubble with a shotgun in his hand. He said something and then fired on the young homeboy, killing him.

The shooter was from a Hispanic gang called WCW, Watts Colonial Wiegand. That night Grape mobilized and went out to take revenge on Bubble's life. Grape killed several of their homeboys and beat many of them down. WCW got themselves into something that they couldn't handle.

The next week, all WCWs avoided school because Grape was looking for them. There were two Butchers from Grape. One was my cousin, whom I found out about through my cousin Rick-Rock—Todd "Butcher" as we called him—and the Hispanic Butcher. I'll call my cousin Big Butcher and my homeboy Lil' Butcher.

Lil' Butcher, Edward, and I were ditching class one day and were hanging out on the balcony when a certain WCW came walking by. We glanced at each other, thinking this guy was crazy. Lil' Butcher strolled up to him and spoke some choice words, asking him if he wanted to die or something. I was walking behind him at this point to prevent him from running. Butcher grabbed him by the collar, pulled him over to the edge of the railing, and manhandled him over the edge.

Lil' Butcher was getting ready to throw the guy over the top, but I stopped him because I saw somebody coming. That was the only thing that kept the homeboy from hitting the ground headfirst. So we let the guy go, reluctantly. It took nearly two weeks before things began to calm down. Police presence was a factor, and I think we had made our point.

At this time, people were dropping like flies—not necessarily people from Grape or PJ, the two that my life revolved around, but Crips and Bloods in general. But I would come to be closely associated with one that would be highly broadcast.

The day that Bubble got killed, another one of our homeboys died as well, about 4:00 that morning. My homeboy Stomper, one of the elite Grape Street Crips, and I were together the day before. I had spent a night over at Wanky's house and got up that morning and went outside after the breakfast Hazel had made for us.

I told Wanky I was going over to the big sidewalk. I ran into Stomper around 10:00 A.M., and the first thing we did was buy some Olde English 800. Stomper wanted to go around to a different family member's house in the JDs, just to visit.

Around 5:00-5:30 that evening we heard that an ex-lady friend of mine, Dottie, was having a house party that night. We reached the place around 7:00 or so, but things really started jumping around 9:00. There were Compton Ave. Crips there, who were huge supporters of Grape. Additionally, Grape and Baby Locos were there. And since Dottie's house was near those 8.9 East Coast Crips, they too started filing in.

They were bumping big songs like George Clinton's "The Atomic Dog" and Roger's "I Heard it Through the Grape Vine." Those tunes seemed to bring out the best in Grape. Things were going well until an 8.9 started talking trash. I guess he didn't realize how many Grape Streets and Baby Locos were at the party.

Blue and purple rags were flying everywhere, and people were throwing up the signs representing their hood. Stomper had gotten too drunk that night, so I decided to stay sober. He got into it with one of those 8.9 East Coast Crips and was standing nose to nose with him. If the homeboy Stomper had been sober, there wouldn't have been any talking, period.

I heard some guys arguing and noticed that Stomper was involved. I stepped up to his side and told those East Coast guys, "What that Grape like, Cuzz? Nigga, y'all in our hood. You wanna get y'all's on or what? F--- 8.9! This Grape, Cuzz!"

At once about twenty of the homeboys came over and surrounded 8.9. When they realized they were outnumbered, they backed off. Respect was given and lines were drawn, and the party continued.

The event began to slow down around 3:30-4:00 A.M. or so, and people were either walking home or getting in their cars and driving off. Stomper and I had walked to the party from the Jordan Downs, which was about a mile west of the projects.

My homeboy, whom I'll call "Tee," drove up to the party at that point, hoping it was still going on. He was in a new car. Stomper and I asked Tee to give us a ride home because Stomper wasn't in any shape to be walking, and I didn't want One Time (our code word for the police) to harass us. Two of my other homeboys also asked for rides: John-John from Grape and my homeboy Wig-Out from Baby Locs.

Stomper let the three of us get in the back, and he got in the passenger seat. I was sitting in the middle. About a minute after we pulled off, Stomper made the statement, "Man, I feel like I'm gonna die," while holding his head with both hands.

Thinking that his head must be hurting from all the drinking he'd been doing, still I said, "Cuzz, don't talk like that." Not long after that, a spot light shone on us. It was the L.A. sheriff who ordered us on the loud speaker, "Pull the car over."

Instead of pulling over, Tee peeled out! He really punched it. That began a high-speed chase. We were all asking Tee what was going on and why he didn't pull over. He wouldn't tell us, probably because it wasn't a good time to be talking. We got to 97th Street, I believe it was, and Tee hit a hard right and headed east.

By that time, other cars were streaming toward us as backup. Tee turned right, heading south on Grape Street. That took us to 101st and Grape, into the Jordan Downs. By now there was a police helicopter chasing us too, along with additional police cars.

It had been raining somewhat that evening, and water had puddled under the light pole on the corner. When Tee turned into the projects on 101st and Grape, the car did a 360 degree spin. Tee jumped out and ran, and Stomper was attempting to do the same. We tried to grab the homeboy Stomper because he didn't have any reason to run.

But he slipped away, against our pleading with him to stay.

Tee pulled out a gun and started shooting as he tried to escape. The next thing we knew, guns were going off from everywhere. Tee was shot, if I recall correctly, in the back and buttocks, but he would survive.

Meanwhile, Stomper was ordered to halt, which he did. With his hand in the air, he allegedly turned around too fast and was shot in the face with a shot gun, knocking him under a parked car. Stomper did not have a weapon on him; I know that for a fact because I had been with him for about eighteen or nineteen hours.

The three of us were piled in the back seat, hoping not to get caught in the crossfire. I could barely see Stomper's body lying partly under a car in the parking lot, and he was now dead. After things were under control, we were ordered out of the car one at a time.

Because I was in the middle, I was the last one out. My home-boys were ordered out on each side of the vehicle. When it was finally my turn, it was like entering a land minefield. I was to step out very carefully with my hands raised to the sky.

They told me not to make a sudden movement or move too fast, or I was a dead man. When I crept out of the car, not only was the helicopter's light directly on me, but every gun out there was as well. I asked God not to let me trip or sneeze as I was climbing out; that's how close I felt I would be from death if I made the wrong move.

Before we got out, John, Wig-Out, and I went over our stories and swore not to say anything different. We had no need to lie or cover anything up because we knew we hadn't done anything wrong, and we definitely had no clue about what Tee had done.

I was wearing my cream colored golf hat, light gray khakis, my white all-stars with blue shoe strings, my blue rag hanging out of my pocket, and a brand new Pendleton. I had to lie face down in the street in water. Oddly, I was more concerned about messing up my Pendleton than I was about going to jail at that point.

Three or four officers ran over to me. One was nick-named "Kojak" by people in the street because he was bald-headed, about 6'5", and around 250 pounds of solid muscle. He had a thick dark moustache and a reputation for being one mean man. He hated gang bangers, or so it seemed from our perspective.

He came over and put his size 15 in my neck and told me

to try to get up and run—insisted he would give me a chance. But I wasn't going for that; I thought, *"This fool is crazy!"* He cuffed me, picked me up with one hand, and took me to his car. On the way to the station, he suggested to his partner that they drop us off in the Nickerson Gardens and handcuff us to the baseball diamond to let the Bounty Hunters take care of us when they woke up, but his partner didn't go along with it. And I don't know how serious he was either. Maybe he was just playing mind games with us.

It turned out that Tee had robbed a man at LAX airport, took a quarter of a million dollars, killed him, and put his body in the man's own trunk. The car that we were in was stolen as well. Tee never told us anything about that.

When we got to the station, we were all separated—put into three different rooms for questioning. We kept to our stories and never strayed from them at all. I don't remember when John-John and Wig-Out were released, but I was released to my mom around 5:00 that afternoon. They could not stick us with anything, so they had to let us go.

The next day at school, my homeboys came up to me to see if I had heard about Bubble's death the night before. I couldn't believe it! I was completely shocked. My homeboy didn't bang; he was simply about having money. But unfortunately, he was caught up in something he had nothing to do with; and in the game of the streets, even the innocent are sometimes victims.

Unfortunately, my homeboy Stomper's death put my name out there even more because I was the last one with him, having spent the last eighteen to twenty hours with him. News of the incident spread all over Watts and beyond. I felt guilty for a while because I could not control the outcome of that senseless death to my homeboy who had nothing to do with the crime that Tee had committed. Tee and I were both the same age at the time, sixteen. He would never see the streets again, not even to this day, I believe.

Chapter Eleven

By this time, I was far gone from reality in terms of feeling like I must be committed to Grape above everything else. Nothing mattered more to me; I didn't care about anything else. People can learn to stuff emotions—things that show pain or hurt—because they interpret them as being weaknesses. I've heard of soldiers of war having to deny their feelings during combat in order for their training to take over. In a sense, that's how I felt. I couldn't allow feelings to control my life unless they were feelings of anger or rage. But when it came to things like family problems, female problems, and even the death of a loved one or homeboy, I had to deny those feelings and let the street survival take over. If a person is going to gang bang, he must deny feelings of guilt or sorrow. He would show his respect for the death of the loved one or homeboy, and then he would need to move on. So that's what I had to do.

A part of being fully committed to Grape, to the Crips, was caring for the homeboys. I didn't like fighting any of them or getting into it with them. I tried my best to stick by my self-imposed rule as best I could. But sometimes even a guy's homeboys would test him.

Back in the eighth grade, Roscoe and Cisco made me give up my money. At that time I was too afraid to stand up to them. But one day a bunch of us were hanging out on the big sidewalk, sipping on 800, smoking weed, and just enjoying each other like we were family. If you were a suspicious-looking individual walking by us, you could be in serious trouble.

Roscoe came out of nowhere, wanting to slap box with me.

About twenty of us were out there—Marckey, Tank, Big Butcher, Jay-Jay, and others. Roscoe was a huge figure in Grape. He and his brother, who had been killed years earlier, as well as his cousins Cisco, Bubba, and Cecil were all O'Gs. So I politely told him I didn't want to. But he kept insisting and began to make a scene in front of all the Locs (our slang term for the O'Gs or elite.) At this point, I was getting a little nervous because I wondered if I would have anybody's support over Theodore (Roscoe).

But Butcher stepped up. "Clipper, scrap with this nigga, home Cuzz! Show this nigga that you're an O'G too, and you're paying your dues like all of us. You my cousin, and ain't no nigga go jump in." Hearing that from Todd Butcher gave me confidence, and it basically offered me the opportunity to solidify my place among the elite.

Roscoe said something to the effect, "Don't get your cousin knocked out. He gotta show me he's arrived." So I decided to take him up on his test. The homeys gathered around us, probably thinking that the O'G homeboy was going to knock me out.

I thought the same thing—until he took a swing at me. We started off slap boxing with our hands wide opened. Soon frustration grew, and it turned into fists. By the time we agreed to quit, I had won Roscoe's respect and that of the Locs. It didn't stop me from giving Roscoe his due respect, and I wasn't going to stop either. I got high fives and hugs from many of the homeys, including Roscoe. Big Butcher was excited for me, not because I proved my heart in front of all possible nay-sayers but that now I had won everybody's respect.

Someone was about to walk into my life who would become the little brother I never had. David grew up around the Mona Park Crips neighborhood—borderline Watts/Compton. He was the youngest of nine children and the third of three sons. His two brothers were from 7th St. Watts, Chris and Andre; but he basically never fit in because he was their "little brother." David's two sisters, Cathy and Carajean, had moved into the PJs on the opposite end of my building. I was coming from Monk Marv's house when I saw him outside with his nephew Rodney. Somehow we got to talking.

He was fascinated by gangs and wanted to tell me all about Mona Park Crips and 7th St. Watts, not knowing that I knew some MPCs and a few 7th Streets. I told him that I knew the Hilt family, who had grown up in the PJs but had moved over by Mona Park some years earlier.

When David found out that I was from Grape, he became an immediate fan. My closest friends like Edward, Wanky, and Randle, Monk's younger brother, were all naturally funny. I found out quickly that David fit that same mold. I immediately took him up under my wing; and some days after meeting, Edward and I initiated him into Grape and gave him the name "Mousey."

After this, I became to Mousey what Monk Marv had been to me—and more. I taught him how to "hit up" (write) Grape style. We taught him how to dress and the whole nine yards. Grape had a style that was totally unique, and Mousey embraced it.

Mousey

Because Mousey became so closely associated with me, he became an instant enemy of the PJs. He was so committed to Grape and to me that he would sometimes start arguments or fights with the PJs just to see if Grape would come to his rescue. What he found out, however, was that Grape's backup to him was just Edward and I. He had not gotten to know the homeboys enough, and on the streets—as in many walks of life—it's who you know that counts.

Nevertheless, things would begin to heat up. I had gotten

Mousey out of trouble more than a few times within a short span; but this particular time, I would let him find his own way—to a degree, that is. Dinky from the PJs, someone I had known since moving to L.A., had grown up to be an O'G PJ and was fearless. Mousey had been wanting a hard beanie like mine. Now hard beanies (tightly knitted pull-over caps, that stood up by themselves) were hard to find. People had been robbed at gun point over these things. Typically, only the elite were safe to wear them.

Clipper in a hard beanie, the Imperial Courts Housing Projects

Dinky had been talking trash to Mousey and calling his bluff. He didn't want to fight Dinky, but he was caught between a rock and a hard place because Dinky wouldn't let up on him. Every time he saw Mousey, he would say something like, "Hey, Mousey, Clipper's boy! What up, Fake Street?"

Finally, Dinky called him out by taking his hard beanie; he wanted to see where Mousey's heart was. I gave the nod basically and told Mousey to hold his own, but he wanted me to step in and handle Dinky. I kept telling Mousey to "throw 'em up," but he wouldn't. Dinky took his hard beanie and said, "If you want it, you got to take it from me."

Mousey couldn't win, and he lost his hat. He was mad at me because I didn't help him. I could have and more than likely would have won, but it was Mousey's time to get some heart. He didn't realize what I had been going through to win respect, and I wanted him to learn that too.

That wouldn't be the last test, either. I was going over to his sister's house where he was staying when I noticed him in the parking lot. Mousey had become just as addicted to gang writing as I was and maybe even more. He would sneak around at night and write Grape St. Watts everywhere, but I would catch the flack.

That night, about six or seven PJs were across the street by the gym when they spotted Mousey and me. They called out, "Don't be writing that Grape crap on our walls, Cuzz! Y'all gonna get barred out the PJs." Mousey said something that made them mad. But when they came toward us, he took off.

I made sure he got safely in the house; then I came back out and walked up to them. One particular PJ, that I'll call "Dee," stood nose to nose with me. He informed me how he was gong to have to start "serving you Grape Streets. F--- Grape!" Instead of repeating, "F--- PJ," I said "F--- you, nigga!"

We kept going back and forth with each other until one of his homeboys, who had started off banging with me when Edward and I first founded Watts Baby Locos, pulled out his buck knife and threatened to kill me. I guess he figured I was going to freak out and run.

Instead, he enraged me. I charged at him, growling, "Don't ever pull a knife on me, Punk A-- Nigga. I'll make you eat that knife, fool." My young Uncle Stone, by marriage, who had also been a Baby Loco and was now a PJ, pleaded with me to back off. I respected him enough and listened to him.

That potentially toxic situation ended peacefully, and I went inside where Mousey was. His mother Rose, father Yule, and other family members were in there at the time. I told them what had happened and challenged Mousey not to start trouble like that if he was not willing to take the heat because there would be times when I wouldn't be around.

His family grew to embrace me as one of their very own, calling me Mousey's third big brother. Mousey would become my little brother, a guy I loved very much and would have given my life for. He himself would become one of the Locs of Grape, riding off my name for a while until he began to pass the test and became fearless as well.

On March 18, 1982, the Crips would suffer a huge loss. One of the biggest O'Gs of all time, a Crip's Crip, Bone from Grape Street Watts, had been killed. I found out he was my cousin by marriage, through Rick-Rock and Todd Butcher.

It was on a Thursday night, and it had been sprinkling for hours. I was in the PJs, hanging out with my homeboy Patmite, a PJ Crip that I grew up with. We were talking outside, when Bone, Bab, and Pop-squali came riding by on bikes. Bone walked with a limp and usually traveled in his powder-blue '76 Chevy Glass House. So I was kind of surprised to see him on a bike and so far from the Jordan Downs.

I caught their attention and asked what was up. Bone said they were just out riding and were on their way to check out some girls over in AGC hood (Avalon Garden Crips). I said, "Stay up, Cuzz! Watch y'all backs and G-careful." Bone replied, "Keep representing Grape to the fullest, lil' Cuzz!" That was the last time that I saw the big homey.

The next day at school I spotted my homeboy Lannie walking in front of Jordan High. I was looking out front there for something when I noticed him. Lannie said, "Clipper, you hear about O'G Bone, Cuzz?! Those Swan slobs killed the homey, Cuzz! All the Locs are meeting later on. Get with us on the big sidewalk." I was completely stunned! I had just seen him the night before. All that day I was in a daze. The nation could have lowered their flags to half-staff—that's how important Bone was in the Crip world.

We got together that evening in the JDs in droves. Everybody was beyond enraged and wanted to bring death to all Swans (a Blood gang who we were told was responsible). But the consensus was to wait and let them forget about it for a week or so. You can't imagine the power we felt that night, and putting those Swans to death wouldn't have been enough to satisfy the rage we were feeling.

All kinds of Crips came to pay their respect to the fallen homeboy: Crips from the PJs, Hoover Crips, Main St. Crips, East Coast Crips, Fudge Town, Mona Park Crips, you name it. A bunch of us visited Bone's mom to pay respects to her and to offer whatever she needed in terms of money or anything else.

I was in Compton a couple of days after that. I was dating a certain young lady named Paula at the time, and it was her family's home. We were in her bedroom with her little nephews and nieces when a news report came on.

There was a violent gang disturbance at Freemont High School, and the cameras showed people being arrested and hauled away. I would find out later that the homeys and the others had decided to go before the scheduled date and kick up big dust. They had gone up there to Freemont, a Blood-infested school filled with Swans and Bishops.

The homeys had gone up there with the help of PJ Watts and others and had terrorized the place. I was tripping out as I watched the TV, recognizing some of the homeys. I kept thinking, *"I should be there too! Why didn't they tell me?"* I knew it wasn't like that, but I had some regret for not being on the scene with my homeboys. They took revenge in a big way, beating up many in the process. One of my guys, I was told, shoved an umbrella down one Swan's throat. Others were stabbed to death or even shot.

Grape sent a serious message to all who even thought about crossing us the wrong way. Bab escaped injury. Popsquali suffered a gunshot wound to the arm, I believe. But Bone, as we understood it, had been cornered under a light pole by a van full of Swans who shot him numerous times, killing him on the spot.

Things cooled down after that, and life as we knew it went on. When I first started gang banging, I considered Twins, Bone, Tank, Darcel, Cisco, and all the O'Gs to be walking gods, deities who could do no wrong. They were the very standards of toughness and the embodiments of what it meant to be Crips. From the founders Big Tookie and Raymond Washington on down to them, they and others carried the name Crip like true soldiers. If they would have asked me to strap on a bomb and run into a pack of Bloods, I probably would have done it. That's how caught up and dependent I was on Grape.

But by now, I had earned so much of their respect that they became my peers. I got to know many of them as people, witnessing some of their family problems up close and even being part of some of their family activities. This was notably true with my homeboy Tank's family, who invited me to their Fourth of July picnic on one occasion.

I felt like I was becoming part of the elite . . . until I was put to another test by one of my own homeboys that I had always revered, the Gemini Twin. I had borrowed my friend Thomas' bike to ride over to the JDs on my word that I would bring it back that night. That evening, before I got ready to return to the PJs, I saw two of my homeboys Twin and Binky. Twin asked me to let him use the bike for a minute to drop off some dope. I told him that it wasn't my bike to lend and that I was about to head back anyway. As much as I admired Gemini Twin, I had given my other homeboy my word.

Twin wouldn't take no for an answer, so he tried to convince me that he would come right back. Because he didn't respect my decision, I began to suspect that his motives weren't quite right. He grew impatient and then moved my hand out of the way and put his right leg over the bike as if to force me off.

I asked him to raise up, to back off. But he continued, saying, "I know you don't want to get knocked, homey. You can give me the bike or get dropped." At this point I lost all respect for Gemini; the admiration I once had was over.

Twin told Binky to show me the gun. Binky raised up his shirt with a conniving smile, and I got the message. Binky lost my respect in that moment as well. At once I sensed that not all the O'Gs had respect for me. But I told Twin and Binky to take the bike and to shove it up their butts, and I watched them ride away with a grin.

I couldn't believe it. What they had just done gave me the equivalent feeling of being raped. I walked all the way back to the PJs in a rage, feeling totally disrespected. I was faced with my own self-imposed rule not to fight a fellow Grape. But what was I to do?

The hardest challenge I foresaw that night was having to face Thomas to tell him that his bike was taken. I cared greatly about my word and about the trust a person put in me. Thankfully, Thomas understood and knew me well enough to realize I wouldn't betray him like that.

The next day I was out in the yard with my mom, Aunt Peg, and her friend from next door. My cousin Rick-Rock came by on a moped with his big biceps showing proudly; he was all muscle without an ounce of fat on him. I noticed he was kind of upset. Ricky pulled up to us, greeted my mom and everyone, and told me to get on the back. I didn't have a clue as to what was going on. Then he said, "I heard what happened last night. That was f----- up! We're going to find that nigga, and I want you to take yours back. He ain't getting away with that!"

Before long we got to the Jordan Downs, spotted one of the homeboys, and Rick-Rock asked if he had seen Gemini. The guy told us that he and a bunch of Locs were at Jordan High watching a football game against their arch-rival. When we found Gemini, he was with his brother Baby Twin, Marckey, Darcel, Wizard, Death, Steve-O, and a bunch of the homeys enjoying the game.

Ricky went into the pack and went straight to Gemini Twin. "Twin, that was cold what you did to my cousin, Clipper. He's one of the homeys. You gots to give him a chance to get his back." Ricky was well respected by all of the O'Gs; and when he said something, you could bank on it.

Twin kept trying to tell Ricky that he just wanted to borrow the bike and that I could have just let him borrow it and the issue would have been squashed. They went back and forth for a couple of minutes, and then Ricky drew the conclusion. "You ain't leaving here until he get his, Twin! Simple as that!"

Gemini said "F--- it! If he want to get knocked out, let him! I'll show him where his heart is. He got his chance." About fifty of the homeboys, plus some girls, all left the school and went next door to the JDs. We were in Steve-O's yard.

I was scared to death. Ricky was doing all the talking while I simply listened. Abruptly, Gemini pulled off his jacket and called me out. I glanced at Rick kind of cautiously. I was feeling a lot of pressure, and it was now my responsibility to live up to Ricky's expectations. And here I was—about to fight my homeboy, Monk's brother.

I couldn't imagine how it was going to affect my friendship with Monk Marv, but there was no turning back. Ricky spouted, probably sensing the fear in me, "You better fight him. If you don't whoop his a--, I'm gonna whip yours, Clipper!" So that was all it took. I couldn't have backed out if I tried.

Twin and I squared up and went for it. After that first swing, my nervousness was gone because I managed to slip one in that sent him backwards by about six feet, shocking everyone there—including me. I respected Twin enough to wait until he got up.

But he wouldn't show me the same respect. Somehow we ended up near Steve-O's house where his bushes were. When I felt them behind my leg, I managed to look back to get my bearings while trying to keep him at bay. In that split second by glimpsing back, I lost my visual of him; and when I turned around, he came charging at me.

I fell backwards and ended upside-down between the bushes and the building, landing on my right elbow. The fall knocked my shoulder out of its socket, and all I could do was kick him off me. I yelled for Ricky to get him back, and he did. Baby Twin didn't want Ricky to stop Gemini, but that was a disadvantage. Ricky believed that Twin should have given me the same respect that I gave him.

The homeys helped me up, but my shoulder was in too much pain to keep fighting, so I asked Ricky to call it off. I had to knock my shoulder back in place in order to move it. Not one person outside of Gemini criticized me for bowing out. Instead, I was shown love. They told me one by one, "Way to hang in there, Clip-Dog! You held your own, Cuzz."

From that point on, my Grape Street homeboys never challenged me like that again. I'm not saying I never had disagreements or even arguments at times, but no one ever tried to punk me again or to question my loyalty to Grape. Nothing or no one was more important to me, not even Jesus Christ Himself, sadly—as blinded as I was. Still, Gemini Twin and I grew in respect for one another after the fight, and obviously I passed his test; he became like a big brother to me.

The one person I wanted to convince that I belonged more was myself. I was my worst critic, and it was necessary that I pass my own test. Specifically, that was to never be anyone's victim again, to be a loyal friend and member of the mighty Grape gang. I measured my success by how others treated me. If I was given respect, if I was trusted by my homeboys with their lives, then I was passing the test. I had only one enemy that kept me from doing some of the things I wanted to do, and that was my stuttering problem. But in the gangster world, the streets, it didn't matter too much.

Things are usually raised to the next level when a person is out of his element. To be found in the wrong hood was taboo and could possibly cost you your life. On one occasion I had gone to Tank's family picnic; and Tank's cousin Ski-jump, my homeboy Mosco, and I decided to go over to Ski-jump's house in Compton.

We stopped by and picked up some girls first but then decided to go to a certain party that Ski-jump had heard about. But he didn't know exactly where it was or what hood it was in. We drove over to Santana Block Crips' hood and asked some of them. They didn't know. We kept asking around but got no leads.

We ended up finding a house party off Rosecrans near a drive-in theater. The party had red lights and trip lights flashing on and off quickly. So we strolled into the party, not realizing we were not at the right place. After about five minutes, we discovered we were in the midst of Bloods. They hadn't noticed it either at first. Suddenly one of them saw what my homeboy was wearing and called out, "We got some crabs in here, Blood!" Heads started whirling in every direction.

We committed ourselves to one another till the death and stayed close together with the girls who were with us while we all crept out the door. I had a buck knife with me and popped it open; I swore that if we were going to die there, some slob was going down with us. By that time, they were shouting, "Get them Crabs! F--- y'all! This is LPP [Ludas Park Pirus] Blood. Kill them niggas, Blood! Get 'em! Get 'em!"

Until this day, I believe it was a literal miracle that we got out of there alive. I can think of no other explanation. We were a good twenty feet from the pack that came out following us. We were able to get in the car safely and drive off.

Meanwhile, people were coming out with guns—but a bit too late. We rolled away waving our blue and purple rags and taunting, "Grape Street Watts Crips, Cuzz! We're out of here, you slobs!" I don't know if they were bluffing about having guns or not, but they never fired a shot.

We could only laugh about what had just happened, understanding how we had escaped death. We each felt it was strange how it all occurred and without a scratch on us. To celebrate, we got drunk off that Olde English 800 brew, smoked on a few joints, and just kicked it.

Unfortunately, I got too drunk and went into Ski-jump's rest room where I threw up everywhere, including on his mother's plush rug. I couldn't even enjoy the lady friend I had brought along because I was too out of it. Ski-jump and Mosco took me home later that evening, and I lived to see another day.

During this time, my life was picking up steam, and somehow I was kept from death and imprisonment. Two of my homeboys robbed an Asian family on 103rd and Lou Dillon, right there in front of the Jordan Downs. I was headed to the liquor store to buy a quart of 800 when I saw my homeboys hiding behind one of the buildings.

I asked them what was up. They explained they had just got their "jack on" (robbery), and the family they had robbed was talking to "One Time" (the L.A.P.D.). They told me not to go around there.

I told them that nothing was going to happen to me because I hadn't done anything wrong. I suggested they stay covered, and I walked over to the store anyway. When I got close to where the victimized family was standing, I was called over by the police. A certain girl who lived in the projects was pointing me out.

Instead of running, I met the officer half way so I wouldn't appear guilty. He informed me that the "young lady" who was pointing me out (snitching) said I was with the ones who had robbed the family. I reacted angrily at this point because I knew she was lying. She had done so, I believe, because I was so closely associated with the guys who actually did it.

The police cuffed me, shoved me in the car, and drove me to the station. There I was booked and placed in a cell. I was later released to my mother but was scheduled to appear in court. At that time the prosecutor questioned me but had a hard time understanding my answers because of my speech impediment. And the transcriptionist could not make out my testimony and could not enter much of what I said into the machine. My charge was later kicked out after the Asian couple stated I wasn't involved. I would've been looking at two to five years, I believe. Over all, to snitch was a forbidden part of the unspoken code. I would have rather committed suicide before I'd have done something like that. It was truly a detestable act.

Because of the lifestyle, I assumed I would lose my relationship with Lois, the only girl I had ever cared for. I desired to love her, but I couldn't do it the way she deserved and according to what the word actually means. I would've had to give up my gang involvement and be clean, if you will. I saw no hope for me beyond Grape; I simply couldn't imagine it. Because of that, I lost my friend and relationship with someone that I sincerely respected and honored. In a way, I had felt guilty being called her boyfriend: she deserved so much more.

Back in the PJs, things were still uneasy between me and those people. In many ways, the problems between Grape and the PJs usually centered on me. Many of them hated my guts and probably wished I were dead many times over. I can only assume it was because I lived in the PJs while my loyalty was with Grape. But they had forced me to side with Grape by treating me the way they did in my earlier years.

I had been told many times that I would be barred from the PJs if I didn't quit bringing Grape Streets over there. Even still, I would defy this all the time because I felt they were trying to control my life and dictate which people I could bring over to my house.

My response was, "Screw those niggas! They ain't running nothing." Mousey, Edward, and I continued to represent the Grape Vine in the area. One night Wanky and I, along with my homeboy Joe from Grape, were bold enough to go into a PJ party. PJs were throwing up the set "PJ Watts, Cuzz!" and of course we were hollering "Chitty Chitty bang bang. Nothing but that Grape Gang! Grape don't die, we multiply, Cuzz!" Things were going fairly well until certain PJs took offense to it.

We got into a big argument with some of the PJs for disrespecting Grape. It turned into a huge scene that forced us outside. We decided to head back to the JDs on foot because they were following us around the block. They clearly outnumbered us, but we weren't backing down.

I was never the aggressive talker and didn't argue much due to my speech impediment. My philosophy was to say what I had to say and then do what I had to do—or deal with whatever came next. So Wanky and Joe did most of the arguing.

Joe and Bittle from the PJs chose to go at it. My homeboy was knocked out in the middle of the street, and we had agreed that it would be a fair fight—one on one—and Wanky and I made sure that no one jumped in. After that, more words and threats were exchanged, but nothing else happened in terms of fighting.

Later that night we came back to the PJs and found it swarming with Grape Streets. My homeboy Phillip (aka E-Quake) led the way. This guy was absolutely feared. He and his brothers Big Haunch and Crow were all well known and respected by probably all Crips everywhere.

Quake met with Big Ken, who lived across the street from me and was like family. Big Ken was also well respected and known as an O'G PJ Crip. The two of them met to discuss what had occurred and what had been happening between Grape and PJ. We agreed to squash the conflict before things got out of control.

I had been at the heart of most of the clashes between Grape and PJ but not because I manipulated it or wanted it. Because I lived in the PJs and chose to gang bang with Grape, it produced tension between the two. I wasn't going to live a lie and pretend not to represent Grape just because it offended the PJs.

It was ingrained in my character to be honest and real, no matter the cost. The conflicts came because the PJs made me feel so much like a victim and dared me to think and act on my own. Who knows— if they wouldn't have hurt me so much growing up, maybe I would've stayed out of gang activity or would've chosen to represent PJ Watts. But ultimately, I had chosen Grape. They appeared more powerful, and their image was almost mesmerizing. They seemed the embodiment of strength. When I decided to join Grape, I committed my life to it: no ifs, ands, or buts about it; and everybody would know it.

And so the conflicts came naturally because I defied the norm, representing one gang while living in another's territory. Many people had no idea how much of it started and had continued around me over the years. But after Easy Quake and Big Ken talked, things would cool down for a little while.

I would repeat the tenth grade, having failed basically every semester. I probably got a "C" in homeroom and art; but by and large, I failed. Unlike in junior high, I wasn't moved along through high school without making passing grades; and to watch most of my class advance to the next grade was secretly embarrassing, but I had to reject those feelings by reminding myself not to care.

That summer, the Watts Jazz Festival returned to Will Roger's Park. Again Crips from many hoods attended. Everything was going well until a Blood tried to be bold enough to stop at a gas station nearby and pump gas. He was spotted and later killed by a group of Crips.

On the last day of the event, it was decided we would stream through the Hacienda Village from every direction and beat down any Bloods we found. And we did. It was a very chaotic scene, made up of many Crips. That was the last time the festival would be held there because of the gang violence.

Chapter Twelve

Just before my eighteenth birthday, my life would be brought to a standstill. My Uncle Clarence and his wife Aunt Mattie, their sons George and Mark came to live with us for a while, after leaving Arkansas to move to L.A.

My cousin George, who had no clue of the gang banging world and had never experienced a fast lifestyle, would come to know it through me. I would eventually persuade him to join Grape and gave him the name "Moose." He and I would grow close, and I took responsibility for his safety during that time. One night, his mother, Aunt Mattie, and my mother were talking about the people they grew up with back in Pine Bluff, Arkansas and the places where they hung out when familiar names began to come to the surface. They had never known each other in those days, but they discovered they had mutual friends.

One name in particular caught my mother's attention, and she asked if that person used to hang out with Jimmy Douglas. My auntie responded, "Yes!" Aunt Mattie just happened to have her friend's number, someone she hadn't called in years.

Jimmy Douglas turned out to be my real father's younger brother. Aunt Mattie's friend's phone number was still the same, and that friend actually had my Aunt Bobbie's phone number—my father's oldest sister. Immediately, we called her and got my father's phone number in Flint, Michigan. We called him, and one of his kids answered the phone. I was in a daze! I simply couldn't believe it. My father had been found, and a prayer that I had prayed many times had been answered.

I had no idea what to say when he got on the phone or how to present myself to him. The first statement out of my mouth, I believe, was, "What's up?" He asked me a series of questions about my life and how I had been. I hesitated to reveal I had grown up to be a thug.

After a few minutes, my mother got on the phone with him and asked him to discuss my getting out of California for a while because I had been getting death threats and she was scared for my life.

My father asked if I would be willing to go to Pine Bluff because he was going down there to take care of some family business with their restaurant. I agreed to meet him there because I wanted to see him. We worked out a time, and my mother purchased a round trip bus ticket.

I had only gone to Arkansas once since leaving there as a small boy, due to my grandmother's surgery; she had to have her breast removed because of cancer. She unfortunately had gotten to a point where she could no longer care for my step-grandpa, C.B., and herself and had to be placed in a senior citizen home. So that served as an equal motivator to take my dad up on his offer.

The bus ride out to Arkansas through the Arizona desert and towns seemed to take a lifetime. I couldn't wait to see my grandmother with my fully loaded plan not to reveal any signs that her baby had turned out to be a delinquent and criminal.

My cousins Wydale and Arthur picked me up from the bus station. They welcomed me as if they had known me all my life, quickly gathered my things, and took me to my paternal grandmother's house. Her name was Mary Douglas, but they all called her "Ma Dear." My paternal grandfather, George, had died years earlier. Ma Dear introduced herself and told me to call her whatever I felt comfortable with. She seemed as warm to me and loving as if I were a long-lost child coming home. I asked her if I could call her "Momma Mary," and she agreed. I was to be the only one to call her that, which made it my personal name for her. I chose it because I called my other grandmother Maggie "Momma Mag."

One by one different family members came by to see me. Throughout the years, they had heard about William or Uncle William's oldest son, but now their eyes could actually see me. Momma Mary told me how they came to visit me in the hospital right after I was born and how they and my grandpa George held me in their hands. Younger cousins were fascinated by the unique way I was dressed and wanted to know how it was in California.

My father and Uncle Jimmy were not there when I had arrived, but finally they came home. Everybody started telling me how I looked more like Uncle Jimmy but had eyes like my dad. As the evening continued, I did my best not to use any foul language because I didn't want to spoil their joy. Their immediate love for me allowed me to come out of my shell and to begin talking.

My pop "Big William," (in later years)

Yet before long, Uncle Jimmy got on me about my boxer shorts hanging outside of my sagging pants and told me he wasn't going to have such a spectacle in his momma's house or around him, period. Normally I would have told him where he could go and would have dared him to put his hands on me. Still, I knew he was offering correction because he loved me, and so I obeyed him. I was just happy to have finally found my family after nearly eighteen years; it was the first time laying eyes on any of them. I immediately submitted to the authority of my grandmother Mary, my Aunt Bobbie, Uncle Cecil,

Uncle Jimmy, and, of course, my father. I wanted to be on my best behavior and leave a good impression.

At one point, my father had to run an errand and invited me to ride along with him. Going out to the car, deep inside me I didn't know whether to smile or shed a tear because I was finally alone with my daddy, a man I had longed to meet all my life. And now I was walking out to go for a ride with him, Mr. Douglas.

I quickly started asking him about his Vietnam experiences because I was in the presence of a military hero who just happened to be my dad. But in the course of our conversation, my pride entered. I wanted to get a certain point across, so I said, "Don't think that just because we just met, you think you can put your hands on me."

He got the point and replied, "I can dig that." I was highly impressed with how he handled it; he could have gotten defensive, but that would have blown straight up, and he would have lost me.

The more the conversation continued, the more I got to know the man. I realized my father was not only an intelligent individual, but he also knew the street game, having lived in Michigan for many years. That connected us even more. His war stories were very fascinating and his high school football exploits as well. These made him more human to me.

We went around to the family restaurant and a couple of other places, and he introduced me to various people. The first time he presented me as "Maurice," my middle name, the one my family called me. To be honest, that kind of hurt me because it seemed like he was embarrassed to say "my son." But he revised it by calling me his "oldest son" from then on without my having to confront him. Somehow I felt it as an adjustment for him too. When he asked me what I wanted to call him, I replied, "Let me call me you 'Pop' for now." He approved of that. I just didn't feel comfortable saying "Daddy" yet; it felt too "mushy" for me at the time, too intimate.

I agreed to stay with my grandmother, Momma Mary. Each day she fixed me breakfast, gave me spending money, and enjoyed so much being around me. At the beginning, I kept comparing her to my grandmother who raised me at first, Momma Mag. But soon I felt that was unfair and decided to just enjoy her love for me and to return her love by obeying her authority.

Without question, this was a weird time for me because I had to alter my life. Though I couldn't communicate emotional things constructively, I did try to talk. I didn't have anything in common with them because all I knew was a gangster's world, and that made it hard to find topics of conversation. But my family gave me so much attention, the questions never ceased to come; and if I wasn't helping around the house, my father and Uncle Jimmy would lovingly get on me. Momma Mary just wanted to spoil me.

My stepmother Louise, however, was not too talkative toward me. She wasn't easy to figure out; and to me, she seemed uninterested in pursuing a relationship. So I went with the flow and gave her respect because she was my dad's wife. I figured maybe she felt uncomfortable being around me because of the situation between her and my mom—who had both been pregnant by my father at the same time.

I did ask my dad about that, and he assured me it had not been the case. He did his best to protect both of us, to keep things from becoming sour before knowing the truth. Eventually she came around and persuaded me that she had nothing against me. The situation was just awkward and was an adjustment type thing. I trusted her word, and she became a loving stepmom to me.

The time came when I got to visit my sisters that I hadn't seen in about four or five years. Poppa Kimbrough had already died years earlier, but Momma Rena and her son Donny, who was mentally retarded, were still alive and well. Donny was like our big brother, and he used to hold me like a baby when I was small. And I just loved him.

My baby sister Tonya was excited to see me and ran out to meet me when my cousin and I drove up. But my sister Charmaine, who was sitting on the front porch with our childhood friend Gail, said a half-hearted "Hi, when did you get in town?" After I gave my answer, she got up and left as if she had seen me every day.

In truth, Charmaine had a lot of anger toward our mom for taking me to California to live while leaving them in Pine Bluff. In a way, she saw me as the beneficiary of our mother's love and not them, so she directed some of that bitterness toward me, I believe.

I later had the chance to visit my grandmother, Momma Mag, in the senior citizen home. She and I reminisced about the past and laughed like we did when I lived with her. I managed to keep my gang life away from her but felt bad to hide the person I had become.

During that month I was there, I was able to spend some quality time with her; and on one occasion, she indicated it would be the last. She was anxious to see my mom, her youngest child. My grandmother asked me to encourage her to come and visit because she felt like she wasn't going to be alive around the same time the following year. I asked her respectfully not to talk like that.

There was a phone by her bed where she lived, and right away I called my mom collect so she could speak with her mother herself. My grandma restated the same concerns she had shared with me, and my mother promised she would be there before next year.

My time in Arkansas was well spent. After our time together, my father, stepmother, and little sister Tia, all left to go back to Flint, Michigan. I headed for southern Cal in somewhat of a daze, wondering what had just happened. I departed from Pine Bluff feeling more complete, having come to know the man I had only heard about all my life. And in a way, I left there finding a piece of me.

I would stay in contact with him and my family, especially my grandmother, Mary Douglas. She had become the loving hen I had longed for since leaving the grandmother who raised me. The only downfall was that we were separated by many miles, and no way was I going to move to Arkansas.

Chapter Thirteen

You might expect that after such an experience, an important change would occur in my life. I imagine my mother was hoping for that; I'm sure she wanted me to stay down there. But that wasn't going to happen. I jumped right back in the thick of things, missing it all for a month. Edward and Mousey came over as soon as they found out I was home. They couldn't wait to see me, and I couldn't wait to see them.

Edward had already begun to distance himself from gang banging somewhat because he had gotten involved with my friend Albert's sister, Mary Ann. It felt like she was coming between us and taking my brother away from me even though that was not actually the case. It was just that we had not been separated from one another since we were kids. He was the brother I had always needed, so I harbored a bit of anger toward Mary Ann for a while.

But that brought Mousey and me closer. He was quickly becoming the little brother I never had. In those days Mousey and I would spend more time over in Mona Park Crip territory, representing Grape. He also introduced me to more 7th St. Watts Crips. Around this time, PJ and MPC weren't getting along. The mistrust between them was probably worse than ever.

My long-time friends Herbert ("Chico") and his brother Tim ("Wizard") had become Mona Park Crips after moving over there from the PJs years earlier. Then they moved near the JDs and sometimes had to walk through the PJs just to get back to Mona Park hood.

I saw them going home one day and went to chat with them

for a minute. They were kind of hesitant to stop and talk, not knowing what would happen if any PJs saw them. So I decided to walk with them until they got past the PJs.

But somebody had spotted them, and about five or six PJs came running toward us. I told Chico and Wizard to let me do the talking. When they reached us, they kind of looked surprised because we hadn't run. I told them my friends were with me and nothing was going to happen to them.

The PJs and I went at it back and forth, jawing at one another. And at one point, I stood nearly nose-to-nose with one in particular that I'd had a run in with before. Beyond that, nothing took place. But I wasn't going to let my homeboys go down alone. Point black!

Around 1983 and 1984, the cocaine factor took off in the streets. Sherm was still huge; but the "white horse," as we called it, was becoming more and more available whereas in the past it had always been dubbed a "rich man's drug."

I sold sherm here and there; it was a thin brown cigarette called Sherman, dipped in a liquid and potent chemical (PCP). When smoked, it could put you in a zombie-like state. In many cases, you would walk in a sort of crawl, in an almost slow-motion type movement. People have been known to strip nude and climb telephone poles or trees or just walk around aimlessly. I'm not sure if it made their bodies extremely hot or what. I guess it just depended on the person.

My first encounter with it was when I was twelve years old, and some of the older homeboys from Grape slipped some on me, after having dipped a joint in it and not telling me what they had done. But that isolated experience was enough to convince me that it wasn't for me.

Getting into the dope game never really appealed to me. I would step in for a little while, make enough to buy what I wanted, and then pull out. Still, I did learn how to play the game and the rules that came with it.

At certain times when Edward and I were broke, we would come up with a dime to buy some Alexander the Grape candies. We would suck them down to the whites, rub them in baking soda, and then sell them off in the night to crack heads. But the danger was that people could get killed for doing stuff like that if they were caught by the cocaine addicts. Edward and I would pull this off at times, just for quick money. You could say that it was a law of the jungle; it was called survival.

Sometime after my eighteenth birthday, I became totally bored with school. I got tired of having to get up in the mornings, wash my face, comb my hair, and get dressed to go to a place I was convinced would never benefit me. I was in my third year of the tenth grade, and I was annoyed by going just to please my mother. So I dropped out even though I knew it would mean losing a monthly check from the government. The check was not my mother's reason for wanting me to go to school; she really wanted me to succeed.

My mother was very hurt by my choice to drop out of school. She had hoped to see me experience a prom and graduation and all that stuff—which meant nothing to me, absolutely zilch. Embarrassment played a small part in my decision, too, because my classmates from elementary and junior high on up went on to graduate—well, most of them—and it made me feel dumb. So I had to reject those feelings.

Something happened that year that kind of hurt me, but I understood why it happened. My mother tried to have male friends, but I wouldn't accept them—except one, Alvin Green. He was all right.

But I did not trust the others and hoped for the chance to punish them if necessary. That didn't work out either.

A bit later my mother met a guy named Bernard Chappell. I had not seen him until some time after they started dating. He was pretty cool, but I had never communicated that to him or my mom. I did not trust men with my mother because I knew how guys thought. And I felt that hell would freeze over before I'd let a man take advantage of her. But it was something about Bernard that I liked.

One weekend, the two of them and Aunt Peg and I believe my older cousin Evelyn left without telling me. It didn't really bother me because it meant I didn't have to explain my business either. When they got back, they told me that Momma and Bernard had gotten married. My mother did not break the news to me for whatever reason; the others had to tell me. I guess she thought I was going to throw a fit. But I did have mixed emotions.

I felt disappointed because I wasn't given the choice to be a part of the wedding or not. On the other hand, I was happy for the two of them. I later told them that. Unfortunately and for whatever reason, the two did not move in together. It would begin a year-long phone relationship with an occasional visit. I'm not sure if my mother's guard was fully down yet which led to the immediate separation.

For me, life went on as usual. My homeboy Patmite and I started going to Lynwood a lot, representing Grape and PJs. Patmite and I had been friends since I first moved to L.A. when I was eight and he was six or seven. As we got older, I turned Grape and he became a PJ; but the gang stuff never came between us. Actually, Grape and PJ in some way were like cousins who fought a lot but who had cooling down periods as well. There were those whose friendships never took a back seat to anything; we were all Crips. And Patmite was one of them who did not allow outside influences to come between us.

On one particular night Patmite and I had walked to Lynwood and decided to go to the bowling alley where those Neighborhood Crips hung out. I had told Patmite how much NHCs respected Watts, particularly Grape. Patmite took on the chore of trying to win the respect for PJ.

That night we met a very pretty girl there. So Patmite and I decided to put the mack down on her. After we worked to get her comfortable with us, she told us that she had run away from home and did not have a place to stay.

Her name was Tameka. We called her 'Meka for short. It was decided that she would come home with us. Patmite did not have the room, so I took her into my home. We got back around 2:00 in the morning. She was hungry, so I fixed her a hamburger. I then gave 'Meka one of my t-shirts to put on and then put her to bed. I put the covers over her, and I slept on the top.

I did not touch her that night because I wanted to win her trust by making her feel safe. I wondered how I was going to explain that to my mother in the morning. So I slept on it and figured I'd deal with whatever was necessary the next day.

Momma was not too excited about my bringing a runaway into our house. But she reluctantly let her stay with us about three months. The girl had been a virgin before she met me, but that would end.

I soon gave my homeboys Randall, Edward, and Tap a chance at her. My homeboy Craig and I came up with the idea to prostitute her. Craig had the car and guns, and I had the influence over her to pull it off. I called 'Meka inside one day and asked how she would pay me back if I decided to collect payment for all I had done for her. She said, "I would pay you back when I get a job." But I replied, "What if I asked for payment today? How would you pay me?"

Craig and I proceeded to pressure her relentlessly. Finally, she broke and submitted to our will. We told her the plan, and she sadly agreed. Craig and I were proud of the power we had just displayed.

But later on, my heart was moved with remorse over what I had done. Delores had been the only girl I had come to love and respect; but now it was as though scales had fallen from my eyes, and I saw 'Meka the person—the scared daughter of two parents who loved their child and wanted her home.

I met with Craig and announced that we weren't going to make her sell herself for us. He respected me enough not to argue with me and agreed. I got alone with Tameka somewhere in the house and apologized for treating her the way I had and for not protecting her. She forgave me, and our relationship changed.

No longer did I allow any guy to pursue her, and I never touched her again. She had become like a family member. Eventually, I persuaded her to start contacting her parents and letting them know she was all right. I later sent her home with money in her pocket and a few nice clothes. By the end of the three months or so, she had become more like a sister to me. Years later I would see her again, only to watch her run into my arms and give me the warmest hug. And I again apologized.

One particular day in 1983, I woke up to the sound of my mother's voice. She was on the phone with her husband Bernard, and the two were talking about making their marriage work. Bernard had served a number of years in the military and was planning to get a G.I. loan, buy my mother a brand new brick home, and get us out of the projects. That probably wouldn't have worked for me but definitely would for them.

My mother called me into the room, saying, "Bernard wants to talk to you." He wanted to know what I thought about the idea of them finally moving together and him buying her a home of her own. I was very excited for her, and to see the glow on my mom's face as I was talking to him was priceless. The day got off to a good start for her; but unfortunately, it wouldn't end that way.

Later that evening, Bernard was at home reclining in his apartment, when an intruder entered the apartment, robbed him, and shot him to death. That was probably the saddest day of my mom's life that I had ever seen.

In April of 1984, we got news from Arkansas that my Auntie Faye, who had been battling alcohol abuse, had died of corrosion of the liver. Her oldest child and only son, Andie, whom we called "Maine," was at home with her after her release from the hospital to spend her remaining days with her family.

He had been preparing to go to a party one night when his mother intervened and asked him to stay with her in case she needed him. Reluctantly, pouting, he agreed—at least until she went to sleep. Maine later slipped out of his bedroom window and went to the party after all. When he came back early that next morning, he crept in her bedroom to check on her. At once he noticed she looked odd. Fear seeped into his heart as he checked her pulse; and to his horror, he discovered his mother was dead. He immediately blamed himself for not being there for her and being the "cause" of her death.

Aunt Faye and my mom, who were sisters-in-law, were very close and had done many things together. The death also crushed my mother, who did not have a chance to ever see her again.

Having dropped out of school, I was loaded with time on my hands. I found myself sitting around watching "All My Children," "One Life to Live," and "General Hospital." After about a month of that, I realized that I was getting frustrated because they left you hanging a lot, making you feel like you had to be around the next day to find out what Erica was going to do or whatever. I finally decided it was time to cut away from Luke and Laura. It was becoming an addiction.

Financially, it was not easy. I only had two choices: to wait around until the first of the month for a county check or to rob or sell dope to get by. Unfortunately, I often chose the latter. We went on a string of "jackings" (robberies) one time. It didn't matter too much whom we robbed as long as it wasn't an elderly person or a child. I loved to knock out crack heads and winos just to get the change to buy beer and a burger or something.

I had many chances to sell drugs for my older homeboys, who were called "High Rollers" or hustlers. Sometimes I would get some work from them—enough to make a quick two or three hundred dollars—but then get back out of the game. Jacking drug addicts was easy because they were just as criminal as you were, so you didn't have to worry about their snitching on you. The only time you got nervous was if they came back and tried to kill you.

By this time in my life, my heart was quickly becoming like stone, not caring about much except Grape. I had strayed so far from the acknowledgement of God that I really didn't care whether He was out there somewhere or not so long as He didn't try to control my life.

But occasionally, God would find a way to whisper, *"Eric, I'm still watching over you."* On one such occasion, He tried to get my attention again. My homeboy Taco had allegedly killed Bounty Hunter T.C., the founder of Lot Boys, the money-makers within BH. I had just seen Taco earlier that day.

That night, in retaliation, about four Bounty Hunters would make their strike. I was at home in the PJs that evening, watching the guys in the gym playing basketball. At that time I hated sports, with the exception of boxing and martial arts because those two were about inflicting pain.

I had been smoking marijuana and had a slight buzz and was

tripping off the guys' playing basketball. I heard somebody murmur, "Leave." I didn't pay it too much attention and continued to watch the game. But the voice continued. I glimpsed around to see if somebody was talking to me but saw no one. So I blew it off again. The more I ignored the command to "Leave the gym," the more this voice applied the pressure.

At first I thought it was the marijuana talking; but soon I became paranoid and actually did get out of there. The pressure let up only after I had obeyed the strange and unknown voice. Then, once I got across the street, I heard a bunch of footsteps rumbling from around the gym. I turned to see what looked like four guys running in there with weapons, a single light above the entrance illuminating their silhouettes.

I could hear them from across the street, "Where them Grape Street niggas at, Blood?! Tell them niggas they go pay!!" Nothing happened. No gun shots, just silence. They started to exit the gym. As they were leaving, a certain guy, that I'll call "Chris," was walking toward the front entrance. They met him at the door. With guns drawn, they started demanding to know if he was from Grape. Chris said something to the effect, "I ain't about all that stuff. I'm a family man, just trying to have something in life." And he was telling the truth.

I thought I recognized one of the voices questioning him; it sounded like T.C.'s younger brother Norman, a guy I knew from Markham Jr. High. But I couldn't be absolutely sure. I was beside a bungalow in front of my apartment building on the side of the parking lot, so I could hear what was being said fairly well; and since it was dark, I was not seen.

I was straining to figure out what to do and how I could help Chris. I didn't have any guns in the house, so I felt helpless to do anything. All I could do was stand there and watch what was about to happen. I was hoping they would let him go since he didn't appear to be a gang banger. Suddenly, one of the bloods decided that he should die. What seemed like a shotgun went off as a blast of fire exploded from the gun barrel. Chris dropped to the ground, and the guys took off in the direction they'd come from. It took the ambulance what seemed like a century to get there—which infuriated and frustrated the PJs. Chris was later pronounced dead in the ambulance.

Things got hot around Watts after that, and it became a huge issue between Grape and PJ. Why they came in the PJs and killed an innocent guy, I'll never know. It was an issue that had to be worked out between Grape and PJ.

But in considering the event, I realized that if I would've continued to ignore that mysterious voice telling me to leave, in another two minutes I would've probably met the Bounty Hunters at the door. And knowing who I was, they would have unloaded their guns into me on the spot.

Problems between Grape and PJ were always up and down. But I refused to be intimidated. One day Wanky, Tap, and I were hanging out at my house; and understanding the tension between Grape and PJ, we decided to walk over to the Mona Park hood to buy a dime ($10.00) bag of Red Head Sess (a brand of marijuana).

We smoked a couple of joints on the way back and had a buzz. That made us hungry. When we got back to the PJs, we thought of buying some snacks at a candy house. The Martins had a candy store on the inside of their apartment.

Wanky, Tap, and I chose some Welch's Grape Soda, just to rub it in. Once we came out, some PJs were waiting for us out front. They started talking trash and asking us what we were doing in the PJs. Of course, we didn't just stand there and take it: we started talking back and letting them know where we were coming from.

After a few minutes, Maniac pulled out a gun, threatening to shoot us. One of the others swung on Wanky, and another started swinging on Tap. The four started scrapping. Meanwhile, Maniac turned toward me. Wanky yelled, "Let's bail, Cuzz!" Immediately, we took off in separate directions. Maniac chased me, probably twenty feet behind, and fired a couple of shots at me. It was a weird feeling to have bullets flying past, not knowing if I was going to catch one to the back of the head or not—in total suspense.

I made a sudden turn around a building; and by now I was losing wind, causing me to become disoriented. I tripped over a patch of grass or something and fell forward, rolling over onto my back. When I glanced upward, Maniac was standing over me with the gun pointing toward my head.

Just then, the L.A.P.D. was ripping around the corner with their spotlight searching. Maniac took off at once. I lay flat on the ground, hoping not to be seen by the cops. I could have easily flagged them down and told them that Maniac was trying to kill me, even to point them in his direction. But that was out of the question. A guy always understood from the streets and as a gang banger that it was better to seek revenge than to snitch. That wasn't even in my DNA, if you will.

When "One Time" (the police) passed by, I got up and left. I later ran into Wanky, only to find out that he had gotten away, rushed to my house, and gotten a seven shooter riot pump that I had upstairs in my bedroom closet.

He had found a pack of PJs gambling or something and shot into the crowd from a distance. The pellets from the shotgun shells flared out, sticking to several of them. One in particular was hit in the neck with some. We found out later that one of them was O'G Big Ken.

I had gotten the gun from Wanky and saw one of them in front of the gym. I ran toward him, and he took off. Before I realized it, the L.A.P.D. was circling back around, and I managed to get away without being noticed.

Wanky and I ran over to my cousin Lisa's house, where Wanky had been trying to talk to her, and her daddy Jerome gave us a ride to the Jordan Downs. I was sorry for bringing that tension to them because I certainly didn't want Lisa and Shanta or any of them to get mixed up in all that. But I had no choice. Lisa's mom Aunt Carolyn got on me, but she wanted me safe too.

It took a couple of weeks before things cooled down. Wanky was man enough to seek out Big Ken and apologize, not realizing he was in the crowd that night. Tap had made it out okay. We were not able to communicate after we split up, so it was great to learn he too had managed to escape with his life. I was able to go back home after a few weeks.

Chapter Fourteen

On June 2, 1984, I was upstairs in my room smoking weed with my homeboys Mousey, Randall, and my cousin Wally, when I heard someone banging on the door. I went to the rest room to look out the window and saw that it was my little cousin, Bootsie. From the look on her face, without her saying a word, I understood and murmured, "It's my grandmother, huh?" She said, "She just died." I couldn't help but remember what my grandmother had confided the year before, "I don't think I'm gonna be around this time next year." It was true.

God gave her that impression I assume, and she did die. I went back to the room in an almost dazed-like state. I sat on the edge of my bed, numb. I expected myself to cry but found I couldn't. My homeboys expressed their condolences, knowing how much I loved my grandmother.

I kept trying to recall moments we shared together when I lived with her. Feelings would begin to rise; but when they got up to a certain point, they would shut off. I felt so guilty because I thought crying is what normal people did. Finally, I gave up and went back to smoking the "blunts" (weed) and drinking the Olde English 800.

Momma didn't have money to pay for our bus fare to Arkansas, and we didn't have a lot of time to get there. I began to consider pulling some robberies to come up with the money; but out of nowhere, a check came in the mail for about $1,800.00. That was money credited to God for coming through.

At last, we got down there, and Momma went right to work getting all the funeral arrangements ready. While we were in town, I took in some sites, going by my old elementary school, First Ward, and visiting different relatives, including my cousin, Maine, whose mother had died a couple of months earlier, my Aunt Faye.

Maine had still been struggling with his guilt over sneaking out to the party instead of staying with his mom, who died while he was gone. Nothing seemed to fill the void or cover the pain, and he showed that through the growing problems in his life.

We hadn't been together since our grandmother's breast surgery four or five years earlier. He was very happy to see me, and I felt the same way. He described the night my auntie died and how that made him feel about himself. During that conversation, he began to express his interest in going back to Los Angeles with us.

Many family members had gathered for my grandmother's funeral. Some of these I was meeting for the first time, including my little cousin Kevin Williams, who would later play professional football as a defensive tackle with the Minnesota Vikings. It was great seeing different family members whom I had not seen since I was a child, such as my older cousins Jesse Owens, Exibe, and many others.

During the funeral, I kept trying to express grief or manage a few tears, but I couldn't; the feelings would just not come up. I wanted to cry so badly, but it was elusive. I kept thinking something was wrong with me. This was the one person who I knew had loved me and cried for me, and now I couldn't do the same for her. There I was—living my life to be loyal to my homeboys and to Grape, yet I couldn't shed a tear for my grandma.

At one point I left the grave site and walked deep into the cemetery to get away from all distractions so I could think about moments of the past, but I couldn't. Frustrated, I figured there had to be some way I could show my feelings. Oddly, at that moment I remembered how she used to try to get me to eat greens, but I would always turn my head or spit them out. So I decided I would dedicate myself from now on to eating greens just for her. And the rest is history on that point: I grew to love them.

Maine's guardian, his auntie, allowed him to go back with us to L.A., which excited both of us. It was fun to watch his reactions as we entered into the city limits; his marveling reminded me of my similar reactions when I had first left Arkansas.

I took it upon myself to instruct him in what I had learned

about what not to wear in certain neighborhoods and what not to say or do. I advised him not to act like he was too tough because that wasn't going to work in L.A.

Andre (Maine) was pretty humble about it all and listened to me carefully. I promised I would teach him the game and would back him up till the death, if necessary. Without heaping too much pressure on him, I asked if he wanted to be put in Grape. He said, "yes."

Randall, Mousey, and I initiated him in. I told the guys not to show us any preferential treatment but to lay it on him because he had to see how things worked in L.A. All three of us rushed him in my room for maybe thirty seconds or so.

When we finished, he was red all over; but he took it. I gave him the nick-name "Romeo" because he had been very popular among the girls in Pine Bluff, and I thought that would fit his persona.

Soon we took Romeo out on some jackings. I showed him what it was like to knock someone unconscious: we went to Lynwood one day, and I walked up to a random man and asked him what time it was. When he glanced down to look at his watch, I hit him with a solid right hand underneath the chin just as he was bringing his head back upright, causing him to go to sleep before he hit the ground. I then dug in his pocket, took out his wallet, and checked it for money. All he had on him were a few dollars.

Romeo absolutely tripped out! "Oh, man!" he exclaimed. "You knocked him out, Clipper! You knocked him out!" I put the wallet on top of the man, and we left. Mousey, Randall, and I were knocking all kinds of people out in those days.

Similarly, Edward and I were on the way to Lynwood one afternoon, and another random guy was coming toward us on a 10-speed bicycle. As he approached, we looked at each other and understood exactly what we both were thinking. When the guy got about fifteen feet away, I asked him if he had the time. He responded right away; but once he got about a foot or two from us, I fired on him in the mouth, causing him to fall backwards off the bike. We heard his body slap the pavement.

His front tooth had dug into my middle knuckle, and it started to bleed and swell. We jumped on the bike and rode to Lynwood with me on the handlebars in increasing pain. It got so intense I could no longer take it, so I asked Edward to head back to the projects.

That evening my right hand was terribly swollen, and the pain was almost unbearable. I don't think I slept that whole night but tossed and turned with only one thought: I wished I hadn't knocked that man out. The next day I had to get a tetanus shot at the doctor's office.

We took Romeo out one day to pull a jack and to test his knock-out power. An unwitting guy was walking along the tracks when we spotted him. He must have suspected something from us because he appeared nervous. We told Romeo to go over and knock him out. Complying, he reached the guy and swung, hitting him in the face.

The man seemed shaken by what had just happened but was unfazed as far as the effect. All of us started swinging at him. He was about 6'3" and 250 pounds with a head as hard as a brick. He was knocked back and forward but would not go down. At that point we noticed he was high off PCP from the smell of sherm on him.

We finally let him go, bloodied and all. Still, we were amazed by our inability to bring him down. He was kind of off that "live" as we called it, and it usually made people do strange things. Sherm would cause people to have almost super-human strength. It reminded me of the case of an older friend who was one of the original Crips back when it started.

Larry had many problems and had become a sherm addict. One day he was so high that he was trying to resist arrest. By the time he was finally taken down, five or six L.A.P.D. officers were on the scene, trying to get him on the ground in order to cuff him. So when I smelled sherm on the guy we were trying to knock out, it didn't surprise me that he had resisted us so well.

Romeo was beginning to catch on, but he was a little too gung ho, striving to become an O'G over night, if you will. At one point, I had to give him a heads up talk about not talking trash to people unless he was willing to back it up. He had been riding off my name; people learned that he was my cousin and were giving him a measure of respect for that.

But one day, Fisher from the PJs decided to test his heart. That guy was known for being a big trash-talker and would talk you out of your skin if you'd let him. Day after day he would challenge Romeo to stand up to him. This was the first time he'd been challenged in L.A., and he was up against a whole other breed of people; he was no longer in Arkansas, and he would be reminded of that.

Romeo, who was usually the one most eager to speak, did not want to talk back to Fisher; he kept insisting that he didn't want to fight him. But Fisher strode up to Romeo, instructing him to stand still so he could knock him out. He had Romeo scared to death, so my cousin started walking fast toward Aunt Peg's house.

Fisher was bold enough that he came inside the doorway after Romeo. At that point, he was scaring my little cousins, Sharon, Michelle, Gloria, Nicki, and little Fred. I stepped in and told Fisher, "You better get the hell out of my auntie's house, or I'm gonna have something to say." He complied, while still talking trash and challenging Romeo to "fight like a man."

Finally, I got tired of hearing his mouth, so I urged Romeo to "fight that nigga, Cuzz! Show him what that Grape like!" Randall was encouraging him the same way. I got just inches from Romeo's face and told him either to fight the guy now or keep letting Fisher punk him. Romeo finally agreed, much to Fisher's delight.

By this time, Fisher had managed to push back into the house. He took the first swing at Romeo. I'm not sure if he landed the punch, but that was enough to finally get Romeo into it. He started swinging back, and at a certain point he just seemed to say, *"Forget it! Whatever happens, happens."*

By the time we finally broke them up, my cousin was earning his respect from Fish. Of course, my auntie's house was kind of banged up, but we cleaned things quickly while laughing and celebrating Romeo's apparent victory. And from that day on, Fisher never tried to punk Romeo again.

That fight seemed to light a fire in Romeo because he began to show his heart in expanding ways. He was no longer easily intimidated, either. When people talked trash to him, he was more willing to talk trash right back to them.

People began to notice that and gave him a little more respect— so much so, in fact, that a particular guy I knew offered to give him some marijuana to sell. He told Romeo to return a certain amount back, and he could keep the rest. We were expecting it to be around a pound of weed or something, but he came back a couple of days later with a 40 gallon Hefty trash bag filled up with red head sess.

Randall, Mousey, and I suggested that Romeo sell joints as opposed to nickel and dime bags because he would get more money out of it. He asked us to help him roll the joints and sell them, and we did. I remember one day we bought a bunch of zigzag papers and rolled a good two to three hundred joints and sold them in a couple days. And that didn't even begin to scratch the surface of what we had.

Pretty soon Romeo decided to forget it. He said, "Screw that nigga! I'm keeping everything. We go get high!" That was cool with us; all of us copped (took on) the same attitude. When it came time for the guy to pick up his share of the money, we wondered what Romeo was going to do, whether or not he was going to stick with his word.

They guy came over, and he and Romeo went to talk in private. Romeo announced, "Cuzz, I decided to keep everything. I ain't got nothing for you." The guy tripped out. He couldn't understand why Romeo had betrayed him like that. Romeo basically laughed in his face and dismissed him, and the three of us stood stiffly behind Romeo, no matter the cost.

We were getting to the point where we felt invincible. Romeo proved to us that he was in it for the long haul, having basically punked a guy who had been in the game for years. He had come a long way in such a short time.

At that point, the four of us made a vow to one another that no one was going to cross us and get away with it. We promised on our lives that we would back each other up even to the point of death—and we meant it.

Randall, Romeo, and me

People began to take note of that, particularly in the PJs. Girls began to want to be with us, and my bedroom was always a meeting place to hang out, smoke weed, listen to Motown oldies, and just to pass time. Even certain PJs began to hang with us, especially my homeboy Patmite, who was always welcomed in our circle.

We began to go out more to Lynwood and other places just to pull off robberies or to represent Grape. If some PJs came along, we would express Watts to the fullest. I felt like Grape needed to be displayed more outside Watts.

House parties were always a magnet to us, particularly in Lynwood or Compton. We loved representing in the parties, "Chitty, Chitty, bang, bang. Nothin' but that Crip thang." I can't describe force-fully enough the power that we felt with one another. Even Mousey had come a long way; his confidence level had reached new heights, and he had developed knockout power.

Edward was not around us as much as before because his life had taken on responsibilities: he was beginning a family of his own. As I mentioned, I had been kind of jealous toward Mary Ann, his girl-friend, because I had a weird notion that she was taking away the only brother I had known, which wasn't actually the case in reality.

Edward (in much later years)

Still, he would always find time to break away to be with me and the homeys, and we would pull off the same stunts as in earlier times. He would just as well represent Grape. I loved those times when he would make time to hang out with me.

I was living a suicidal life in a sense because I didn't care what the situation was or who I had to confront. I was determined to represent Grape to the max with no fear ever involved. In truth, loyalty to my homeboys meant more to me than life itself, so I was always ready to defend what I cared about.

Chapter Fifteen

At this time we decided to buy some buck knives just to carry with us in case somebody tried to cross the line. A movie called "Scarface" with Al Pacino came out, and everybody in the gangster world was going to see it. About eight to ten of us went to see it in Huntington Park, including PJ Patmite, Cancer, and Lizard.

The bus that travels straight to Huntington Park from the Imperial Courts was about a forty-five minute ride, and we had to go through a Blood territory to get there. The Pueblo Bishops hung out at a certain pool hall, or game room, on the corner of Florence and Mona Boulevard. Unfortunately, bus number 254 had to make a stop right there at the light in front of the pool hall. On the way to the movie, no one was hanging around there—a situation that was not normal. With relief, we went to the movie and had a good time; but on the way back, the place looked packed. Bloods were coming and going, sporting their predominant red colors.

We pulled up to the bus stop, which was on the same side of the street as the pool hall. The bus windows were tinted, so they were not able to see us. We were sitting there and checking them out, laughing because they had some Crips within fifteen feet of them and didn't even know it.

But Romeo decided to pull out his purple rag and hang it out the window, mocking them with, "What that Grape like, Cuzz?" A couple of them heard him and yelled into the small building that we were out there on the bus.

At this point our adrenaline was soaring; and we knew that

whatever happened, we had to survive as a unit. That was just automatic. Our homeboy Mousey told the bus driver to pull out, but the man was so scared that he couldn't move. Women and children were screaming and crying because by now twenty or thirty angry Bloods were struggling to leap on the bus. They were even trying to pry open the windows and were throwing trash cans, bricks, or whatever they could find to help them gain entrance.

A couple of us, including Edward, were stationed at both doors to prevent them from opening them up. One particular guy managed to get both hands between the parting doors and was trying to wrench them opened to the halfway point so they would open automatically the rest of the way.

Fortunately, I happened to notice him. I pulled out my buck knife—about a six inch blade—and thrust it into the back of his hands two or three times. Obviously surprised and in severe pain, he jerked his hands back as fast as he could with blood pouring from them. My thought process was—either him or us.

Mousey, Randall, and Patmite threatened the bus driver with some consequences if he didn't drive off, and the man finally shook off his paralysis and peeled out. I guess he had never encountered anything like that before and was frozen in fear. But we had to force him to act; otherwise we eventually would have been overtaken. And only God knows what the outcome would have been had they gotten onto the RTD bus.

When we got out of harm's way, we all relaxed and got some laughs out of it, especially because of Edward's sense of humor. We felt like we had scored a victory because we were cornered by Bloods—in a Blood neighborhood—and got out of it alive. All they received for their trouble were some cut up fingers and some taunts from Grape and PJ.

We also scored points with some PJs who were with us because they got to see us in action and, even more, our willingness to die for one another if necessary—even for them too, who were in our company. In fact, those who were with us never again fought us or joined their PJ homeboys against us. And that was huge.

In so many ways, we had kind of launched a campaign to win over the PJs, to get them to realize that Grape wasn't their enemy but that we weren't going to take anything off them or anyone else, either.

They also learned that if they were with us in whatever situation, we had their back to the fullest. And some came to trust that.

We were becoming friends with a number of PJs and were beginning to gain their respect and friendship. Despite my past problems with them personally, I wanted them to understand my intentions, namely that I would not treat them the way they treated me. Vengeance was not something I sought.

I once kept several of them from being shot by a homeboy of mine in the Jordan Downs when a couple of the PJs came through that territory on bikes. If I wouldn't have asked my homeboy to let them go, one or both would have been put to death, never even realizing from what direction they'd been shot. But I made sure that they and whoever else understood that those days of punking me were over.

As was my policy, I never would disrespect them if they were alone and I was in a pack of Grape Streets. I was always the same in the crowd and out of the crowd. They were beginning to come around to the fact that I was real in every sense of the word; there was no pretending in me.

One certain guy named Fred from the PJs had become real cool with us. We often kicked it together along with his brother Renzo. Fred was seeing a girl over by the Carver Park Crips' hood. He had been hanging out with her one evening when he decided it was time to go home.

Fred had ridden his bike over there, and it was a real clean one. Some of those CPCs saw him leaving and decided to put him to a test; they didn't recognize him from their hood and wanted to find out who he was. About three or four walked up to him and began to "sweat" (bother) him. Freddy informed them he was a PJ Watts Crip and they'd better back off.

Well, predictably, they ended up robbing him of his bike, which obviously made him mad. It always felt like I was being spit on—or something to that effect—when people would take something from me, and I related to that. Fred managed to walk away without any physical harm, but he was seriously offended.

It was about a mile and a half to reach the PJs. When he arrived, he tried to rally up some of his homeboys to return to the Carver Park Crips' hood with him to retrieve his bike but, even more than that, to get his respect and respect for the PJs.

He went around explaining what had happened to him, but nobody stepped up to the plate to help. Of course, that devastated Freddy. He simply couldn't believe the lack of support and started walking home disappointed. He lived in back of me; and Mousey, Randall, Romeo, and I just happened to be hanging out in front when he came by.

Freddy stopped and described how disappointed he was and was venting how, even if he had to go back over there himself, he was getting his bike. Without a second of hesitation, we stated that we would return with him. Mousey said, "Let's go get them niggas, Cuzz! They can't f--- with our homeboy Freddy! We from Watts." All of us fully committed ourselves on the spot.

We dressed up in dark colors. I think I had on some black Dickie khakis, a black sweatshirt, my black hard beanie, some black shoes, and a blue rag tied around my face. Freddy produced a couple of guns to take with us. The five of us crept back over there, down residential streets under the cover of the night.

When we arrived, we found a house party going on. Right across the street sat an elementary school with a wide open field directly in front of the house. Freddy and Mousey, I believe, went over by his girl's house where Fred remembered seeing the guy with his bike go inside. The rest of us stood about three hundred feet from where the party was being held. In addition to Freddy's guns, we also had a .25 automatic that we had gotten in exchange for some drugs. We saw people coming and going out of the party, and we yelled, "What that Grape like? What that PJ like, Cuzz?" as we represented Freddy, who had gone to look for his bike.

We fired a couple of shots in that direction but without hitting anybody, we believed. Immediately they came back blasting shotguns randomly into the area, not knowing where our shots were coming from. And because we were in dark colors under the night sky, they couldn't see us.

But because they had guns and were using them, we hurriedly decided to break up. We agreed to meet at a particular location. Romeo and Randall took off together, and I went by myself. Fortunately, we all managed to gather within an hour and a half.

Freddy and Mousey did get his bike back which had been our objective in the first place. Romeo and Randall came across some

CPCs and had to get out of that situation; meanwhile, I didn't encounter any problems and was able to get back to the PJs in safety.

The six of us celebrated for Freddy and were glad we were able to help him out. He exclaimed, "Cuzz, y'all helped me when my own homeboys didn't even help. I don't care what they say about y'all, y'all all right with me, and I'll go to bat with y'all anytime." We smoked a little weed, drank some 800, and left it at that.

Chapter Sixteen

Around this time, my mother began dating a guy who I thought was cool—at first. He had lived in Chicago and was pretty knowledgeable about the Black Panthers, the Black Stone Rangers, and the Mafia; so when he'd come over and I happened to be there, we would discuss these things that had always fascinated me. Their allure was mainly the reputation for power and evil these organizations held.

But after awhile, I began to notice a different side of David. He was a heavy drinker like my mom. By this time she had become an almost severe drinker, which made me ashamed on the one hand but served as a justification to not involve myself emotionally with family issues on the other.

The two would get drunk a lot, but she was always spending her money to support both their habits. This was quickly becoming a problem in our home, particularly every time David would come over. Behind the scenes, I think my mother was not only feeling guilty for not fulfilling my grandmother's request for her to come visit before her death, but she also had lost not only her best friend and sister-in-law a couple of months earlier but a husband who was murdered execution style a year before that in his own apartment. And to be honest, I was putting her through a lot of fear and stress myself. But now, David was beginning to make it all worse.

In August or September of that year, Uncle Charlie was killed in his home. We were all pretty close to him, and it was a shock for him to suddenly be gone. But as with the other deaths in the family, they were just passing tragedies that had no life-changing power over me.

I continued to live as I saw fit, and being able to control the outcome of events around me was incredibly important. My mother seemed to sink further down in her drinking. I would come home at night and sometimes find her and David flat out drunk with the front door unlocked, a serious lapse in such a dangerous environment.

I would mention to her it later, and she would mumble what she figured I wanted to hear. Yet I would come back another day to find the same thing again with both of them stretched out on the couch and loveseats, asleep. I began to see David as the problem and started holding him responsible for my mother's continuing decline.

David

Sometimes he would make me burning mad because he didn't seem to care how he was pulling her down. I noticed him beginning to show a pattern of using her to support his habit and how she would let him. I just couldn't understand that.

After awhile, I started getting in his face, stating that if he didn't get out of my mother's life, I was going to put a real hurting on him. But every time I would confront him, my mother would jump between us and order me to leave him alone. I'd tell her to screw him and herself and walk off.

I soon came to the conclusion that he was controlling her and I needed to remove him from the scene. I decided to set him up by pretending to like him, then get him out somewhere remote, put the gun to his head, and fire every available bullet into his skull. That's how much I had grown to hate the man. I made plans to do this along with Randall, Romeo, and Mousey. Randall got a gun for the job.

When it came time to do it, though, I got to thinking how it would damage my relationship with my mother forever, and this realization broke my will to do it. I didn't want to hurt her that badly, so I called it off. But my homeboys were more than willing to follow me at my word, and understanding that pleased me. David had no idea how close he came to dying, and I never told him.

Instead, in frustration, I chose to put up with him for the time being and to just keep an eye on him. But I had to get out of that emotional mode of caring about my mother's safety because I had begun to believe David would be the cause of her death. It was beginning to get in the way of my living.

I tried to remain detached, but it wasn't always easy. David soon moved in with us, and that made me want to stay home even more. But Randall and the guys found ways to tear me away from the house—which helped a lot. We would go to Lynwood quite a bit to find house parties or girls.

One particular girl named Tricia Ann (short for Patricia Ann), her sister, and some friends of theirs along with Mousey, Edward, and I had met in Lynwood one night; and we began to visit them frequently. Tricia Ann and her two sisters basically made their home open to us any time we were in the area.

Before long, Tricia Ann became very interested in me and had begun to claim me as her "boyfriend from Grape" before it was even official. Her mother was very nice, and I made the guys respect her even though my intentions were not always right.

One night we had determined to go over to their house before a planned party and hang out for a little while. We thought of getting a couple of 40 ounce bottles of Olde English 800 to drink while we waited for the party to get into the flow. But like many times in the past, we were not planning on spending any money to get them.

We had stolen from this particular store on a number of occasions and had intended on doing it this time as well. When we arrived, the idea was to spread out so the clerks couldn't keep an eye on all of us at the same time. One by one, each of us loaded up on 40 ounce beers, chips, cookies, wine coolers, and whatever else we wanted to take.

Each of us headed for the door. I was the last one, and the store manager and his young attendant figured on making an example of me, believing I would be weaker without the rest of my homeboys. I had about three bottles in my arms along with Oreo cookies, honey buns, and whatever else I craved.

They stopped me just as I was approaching the counter and accused us of stealing. I pretended to the best of my ability not to know my homeys. I said, "What you talking about? I don't know those niggas! I'm by myself. Y'all wanna act like that? I'll take my money and spend it somewhere else." I was putting up a big front at this point, but the manager wasn't buying it. The young guy was speechless.

The manager, who was Asian, said, "Put the stuff down! You're going to jail!" He ordered his employee to lock the doors. Before I knew it, he swung a golf club at me and scraped me across the lip. I happened to back up just in time to avoid anything worse. At this point I was filled with rage because he had tried to hit me. I dropped every thing I had, grabbed the man by the collar, and started punching him in the face. I must have hit him about five or six times, resulting in blood shooting out of his mouth. The other guy pulled out a .38 special and held it by his side; but he was frozen in fear, apparently too scared to use it.

I let the guy go and strode to the door, unlocking it with the key the attendant had left in the lock. I yanked it open while realizing this guy wouldn't have the heart to pull the trigger. I cracked an evil grin and told them to screw themselves, then left.

Our meeting place was over at my girl's house. When I arrived, Randall was the only one who had not returned, so we were getting ready to go back to search for him—when he came banging on the door. He was glad to see me and asked, "Clipper, what you do to that nigga? His whole face was all bloodied." Randall had gone back to look for me and peeked through the window. The guy was wiping his face with a towel that was soaked with blood. We got some laughs out of what had happened, drank our beer, and enjoyed the evening at my girl's house because the Lynwood sheriffs were looking for us after that. Once things cooled down, we went back to Watts where we belonged and called it a night.

That October, my young cousin Charlie Brown was gunned down in a drive-by shooting. It was a serious case of mistaken identity: some gang bangers from a particular set near his home thought he was someone else. Charlie Brown was a neat kid, never in any trouble as far as the streets were concerned. He simply caught someone else's bullets, ending his young life before it ever really got started. I think he was about fifteen at the time. He was the fourth family member who had died in six months and the fifth in a sixteen-month span, including my stepfather Bernard, who had been brutally murdered the year before.

It seemed like the death of such a young, innocent kid as Charlie Brown should have gotten my attention; but as with all the previous ones, I mourned silently for a moment and then continued my life as I had been doing. I was never taking into account that life is truly like a vapor, here for a while and then gone.

Still, I sensed that somehow my life was reaching a climax. I couldn't allow myself a pinch of fear; I desired, however, to be a leader by my actions. My stuttering condition would not let me lead verbally because that would demand a voice that spoke up, argued on behalf of what we believed, or asserted itself in the heat of a crowd. I couldn't compete with all that; but when I did speak, people knew I would back up what I said to the max.

So opening up my heart to anything other than Grape was a threat to what I regarded as my destiny, and that was to be the truest and the hardest Grape Street Watts Crip that I could be—at all costs. In other words, even the death of a loved one was not enough to awaken me to the truth.

We were beginning to pull off more and more jacks (robberies), and we never went without money and marijuana. Occasionally we would sell crack but very seldom. If we were really desperate for money, we could always go back to sucking the Lemon Heads and Alexander the Grapes down to the whites and selling them as "rocks" (crack) to those sprung out crack addicts. The problem with that scenario was that sometimes we might inadvertently mess with the wrong one, who would come back and try to kill us. Nevertheless, that was a part of the street game—called survival.

One evening, Randall and Romeo attempted to jack some crack heads for money, but I decided to stay in the house that night. Later that evening, Romeo came home scarred up with his shirt ripped in several places. He explained that he and Randall had tried to jack some crack heads in a van, guys who had come over to the PJs to buy some crack.

We had a .25 automatic that didn't work properly for whatever reason, but the two had taken it anyway to pull off some robberies. Romeo was carrying the gun and had pushed inside the van near the back and was demanding that they all empty the money from their pockets and purses.

The driver had the presence of mind to take off in the van. Randall jumped away as it peeled out to keep himself from being hit while Romeo fell backwards, dropping the gun. He had been standing up at the time.

The group consisted of four men, including the driver, and two women. As the guy behind the wheel floored it around the corner and down the street, Romeo—in the back fighting for his life—was up against these five people who were trying to beat him to death.

He managed to knock out a side window and force his way out of the vehicle, scraping different areas of his body as he was kicking off his attackers. The van was slowed by another driver, I believe, and was moving about twenty miles an hour when he jumped out in the middle of the street.

On another occasion, some crack heads pulled out a gun and started shooting at Romeo, Mousey, Randall, and a couple of PJs. Again, I happened not to be with them on that particular evening. Romeo had his shirt wide open while he was running and later realized he had a bullet hole in his shirt, missing his flesh by about six inches or so.

These two triumphant near-death events made my cousin somewhat prideful. He had begun to assume he was invincible. All of us felt that way to some degree, but he was starting to turn it against us. In a way, we felt a measure of pride that we were the ones who had shaped him into the gang banger he'd become. In truth, we rejoiced in how he'd turned out, but now he was using it against us—the very ones who would die for him and with him, if need be.

Romeo started testing us by trying to see if we were tough

enough to take him on. Mousey, Randall, Edward, Patmite, and I were beginning to get turned off by him, even refusing to fight him over stuff while he tried to provoke us.

I noticed my homeys were beginning to stop coming by the house because of Romeo. Yet since he was my cousin, living in my house and even staying in my room with me, I naturally took on the burden of trying to persuade him to back off. He tried to fight me at Aunt Peg's house, but all I did was walk away from him, went into the rest room, and considered how I should deal with him.

I just couldn't understand why he was turning on us; and it seemed no amount of talking would induce him to "raise up," to back off from his antics. One day over at Aunt Peg's, I had to get in his face aggressively. I said to him, "Romeo, you better raise up, Cuzz, before I put you on your Mother F------ back! Nigga, we made you! Don't come out here thinking you can run nothing. You gonna get f----- up, nigga!" He kept talking trash, but he stayed a comfortable distance from me.

Around this same period of time, another uncle had gotten killed: my mother's brother, Israel, whom I didn't know basically. My mother's drinking was at an all-time high. My older cousin Evelyn, whom we called "Elma," had moved in with us from Pine Bluff, Arkansas. She had taken in our step-grandfather after my grandmother Mag died in June of 1984, that same year. The two of them were living with us as well in a two bedroom apartment in the projects.

She didn't have a job yet, and my grandpa C.B.'s checks had not started arriving. So my mother had six people to feed, including herself. Romeo and I basically robbed, stole, or did whatever was necessary to survive; and this kept some of the weight off my mom. But now this new tension between me and Romeo was beginning to heat up.

The two of us got into a fight in my room that day because of how drastically he had changed in such a short time. Normally, we needed to be breaking up fights between Momma and Evelyn, who were quick to throw blows at one another, especially when they were drinking. Or it was my mother pulling butcher knives on David, trying to kill him.

But this time, it was Romeo and I causing the conflict. He swung on me and I went for him, holding nothing back. I dropped him onto the bed, but he bounced back upward and tried to bear hug me and slam me to the ground. I was stronger than he expected and ended up on top of him, getting ready to hit him in the face.

Just then my mother and Elma burst through the door after hearing furniture fall over and bodies slamming into the wall, and my mother ordered me not to lay a hand on him. I obeyed and got off from on top of him while talking trash as I got up. "I told you, Cuzz, to raise up!" He yelled back, "F--- you, nigga! Let's go for it again."

But somewhere in me, I remembered my love for my cousin. I had sensed the problem was something more than us, but I couldn't communicate emotional stuff very well. This fight was the culmination of all he had been acting out. A couple of days earlier, we had been in my room—Romeo, Randall, Mousey, and I—when he was in one of his moods; and I made the comment, "You act like you got death on you, Cuzz!" Romeo replied, "I do, nigga!"

I stated that because, when I connected with those feelings, I remembered I had a Bible that I'd gotten years earlier from Bible club with World Impact. I offered it to him, suggesting he find some help from God. What was his response? He grabbed it and threw it against the wall on the opposite side of the room.

That's when I said I thought he had death on him. Despite all the crazy things I had done, I still retained a measure of fear of God in me; otherwise I wouldn't have made such a statement. It was just eerie to see my cousin take God's Word and sling it up against the wall without fear or hesitation.

After our fight, I felt compelled to take the initiative in mending our relationship. At that moment I sensed he needed me more than ever. Even as I write this, tears are pushing into my eyes as I recall the scene. We forgave each other and hugged one another, promising never to fight again.

Romeo confessed that he regretted how he'd been treating us and that he was wrong to take out his feelings on us, his best friends. With a blast of emotion, he admitted he was sorry for leaving his mom to die alone just to go to a stupid party. He told me he was angry with himself and the world and life itself, not with God, and that he would step up to the plate and apologize to the homeboys, too. That day a new sense of love for one another began, and things were good within our circle from that day on.

Shortly after our incident, Romeo began to voice his desire to go see his sisters and my Uncle Floyd, his father, in Kansas City, Missouri. I didn't want him to leave, but he had set his heart on it. I had no choice but to support him to the fullest; we all felt that way, even to the point of pulling off a few jacks to get money to help with his ticket to Kansas City.

Romeo's last few days were spent saying goodbyes, smoking weed, and enjoying the company of Randall, Mousey, and me as well as the family. I got a ride for him to the AmTrak train station, and the two of us sat together in the waiting room until it was time to go. It was a sad day for both of us. Romeo was more to me than just a cousin, and on that day he seemed like my younger brother leaving home.

After Romeo's departure, life slowed down a lot. The four of us in particular were very close, so Romeo's absence left a big void within our circle. Personally, I didn't know if I had helped him or hurt him except that I did assist him in becoming street smart and courageous in the face of fear.

But after a couple of weeks, it was time to move on. We continued to go to Lynwood, Compton, and other places in L.A., representing Grape to the fullest. My mother and David continued to drink and live their lives, and my grandpa C.B. was becoming quite popular with many of the PJ Crips. He was just a lovable person. He would be full of beer and would try to talk like the younger guys. His favorite saying was, "Yo, freak!" When people would see him outside sitting in the yard, many of them would shout from across the street, "Yo, freak!" or "Yo, pop!" Watching him enjoy people who had been my enemies before seemed to break down old barriers quickly.

Chapter Seventeen

One day I woke up feeling very low in spirit, just gloomy inside. Throughout the day I would have weird mood swings: happy one moment and depressed the next. I wasn't hungry at all, and I couldn't explain why I was feeling the way I was. I hadn't taken any drugs or anything, so I had no answers.

Around 4:00 that afternoon, my mother, David, my cousin Evelyn, and some of their friends were hanging out in the living room drinking, laughing, and talking; and I came and sat down at the bottom of the stairs. I stayed there considering all they were chattering about, and I thought to myself, *"Is this all there is to life?"*

As time went on, I became more and more darkened in my spirit and suddenly felt out of place in life. I began to shout out to my mother, "Momma, we need to change! You hear me, Momma?" My pleas kept growing more intense, but I had no idea why I was feeling this way.

Around 6:30 one evening the phone rang. My cousin Evelyn answered it. Out of nowhere, she let out a loud scream, filled with grief. Momma asked, "What's wrong with you?" And she answered, "Maine is dead!" Romeo was gone.

As soon as I heard those words, the heaviness I had been feeling all day vanished. It was as if God had been using that bleakness to prepare me for the news of my cousin Romeo, almost as if He allowed me to feel the darkness that had been in Romeo all along. I have no way of proving that theory and will not even try. But as soon as I heard of Romeo's death, my focus immediately left myself.

What my grandmother's death and those of the other relatives had failed to do, Romeo's passing accomplished. His death shook me to the core, and it felt so close to home. I had not only spent almost every waking hour with him over the previous six months, but I was beginning to realize that I cared about my family. I began to wonder finally what was *going on* in my family: something was happening to us. Something wasn't right about it all, and I concluded that a very ugly pattern was taking place before my eyes.

Soon a panic began to set in, and I became afraid that the next one in our family to die would be me or, even worse, my mother. Of course, that drove me to take matters into my own hands; I set out to make some changes.

I wanted my mother to stop drinking because I didn't want her to die like my Aunt Faye, Romeo's mother, who was struck down because of alcohol. Every time I saw her drinking, I would insist that she needed to stop. I would not let up, and it began to irritate her a lot. The battles got to a point where she would yell out at me, "You can't tell me what to do! I'm your Momma. You just worry about your own drinking."

This control thing started to pour over into other areas as well. Abruptly, I realized that kids shouldn't be sassing their parents. This was limited to my family, of course. My cousin Michelle rolled her eyes at her mother one day, and that didn't sit well with me. I told her not to do it again. Naturally, that caused a reaction from her, which didn't sit well with me either. I advised her if she got mouthy with me once more, I was gong to slap her. She started asserting that I wasn't her daddy and I needed to shut my mouth. So I slapped her.

That upset her even more, so she ran off to get a butcher knife and threatened to kill me. I felt the anger rise because my life was in danger. I swept up on her aggressively to take the knife out of her hand, but she rushed toward me in the direction of my heart. I grabbed the weapon with my left hand; then she yanked it back, cutting my palm and finger in the process. I stayed with it and finally wrenched it from her grip. She looked both scared and shocked, not knowing what I was going to do next.

I gazed at her with compassion, then turned, walked into the kitchen, and set the knife down in the sink. I loved my cousin and was just trying to teach her to not disrespect her mom as she had done. I didn't hold the incident against her and ended it right there.

In short, my attention was beginning to turn more to family and less to the gang life I had known for nearly eight years. I found myself staying at home more often, mainly to keep an eye on my mom in case David tried to hurt her. Their drinking grew worse and worse. It seemed like the more I tried to control the situation, the more treacherous it appeared to get.

I blamed David for coming into my mother's life and dragging her down to what had to be the worst period of drinking binges I had ever seen. A part of me wanted to murder him, but hurting my mother was a more dreadful consequence.

My homeboys Edward, Randall, Mousey, and Patmite noticed the growing stress on me more than others did because they spent more time with me and around my family. Occasionally, I would go to the JDs to hang out with Wanky, Tank, Puncho, and the other homeboys just to get away from the family issues.

I continued to live a gang banger's lifestyle—smoking weed, drinking 40s, going to house parties, hustling now and then—but something was wrong with me inside. The passion and the wholeheartedness just wasn't there like it had been. These things were beginning to lose their meaning.

Soon I began to ask questions from those around such as my cousins Wallace and Hub and others; but no one gave the answers I needed to hear. In fact, some of them thought I was crazy. My cousin Hub told me I was "talking in circles" and going nowhere. In some ways he was right. I didn't even know what I was asking or what I truly needed to know. I was wanting people to make sense of my life because it was coming apart.

As time went on, I started spending a lot of time in my room, not wanting to do anything with my homeboys—or anything period. It wasn't that I didn't want to be with them, but the ideals and interests we once had in common were collapsing around me. I was not finding any answers to the strangeness I was now feeling inside.

The longer my questions went unanswered, the more frustrated I became. The one person who should have rescued me seemed to be at a loss herself; my mother could not give me the solutions I needed. I felt she couldn't even help herself. In fact, she thought I was beginning to lose it too.

At times I would feel a desperate urge to force her to quit drinking beer. I remember one day coming home: my mother, David, and several of their friends were spread out in the living room with beer cans everywhere. Our rent was due, and I had heard her complaining earlier about not having money to pay for it. At that moment David asked her to give him some money to buy a six-pack of Colt 45 beer. And she gave it to him. I couldn't believe it! This was becoming very typical behavior.

I simply blew up! I shouted, "Momma, you talking about not being able to pay your bill, yet you can buy this nigga's beer? How stupid is that?" I turned to their friends and demanded, "Y'all get out of my house now! Get out!"

My mother started cussing at me for trying to run her life. One of her friends chimed in, "Why you talking to your momma like that?" I went over and grabbed him by the shirt and almost dragged him outside. Then I did put them out—the whole bunch of them—daring any one of them to challenge me, especially David.

My mother became very angry with me and hollered that what I was doing to her was driving us further apart. In my mind, I was trying to keep her from dying like my Aunt Faye, but she was seeing it as an attempt to control her life. Of course, that was true but only because I was beginning to realize how much I really did love her and how greatly I needed her as her son.

My mother didn't understand that the lights in my soul were growing very dim. I was mad at her—even to the point of hating her—because down deep inside I needed her to be my mother. True, Randall, Mousey, Wanky, Edward, and Patmite were my closest friends whom I would share my heart with the most; but I needed her, and she wasn't there.

Nobody seemed to have any answers. I had always prided myself on being a true person, being real; I despised the very thought of being fake. Such behavior had no place in my life, and I was willing to stand on that truth until my death. Likewise, I turned my attention to finding some sense in my existence and felt that I couldn't be the Crip that I longed to be if my life was to lose its meaning and purpose. Finding those answers now became my number one focus.

After awhile I got to the point of exhaustion. My life became dry, burned out. By this time a depression kicked in because I wasn't finding my way. Then anger toward myself became an issue.

I believed I was fighting a losing cause; I had come up against something way bigger than I was and might be quickly losing control. As a punishment to myself, I concluded I wasn't worth anything and denied myself food at times when I was hungry. Day after day I would just hunch in my bedroom or lie across my bed, thinking of ways to kill myself.

My inner voices would taunt me with words like, *"See, you're nothing! Nobody cares about you. If your friends were really your friends, they would tell you what you need to hear."* Such thoughts would make me even darker inside. Other times I would hear a voice muttering, *"If you kill yourself, you won't have to worry about feeling this way anymore. Go ahead! You'd be better off. God don't love you either!"*

Images of hanging myself would pop in my mind at times or of taking a razor blade and slicing up and down my face and chest area repeatedly. I would always try to reject those pictures in my mind; but as the days rolled on, the thought of suicide became more and more appealing.

When I would see my mother coming back from the liquor store or watch her drinking, such sights would trigger depressing feelings. It was a very sobering realization that I could not change her lifestyle. So I got to a point where I just gave up; I basically resigned myself to waiting for the day she would die from either alcohol or the hands of David.

One afternoon I was lying on my back across my bed and just staring at the ceiling. I remembered a book I was given by some strange people one day and pulled it out of hiding. It was a volume on guided imagery, a unique New Age practice. But I didn't know that at the time. The text guided its readers on an imaginary journey through a forest with a long winding path. They were supposed to hold a chosen person's hand but not wander off that path. If any wandering occurred, they had to concentrate on getting back to where they'd veered off.

In my mind, I was being distracted, which made it hard to stay on their little path. After awhile, I got stuck in the imagery and couldn't get out of this non-reality; I began to panic. Just then I snapped out of it and concluded that something was strange about that book—and threw it away.

Soon my suicidal mind-set turned from slicing myself with razor blades to putting a pistol to my mouth and unleashing everything it had to offer. But the twist in my mind was that the bullets would not run out, and I would never die. I imagined flesh being pierced on all sides and the bullets escaping from the back of my head and neck, but still I couldn't be released into death. I felt that I deserved to feel continual pain only and fire-like burns from the nerves being ripped and torn. That's just how much I hated what I had become: a waste of breath.

These mysterious voices would come and go, trying to persuade me to end it all. Usually they were calm, assuring, and persuasive. But occasionally they would shriek at me to stop imagining it, to go ahead and do it. *"Relieve yourself, and quit being a burden on your mother! You're the cause of her drinking!"* the voices would insist. The longer the answers took to come, the more convincing these unseen tongues became.

The one thing that kept me from going through with executing myself and holding out a little longer was something I had heard as a child from my mother and others—that if you kill yourself, you would go to hell.

Little did I know that life for me was about to change. My answers would come like a rushing wind, totally catching me off guard. I had woken up that morning, feeling as dead inside as ever. I didn't feel like doing anything, least of all living.

That afternoon the sun was at its brightest, but it wasn't enough to lure me outside. I was very hungry but refused myself anything to eat. I found myself lying on my back across my bed with my head resting comfortably against my hands. I was staring at the ceiling, lost in my thoughts.

What was the point of living, of having to wake up each day—only to repeat the same things over and over and over again? What was the point of getting dressed? Why do we have to eat? Why do we have to talk to people? Why do people have to go to work or to school? What was the point of living, period? What is *my* purpose for living? And who am I?

No answer was enough. Finally, my thoughts turned to God, the one person I had run from for years, not ever wanting to be confronted by any realities He might observe about my behavior. And when I'd spot anybody from Bible club, I would dash off the other way. People in my family and those in my neighborhood would talk a good talk about "knowing God"; but the World Impact Christians actually lived it, taught it, and believed it. Seeing them reminded me of Jesus Christ, and I would do some strange things to avoid them whenever I'd see them in my way.

But now I was desperate to no end, and I turned my attention to this God I had always heard about, whom I once knew, and who I believed had abandoned me as a child. I wanted to see if He was there. I saw myself standing in the clouds with nowhere to look but up. It was so very real to me.

In my broken state, I called out, "God, where are you? If you're real, I need to know now. If you're really who you say you are, then I need your help. Please help me, or I'm dead." Immediately, I started thinking back to when I was a child when my heart was still tender. I remembered the fun times at Bible club, the Bible stories about Jesus, Moses, Abraham, the disciples, and the many others. I brought to mind the wonderful snacks after every club meeting, the fun times of wrestling, the camp-outs at Rolling J Ranch up north in the mountains. I pictured the tangible hugs that I got each week and the hands that rubbed across my nappy hair from Fred and Mike and the other godly men.

These memories seemed to warm me up, reminding me of the richness I had once had around Christians. Desires for all those things struggled back to the surface, and abruptly I realized how much I missed it all. All of a sudden, I snapped out of it; and I sensed a loving voice saying to me, *"Eric, I'm who you need. Not your mother or the gang or your friends. I'm who you need."* I felt in my heart of hearts that the one I was hearing was God Himself. I was fully convinced of it.

Eventually my thoughts drifted back to where I was—still in my room and on my bed. For some strange reason, I felt an urgency to go to Kim Seebach's house just down the street. He was one of my Bible club teachers back when I was attending. He and his wife Yvonne and their two beautiful children had moved directly across the street from the PJs several years earlier.

Kim never failed to call out if he happened to see me, "Eric,

I'm praying for you, brother! We love you, and you're welcomed back anytime." I would generally nod in acknowledgment, mutter what I imagined he wanted to hear, and get away from him as quickly as I could. But now I felt compelled to go to his house and knock on his front door.

So I got up and prepared myself and left for Kim's house. It was about a five to ten minute walk from one end of the projects to the other, from my side to Kim's. I tried to figure out what I was going to say, but the answer never came. I wondered what he would think when he opened his door and saw me standing in front of him. *"Will he believe me and take me seriously?"* I thought to myself. The closer I got, the more nervous I became; and my hands began to sweat. I kept having impulses like, *"Don't go over there; he's too busy for you. Turn around. Go back! Don't waste that man's time."* But like a powerful magnet that's found in junk yards, I felt myself pulled—as if I were destined—and needed the help to get there. And I did.

When I arrived, I pulled in a deep breath and knocked on the door. Kim opened it, and when he saw me, he exclaimed, "Eric, what a surprise! What brings you here?" as he gave me the grandest hug. All I could respond was, "I don't know, I just felt like I had to come."

Kim invited me in at once and called to his wife, "Honey, look who's here!" He asked if I was hungry or wanted something to drink. I admitted, "Sure." Kim had no idea that I hadn't been eating well and was quite hungry. But God knew.

Yvonne fixed me some lunch and something to drink, and we made casual conversation while I was eating. When I finished, Kim invited me into his study where we sat and talked for about two hours.

He began by asking me what brought me to his home. I said, "I don't know. I just felt like I needed to come here. I used to break my neck to avoid y'all Bible club teachers, but now I'm in your house. All I know is that I'm hurting, and I guess I need help. I don't know."

Kim asked me to describe what had been going on that was making me feel like I needed help. I confided that I'd been thinking about suicide off and on and that my mother had been drinking far too much, and that was hard. I couldn't explain a whole lot because I myself didn't really understand it and couldn't quite articulate all I was feeling.

I guess Kim picked up on the severity of my problems and

understood I was undergoing a crisis in my life. He began to share the Gospel of Jesus Christ with me as if I had never heard it before. And amazingly, it was like new to me because I was not hearing it with a child's ears; instead, I was now receiving it from a broken man's perspective, one desperate for truth.

Kim counseled that I needed to make a choice to accept Jesus into my life that day and to give up my current destructive way of life. He challenged me as if he were a loving dad, hoping to get his son ready to face the reality of where I was heading. Or he could also allow me to reject his advice, to walk out of his house. Kim said I was at a cross roads: I either needed to surrender my life to Jesus Christ or walk out of his house and keep trying to run my own life.

When he shared that with me, fear took root: I got the point loud and clear. I realized that I had no more ideas and no one else around me did either. I sat there in my chair, staring at the ground or up at the ceiling, facing the fact that *I had to give up Grape,* my homeboys, and the will to rule my own life. I understood that Jesus must be Lord and not just Savior. As I sat there staring in deep thought, I broke down and began to weep.

It was as if I had swallowed the ocean as a child, and it could no longer be contained. In the privacy of my own will, I came to grips with the reality that life as I had known it, around which I had built my whole identity, would no longer be the same.

The tears seemed to spring from my bowels as I quickly crouched into a fetal position and wept. Years of shame and hurt splashed to the surface of my life as I surrendered it all. I knew Jesus was proud of me as I willingly obeyed His call by making the first step of obedience.

After about five minutes, I dried my eyes and glimpsed up with the simplicity of a child. I sighed in relief and then told Kim I was ready to submit my life to Jesus. Kim led me in a sinner's prayer of confession; and I gave my heart, my will, and my life to Jesus Christ as my personal Lord and Savior.

When I came up from that prayer, the burden and weight seemed to be lifted from my shoulders. And in their place, I received a child-like joy. I felt clean for the first time as if I was guiltless from a lifetime of offenses against a holy God.

Kim led me into the living room where Yvonne and the kids

were waiting and announced I had given my life to Christ. Yvonne was thrilled for me. Of course, the kids, who were under five years of age, were happy because the adults were.

Kim and Yvonne Seeback

They gave me a Bible and suggested that I spend some time in the gospel of John for starters. Kim warned me that Satan would not take my change lightly, that he would start throwing all kinds of darts and temptations at me and would try to block my growth in Christ. He explained the need to be discipled in the Word and to be willing to accept accountability from someone else. He offered to be that person, and certainly I agreed. I thanked them for the amazing help and then left their house with the commitment to meet regularly.

When I got down the way a bit, I noticed some PJ Crips across the street shooting dice. One of them spotted me and yelled, "Clipper, what up, Cuzz? Check it out." Immediately a fear set in. I thought, *"What will they think if they see this Bible in my hand?"* So in a slick move, I switched the Bible into the other hand—out of view—and hurriedly stuffed it in my pants.

Yet in my spirit I heard God say to me, *"I'm not ashamed of you. Why are you ashamed of me?"* My heart was broken as I thought back to how God had just changed me at Kim and Yvonne's house. Convicted, I pulled out the Bible, held it in full view, and proudly strolled over to the dice game. We all exchanged some small talk until one of them noticed the Word and blurted, "What you doing with a Bible in your hand, Clipper?" I admitted without shame what God had just done for me. The gladness began to bubble over as I shared this truth; and one by one, they each found an excuse to leave. The dice game was over; and I left with joyfulness because I knew I had made Jesus happy by obeying Him.

I couldn't wait to get home and tell my mother the incredible news. When I went inside, I called out to her, "Momma! Where you at?" After locating her, I announced I had given my life to Christ and was transformed. But she didn't show the kind of emotions I was expecting. I hoped for a shared excitement, but it did not come. Still, I didn't let it get to me.

The joy of feeling clean inside and guilt-free overshadowed any disappointment with the nay-sayers. I shared it with my closest homeboys Chepo (Edward), Mousey, Randall, and Patmite as well as my cousins Wallace and Hub and Lisa; but no one could believe I was serious. As the days went by, I started getting very awkward reactions from people because this God stuff was so strange coming from my mouth, the Clipper. They all thought I was going crazy or something.

Many doubted the sincerity of it all, thinking that I wouldn't be loyal to this newfound faith in Jesus; they believed I was too loyal to Grape to all of a sudden give it up for some silly "religious reason." Looking back, I can definitely understand why many felt that way because Grape had been number one in my life for so long.

Kim suggested I start spending time with and getting to know other Christians. He also recommended that he and I meet at least once a week for one-on-one Bible study so he could disciple me as a new believer. I trusted Kim's judgment and agreed.

He set up a day for us to meet, and we began concentrating on the New Testament book of John. The scripture began to take on a new meaning for me; it seemed to come alive because it started speaking to me on many different issues. But it was the love Christ demonstrated toward people that stood out to me more than anything else.

I identified with this greatly because He had shown love to me unconditionally. God had forgiven me for all that evil I had done. He had taken away my heart of stone and was giving me a heart that cares.

Through my weekly Bible studies and spending time with other Christians from World Impact as well as being over to Kim and Yvonne's, the Lord was teaching me how I should value people and how He wanted me to treat them. Every little detail I learned from God's Word excited me. For example, I discovered how patiently Jesus dealt with Peter when he acted before considering what he was going to say.

I related to Peter somewhat: I realized I would need the same patience. Peter became the major person of the Bible, other than Jesus Himself, to impress me. Even though he was the one who often got himself in trouble, he was the only one willing to take chances. I identified with that. And perhaps this is why Jesus chose Peter to be the leader of the disciples and His church, knowing what He would do in Peter's life later on.

Many of my homeboys, when they found out what had happened in my life, no longer felt comfortable around me. My way of living was now cut off from theirs. We no longer shared the same interests, and some began to feel the difference. And there were those who counted me out, scoffing, "I'll give you six months, and you'll be back."

Some criticized me for "walking out on the set." By this time, the honeymoon period was beginning to wear off, and I was starting to feel the changes as well. I got a little irritated by the guy who said I was walking out on the set; he was implying in effect that I was abandoning Grape and the homeys. I fired back, "Cuzz, what up with that? I ain't running out on Grape. You know that I ain't no punk. But where was Grape and everybody else when I was thinking about killing myself? Nobody had no answers for me except Jesus. He didn't run out on me, and I'm not running out on Him." That was the end of the conversation, and I left.

A part of me, though, was getting tired of people's criticism of what I had decided for my life—or rather what God had decided. A loneliness began to set in, and I was beginning to question the decision I had made to stop gang banging and give my life to Christ.

My homeys didn't want to be around me anymore because I was always witnessing about what Jesus had done for me. I started to wonder if it was worth giving up the life that I had known for almost half my years.

None of my friends or family understood my intentions, and I couldn't make them see it. A few individuals were happy for me, but they were basically the older people who had begun to appreciate the good changes in me. It seemed like their opinions should have mattered, but those who "counted" were my peers. And yet I felt strange around them all of a sudden.

I was able to share these concerns with Kim, and he explained what every Christian had to go through. It wasn't that my friends were running from my company but that the reality of the Christian life meant I belonged to Christ now, and Satan knew he'd lost the victory over me. When I gave myself to Jesus, bowing to Him on His terms through His death and resurrection, God put His claim on me through the Holy Spirit. I represented Christ from that point on.

Kim reminded me how I used to run from God, how every time I came in contact with a Christian, I avoided that person at all costs. It wasn't anything personal; it was just that believers reminded me of my evil lifestyle and the independent way I was trying to function apart from Christ. I didn't want God telling me how to run my affairs, and that is what people around me were dealing with.

Further, Kim encouraged me to pray for my homeboys and family and to love them every chance I got. But at the same time, he advised me to spend more time around other Christians who would be a support for me. The real enemy was Satan—not those who were being critical of me or simply doubting the reality of my transformation.

Our talk gave me clarity and made me understand that I was in a spiritual battle. It provided me with a new sense of steadfastness and dedication as well as a renewed commitment to the Lord. I didn't know the mind of Satan, but I did more fully appreciate that he is relentless and merciless and will never take days off.

Chapter Eighteen

A particular guy who lived in the PJs and was not involved in gang activities growing up saw me walking by his house one day. He stopped me and remarked, "Hey Clipper, I notice you're different now. What happened?" I told him simply that I was a Christian now. He said, "Uh-uh! You're lying!" I maintained that it was on the "up and up." I was telling the truth.

He said his name was Keith and that he had always watched me gang-bang and looked up to me. I knew he and his family were Jehovah's Witnesses because I used to see them going door-to-door and passing out *Watch Tower* magazines. He admitted he was kind of tired of it and wanted to get out on his own as soon as possible so he could join a gang. His style of clothing and everything had begun to resemble that of a wannabe gangster. Flags went up when I heard that. I certainly didn't want to be his excuse to take up that lifestyle! He had been sheltered all his life and restricted from being a part of school activities, holidays, etc. I could see the guy was basically on the verge of rebellion.

I felt an immediate sense of responsibility toward him, a need to warn him against entering the criminal world like I had. So I suggested he and I get together and hang out more. He agreed.

In a very short time, I got acquainted with his mother, two brothers, and three sisters. They all remembered who I'd been in my gang banging days; but I hadn't known them except for having seen them in their yard or passing out magazines. They all took an interest in me quickly, being drawn to and curious about my rejection of the gang lifestyle.

His mom, Ms. Barbara, told me I was welcomed in their home any time and that she would even feed me. Keith and I spent more time together, and I began having an impact in his life as far as steering him away from the gangs was concerned. Ms. Barbara, true to her word, included me in evening meals. Sometimes I would be so drained from trying to persuade my mother to quit drinking that Keith's home became a place where I could go and fall asleep on the couch.

But my faith would soon be tested. Keith, Danielle—his oldest sister—and I started having doctrinal conversations involving the differences between Christianity and Jehovah's Witnesses. I was able to hold my ground against them and often left them off-balance. I guess I had been a good student and had learned enough to represent a believer's point of view.

However, one day Keith and I were hanging out when out of nowhere he asked me, "Hey, Clipper, you're a Christian, right?"

I answered, "Yeah."

"Do you believe that Jesus is God?"

"Yeah, He is God. Why you ask me that?"

He said that he wanted to see what I believe.

I asked him, "You believe He's God?"

"No! He ain't God. He's the Son of God. He's also Michael the archangel."

"No, He ain't! Where you come up with something like that?"

"He is! Let's go ask my mother."

At this point I felt challenged and, to be honest, somewhat intimidated because I didn't know a lot about the Bible. I was basically riding on the faith of Kim Seebach—which wasn't his fault. That's just the way it is with a new Christian. Still, I knew I couldn't show Keith that I was shaken, so I had to accept his challenge to face his mother, a seasoned Jehovah's Witness. I followed him into his house like a sheep being led to the slaughter, having no clue about what would happen.

When we walked into the living room, to my horror Ms. Barbara and three or four older women were in the middle of a Jehovah's Witness Bible study! My heart about jumped out of my chest, but I managed not to show any fear—a handy skill I had learned from gang banging.

In front of them all, Keith, who was almost foaming at the mouth, said to the ladies, "Excuse me, Momma, but Eric said that Jesus is God. Tell him he's wrong." Without hesitation, the questions began to roll off their tongues, which completely overwhelmed me. They started throwing their scriptures at me from every angle to support their viewpoint. And then they demanded, "Can you prove your position?" I could only say, "All I know is that Jesus is God. He's God." Unfortunately, I wasn't able to back up my claim, which made them look good.

It was like some female lionesses had just captured their prey and left me there with just my bones on the floor. I didn't dare admit this in front of them, but they raised so much doubt in my mind that I lost my confidence as a Christian. I crept out of there so defeated inside that it made me question all over again whether God was who He said He was and if He was strong enough to keep me secure.

Keith, just being himself, couldn't wait to get me outside to find out what I thought now. I stuck with my guns and affirmed that I still believed Jesus is God. I had to keep that edge; I could not appear weak in front of him. But little did he know I was totally devastated.

I made up an excuse to leave, just to get away from them. I needed to find Kim and have him to answer that question, "Is Jesus God or not?" and to prove it to me so I would know for myself. I couldn't stand not being certain of the truth. It was the story of my life: an urge that drove me always to look for security. I think the traumatic separation from my grandmother at age six removed my bedrock feeling of stability. But now God was redirecting that drive to rely on Him—and Him alone—for my safety.

I met with Kim, and he reassured me that Jesus is God and gladly showed me passages in John 1:1, John 14:10-11, and Colossians 1:15-20 that gave me the answers. That day I decided I would never rely on the faith of others but would know the truth for myself. It was so cool to learn that Jesus is who He says He is and that God's Word could not be shaken as I myself was shaken.

That renewed confidence led me to go back to Ms. Barbara with the necessary answers. I had learned that I didn't need to have the answers ready right there on the spot but that I could go away, dig them out, and then return.

Though many of my homeboys had fallen away, my core

friends never gave up on me. Mousey insisted, "Clipper, you're my best friend. You're like my big brother, and you never walked out on me. I might not be ready for religion, but that ain't going to stop me from being your ace homeboy."

That meant a lot to me. Mousey had become the little brother I never had. I had risked my life more than once to save his. I made sure this guy was fed, clothed, and prepared to deal with the streets. So hearing his declaration meant the world to me, and he stood true to his word. Randall, Edward, and Wanky remained firm as well.

I had begun to spend a lot of time in God's Word, but I still had a few hang-ups that I hadn't yet released. Although I wasn't as involved as I had been, I continued to find quiet times in Olde English 800 beer and marijuana. This was the case one particular evening at home. My mother and David were gone somewhere, and I was at the house by myself, enjoying the moment.

I had bought a 40 ounce bottle of 800 and a dime ($10.00) bag of red head sess. I rolled up about five or six joints the size of a Sharpie marker, lit one up, and sat on the couch with my Bible in one hand and a joint in the other.

Somebody had told me that if you smoke a joint before you read your Bible, it would help you understand it better. That kind of made sense to me because marijuana made me alert. In an almost panic state, I took a drink of my 40 ounces of 800, hit the joint several times, and randomly opened up to the first chapter of the book of James.

When I came to the verses revealing how God cannot be tempted by evil, nor does He tempt others that way, it was as if I'd stepped into the very throne room of God. It was like I had suddenly emerged into pure holiness. I felt convicted: I seemed so dirty and perverse by what I was doing.

At once I put out the joint and stuck the top back on the 40 oz. It was as if the Scriptures echoed from heaven itself, and God prodded in a gentle voice, *"Eric, why are you doing this to me? This is not from me."* I closed the Bible, got up with the joints that I had in a ziplock bag, and walked to the sink in the kitchen. One by one, I tore the papers apart and dumped the weed down the drain. I also poured out the beer.

Immediately after, I begged God to forgive me and apologized for contaminating His Holy Word, the Bible. I promised to never smoke weed or drink beer again if He would forgive me. In my heart I knew God had done that indeed, and a sense of peace between us was restored.

I did okay for a couple of weeks but found a way of justifying my smoking weed once again. A dance called the "Pop Lock" was pretty popular in that day. It wasn't exactly break dancing, but it was similar—without the spinning and flipping on the floor.

My thing was ticking and the wave. We had a big mirror in our downstairs hallway, hanging on a closet. I used to get high off some weed and would practice ticking and waving while listening to George Clinton's "The Atomic Dog" or whatever I chose. So I rationalized in my mind that it would be okay to smoke weed so long as I only did it for dancing purposes.

So I found myself dancing for about a week while ignoring the Holy Spirit's voice urging me to quit. During that time I couldn't pray or read my Bible; I made excuses not to meet with Kim as well. It was driving me further and further away from being in tune with my Lord, and I frankly felt miserable. But at the same time, I noticed I was improving in my pop locking.

I began having certain weird experiences at night as if someone were calling my name from a distance. This occurred especially in my room—something that started to freak me out. The voices soon began aggressively attacking me, calling me a fake Christian. I would hear them yelling and screaming all sorts of profanities at me and asserting, *"You're not a Christian! You're fake! God don't love you, and you're going to die and go to hell! God is really Satan, and Satan is really God!"*

These voices would only come out at night when I was alone. Once they would start, I would try to pray or read the Bible; but the screeching would just drown out my words. I was becoming very paranoid and dreaded nightfall. I was averaging about an hour and a half of sleep each night because the demonic speakers would shriek into my head and wake me. And sometimes I wouldn't even sleep at all.

This went on for about two weeks. I tried to confide in my mother and different friends, but everybody thought I was going crazy; nobody believed me. During this stretch of time, I had several nightmares about Satan. During one in particular, I dreamt he came to take me to hell with him, but I started hollering out to Jesus for help—

and I woke up.

At night I could sense a demonic presence in my room even when wide awake. The hairs on my arms would seem to rise. In an attempt at escape, I would get up and leave the room. I could not pray to Jesus without being intimidated into stopping. At the end of that two-week period, I think I was on the verge of either killing myself out of fear or out of pure exhaustion. I wasn't planning to check myself into a mental institution, and I shied away from telling Kim about my experiences because I didn't want him thinking I was crazy too. But I was extremely tired, and my trust in God's power to help was nearly depleted, bankrupt.

The last night I would be dealing with those things would be pivotal: I would either be rescued by God Himself somehow, or I would find a way to end my life. After all, the voices were telling me to do just that.

It was a Sunday night. My mother and Aunt Peg had decided to go out, and David was gone somewhere. Elma and my grandpa CB had moved out, and that night I faced being left in the house alone. Aunt Peg's kids had stayed over at their dad's house, so her house (across the street from us) would be empty as well. I decided I couldn't face my empty house by myself, so I asked Aunt Peg if I could stay over at her place and watch cable. She gave me the green light; and I grabbed my Bible, hoping against hope that I would be able to read it in a different environment—away from my bedroom—and scare the demons away.

After about a half hour, once everyone had finally gone, I was sitting there watching TV when I heard somebody shouting, "You're going to die and go to hell!" All of a sudden the voices began to yell out evil rantings at me, mercilessly once again. That shattered the notion that they were only in my house. The fear really began to set in then.

I turned up the volume on the television as loud as it could go—but still heard the voices. I turned on the stereo sky high, hoping that would help—but it didn't. In sheer panic, I jumped up and ran out into the night, leaving the door wide open. That's something you don't do in the projects; it's like advertising in bright neon that you're offering your things to be stolen. But I cared nothing about that at the moment.

I wanted to find someone, anyone, just to be with a human person. It didn't matter. Friend or foe. In about a hundred yards, I ran into a guy named Larry, whom they called "Grape." He was not from Grape Street Watts, but he had been among the first generation of Crips back when Big Tookie and Raymond Washington had first started the gang in the late '60s.

He had gone through a lot of personal things and had become addicted to PCP, or sherm, as it was called, from the use of the Sherman cigarettes. Larry was kind of high then because he had the characteristics of a person under the influence of the "bomb."

I stopped him and started asking him how he was doing and a series of other questions, whatever, just to keep him with me. I was prepared to stay out there all night, if necessary, and really didn't know what was going to happen from that point on.

After awhile, Larry began to focus on who I was. It was a weird night because hardly anyone was outside, and it wasn't even 11:00, a very rare event. He asked me a question that I didn't expect: "Clipper, I notice you done changed. What's up?" This was a man about thirty or older at the time.

With a sense of urgency, I told him precisely what led to my change and that Jesus Christ had given me a joy no one or nothing else was able to do. The more I shared with Larry, recalling the excitement I'd had about reading God's Word and feeling like He'd given me a purpose for living, the more confident I became that God still loved me.

Right before my eyes, I watched Larry's chemical high decrease until he was totally coherent and clean. The man began to express a depth of pain and a void of Jesus in his own life and how much he needed God. On the spot I was able to invite Larry to give his heart to Christ and referred him to Kim and World Impact for further help.

I also told him about my satanic oppression, how I had been terrified and suffering, and how it had kept me from praying and fellowshipping with my Lord. All at once I blurted, "Larry, I'm going back in that house; and if I have to die tonight, I will not doubt my Lord again. He is with me. I'm gonna face it." I gave him a hug and walked back inside.

Everything was still blasting loud in there. I'm surprised the neighbors didn't complain, though they probably thought it was a house party or something, an event subject to breaking out anytime in the projects. But I turned off the radio, locked the door, and turned down the TV. I grabbed my Bible, lay down on the couch, and put the Word under my head as a pillow.

The threatening voices returned, and I could hear the usual negative charges and criticisms. But this time, I could also hear God murmuring gently but absolutely, *"I will not leave you."* I asked Him to please help me sleep. That's all I wanted. Amazingly, I was able to fall asleep almost immediately and slept soundly. That was the last night of my satanic oppression, and God gave me the victory because I trusted Him finally to help me. I also repented from smoking weed and extended my faith in God to help me quit. And I have not had a single temptation to drink or smoke since.

Chapter Nineteen

God was beginning to do some incredible things in my life. To others they were probably not that big a deal; but for me, everything God was doing in me and through me was revolutionary and filled with goodness. He was transforming a heart that had become like stone into a tender cushion that cared for people. That was overwhelming to me.

I stopped at a small restaurant one day, called Jordan's Café, a family-owned business that bordered the PJs and Bounty Hunter territories, both Crips and Bloods. Upon leaving, I spotted a certain Bounty Hunter that I had gone to middle school with.

Jerome McKnight had been kind of cool at first. He was in the eighth grade when I was a seventh grader. Although I had already started gang banging, he—like Bounty Hunter Norman and others—had not. But later on, he became a Bounty Hunter; and we grew to hate each other. To be honest, if we'd had the opportunity in those days, I would have killed him, or he would have killed me.

Just as I was walking out the door, he and one of his homeboys were coming in. They were what we called "slobbed down"—"slob" was a derogatory word we used for Bloods. He had his predominate color red on, identifying him as a Blood.

They looked shocked to see me come out. A part of me wanted to get defensive, assuming that they were going to try something fierce since I was out-manned. Jerome said, "What that is, Blood?" I replied, "What a Jerome? I ain't about that no more, homey. I'm done. It's about Christ now for me, man. Y'all stay up." Then I strode away, feeling like God had won through me.

Jerome and his homeboy stared after me with surprise by my response—and rightly so. If it had been on the old terms, something violent indeed would have happened. That taught me that a power beyond my own was at work through me. And as I walked away without a fight or shooting, my heart felt compassion for them. I sensed that Jesus loved them as much as he loved me.

I remember running into a couple of homosexual men at a bus stop. Any other time, as once when I drop kicked one at another bus stop in downtown L.A. because he was leering at me sexually, I would have done something evil to them or said something hateful. But again, I felt like Christ loved them too, so I spoke to them respectfully.

If they would have presented me with the opportunity to express my view of that behavioral preference, I would have shared the biblical truth. But the timing wasn't right. I felt in my spirit that God just wanted me to greet them respectfully because Christ died for them, too.

At this time I got a job at a local grocery store across the street from the PJs called the "Pink Store" because of the color of the building. My job was to stock the shelves. People would come in and see me and exclaim, "Clipper got a *job?!*" or something to that effect. At first it was almost embarrassing to be seen working, earning an honest living. But it felt so much better to be going to work each day and earning $135.00 a week or so than to be putting dope in people's bodies or knocking someone out for quick money—something that, if done regularly, could bring in much more. The difference was that I was now guilt free and totally under God's approval. And as time went on, I grew into it and the initial embarrassment went away.

I eventually had the privilege of leading a number of friends to Christ: Randall, Derrick Evans, Zap, and a couple of others. I would connect the guys with Kim Seebach to either make their commitments to Christ or for discipleship, something I was ready to do. But Randall and I really began to hold each other accountable.

Mousey wasn't "ready" to give up his life yet, but he didn't let my choice to give mine to Christ keep us apart. He often mentioned that "I respect what you chose to do, Clipper, and it doesn't matter what the homies are saying about you; you've been there for me when no one else was, and I ain't walking out on you now. When I'm ready,

I'll be ready, and you'll know."

Edward, my closest homeboy because of our long-time friend-ship since back in grade school, came around as well. I wanted all my homeboys to find Christ. Many sheepishly dismissed the offer to bow before the loving Savior, but all began to respect my decision. They knew I was a die-hard member of Grape Street Watts and still did what I could to represent. Though some continued to think I had abandoned Grape and the homies, none attempted to retaliate.

I heard about a welding school in Downey called the Pacific Coast Technical Institute, and I decided to enroll. Eventually I would bring on board Randall, Edward, David (whom I called Dave-Bo), and my homeboy Larry (aka Sprancy from the PJs) as well.

A part of why I did this was because they offered you fifty dollars for every person you got signed up. But the bottom line was, I wanted them to have a chance like I had. It was a six month course, and both Edward and I went on to stay for seven. I would eventually win an Arc welding machine for near perfect attendance.

About four or five months into it, Edward and I—who would complete the program, plus that extra optional month which was basi-cally for practice purposes—went out and got a job at a factory in Cer-ritos. We were later let go; I guess our work ethics weren't what they wanted.

We got another job in Cerritos, I believe, in a plastic wrap factory. Our daily schedule consisted of leaving the house about 10:30 A.M. and taking the RTD bus ride to Downey, which took about an hour. We would leave the welding school and get home about 6:30 P.M. In other words, we were at school from 12:00 to 5:00.

After we got home, ate, and rested, we would leave again around 7:00 P.M. for another one hour bus ride. We would work from 8:00 in the evening until 8:00 the next morning. Then we had to be back at school by 12:00 noon.

This was our routine for two weeks. We would work a twelve-hour shift, nonstop, except for restroom breaks, eating "lunch" while we worked. Needless to say, that kind of schedule wore us out, so we decided to give our day's notice and quit. We found another job after that and worked for a while. I had quit my position at the Pink Store because I wasn't getting enough hours.

Finally we graduated from Pacific Coast Technical Institute

and were pretty excited about finishing the program. But working those several jobs during that time seemed like I had been laboring away for a lifetime. The only previous work experience I had was one summer with the Imperial Courts Housing Authority picking up trash around the projects and a few other non-skilled things as well as with the Catholic Youth Organization serving lunches to kids and playing games under the management of Ms. Maxine Waters, who is now a democratic member of Congress.

Soon we were out of work and out of school. We had graduated after a great deal of effort and commitment, and we decided it was no longer worthwhile to take the long bus rides to Cerritos. Still, Edward and I kind of grew up further during those trips, and our friendship became even more solid; we kept each other focused, and of course he kept me laughing as well.

I was out of work for several months, but I was approaching my one-year anniversary as a new Christian. As a "birthday present," I was offered a job in Hawthorne at a trophy shop. It was owned by a beautiful Christian family, who just happened to be white. The owner and founder was a former N.F.L player with the Green Bay Packers, but his parents basically ran the shop. It was named Rex Trophies after his father, Mr. Rex. The members of this family were supporters of World Impact, and Fred Stoesz had contacted them and got me and Randall a job in their shop.

My friend Alex, whom I grew up with in the PJs, was offered a job at another trophy shop that was also in Hawthorne. Our bus ride for the three of us took about forty-five minutes. God had truly done a work in our lives, particularly with Randall and me—who had been enemies of the Bounty Hunters for so long. Now we had to commute past their hood, the Nickerson Gardens. Yes, we had some fear; but for the most part, we were willing to trust Christ with our lives. Nothing would ever happen.

This family was very patient with us and really helped us learn the business. They also hired another Christian from World Impact. Her name was Anita. It was very tempting to do what we called "to bus game" at her—to use persuasive words to get someone to fall for you or to get what you want from her. But God taught me that Anita was my sister in Christ, and I was to respect her. Anita, Randall, and I became very close friends, and we were committed to protecting her on the bus when we would ride together.

This family, in particular Mr. Rex and his wonderful wife Ms. Yvonne, showed us so much love and respect that we were amazed because they were a very close Christians family and rich but very, very caring. Ms. Yvonne, the grandma of the family, in particular treated us like her own grandchildren even though we were black and they knew Randall and I had come out of a life of crime and gang activity. They trusted us. Never once did we betray them.

Their son, Bob, who owned the shop, had developed throat cancer and went through a lot of suffering. They rallied around him as a family and loved him. I concluded it was extremely desirable to have a family like that, and incredibly they included us into their family activities during this time.

I went on to hold this job for four months and felt like I could have put in years at Rex Trophies. But Kim was hosting an evening at his home for parents of male teenagers in his Bible clubs, and it would be offering a chance to see a promotional video of World Impact's Christian Leadership Training Center, called "The Ranch," located in a place called Florence in central Kansas.

All I knew about Kansas was Dorothy and Toto from the Wizard of Oz. I was invited to see the video, but I was reluctant. I had already begun considering the military and had started taking evening classes for my GED. My desire was to get my mother out of the projects and build her a brand new brick home like she had always wanted. Kim did not give up easily because he truly felt God wanted me to come. He also invited Randall, who had given his life to Christ as well and was being discipled by Kim. I finally agreed to go and watch the presentation about the ranch to discover what kind of program it offered. Alex was also there.

The video presented some good things, but the idea of leaving Watts for Kansas—a wilderness sounding place—and leaving my mother alone with David was out of the question. Actually, I had planned to get him out of the house before leaving for the military if accepted.

Kim later asked me what I thought about the ranch. I said, "I guess it's all right for those who want to go." Without coming out and blurting, "Nope! Not gonna do it" or something, I elected to *imply* that my choice was not to go. I didn't want to disappoint Kim, who had become like a father to me; but at the same time, I didn't want to pretend to be all excited about it either.

I would go on to drop out of night school because the material was too hard to grasp. And when I decided to take the test to enter the service, I couldn't pass. Three times I attempted, but I couldn't do it even though my score got better each time. Those doors seemed to be closing.

Meanwhile, God had started to impress upon my heart that He wanted me to go to the ranch. I tried to ignore that tugging from Him, choosing not to give up my chances of going into the military. Of course, God wasn't in the business of just going away quietly; He continued to knock on the door of my heart, telling me that it was His will that I go to Kansas.

Eventually I could not resist His direction any longer. I came to the realization that the Lord had other plans for me; I had to understand that it was not about me—but Him. And with agonizing humility, I bowed my heart and will and told Him I would obey.

I went to Kim and announced I was choosing to go to Kansas—not because he wanted me to, not because I wanted to, but because I believed it was God's decision for my life. Kim was simply thrilled, suggesting that the military wouldn't have brought me peace in any way and sharing how glad he was I had obeyed our Lord.

Alex had already decided to go himself, which made it easier to face leaving my mother all alone and my beloved Watts. Then I revealed my sudden change of plans to my mother and family as well as Randall, Edward, and Mousey. At once I started campaigning to take them all with me, but only Randall agreed to go.

Sometime in the spring of 1986, Alex, Randall, and I along with two other guys—Glenn Enriquez and Saul Aur—had to move into the "single men homes" for two weeks with the men on the World Impact staff. We had to get a feel for living with other guys in close quarters and sharing the responsibility of preparing meals, cleaning, and meeting for devotions and one-on-one accountability. We were asked to promise them two weeks without going home before making our final decisions. This arrangement was designed to see if it was something we could commit to—not for two weeks but for two years.

My bosses at the trophy store, Mr. Rex and Ms. Yvonne, and their whole family were excited for Randall and me since we had faithfully worked for them about four months by this time. They made it crystal clear that if we wanted a job after the two years were over, it would be available for us. And we would continue to work there at Rex Trophies even while we lived in the guys' house for those initial two weeks.

Others weren't so supportive but had no evil intentions. One among this group was my mother, who thought I wasn't going to leave L.A., but she did bless my decision. Others doubted my seriousness, claiming that it wasn't going to last; these gave me about six months before I'd be ready to return home.

We completed the two-week program—which seemed like it lasted months. It was tough because I was still in L.A. but wasn't able to go home. After work, Randall and I would catch the bus and go straight to the guys' house; and we were expected to assist with Bible clubs, wash our clothes, help with meals, and meet with our one-on-one leaders. It was actually a good experience, and it gave us a taste of what to expect out in Kansas at the ranch.

One day I was coming home from work, and one of my O'G homeboys from Grape, whom I had once idolized, was in the PJs right by my house with a couple of my Baby Loc homeboys. He was talking with Big Ken and another PJ outside by his low rider.

Kenny (also called Crow) saw me coming and called, "Clip-Dog, what that Grape like, Cuzz? Where you been, Cuzz? What, you don't wanna kick it with Grape no more?" People were noticing I had separated myself from even friendships, not because I didn't want to be with them but because we no longer shared the same lifestyle. But many of them couldn't understand that and saw it, I believe, as a betrayal.

I answered him honestly, "Crow, I ain't about that no more, homey. It's about Jesus Christ for me now." Crow replied, "Well, I'm gonna Grape until I die." I understood exactly why he said that since I'd had the same attitude just a year or so earlier. I asked him, "What you gonna do when you have to stand before Jesus on judgment day—claim Grape?"

That pretty much ended the conversation. I said to them, "Stay up, homies" and walked away, having spiritually witnessed to one of the top O'Gs from Grape, a guy I had once worshipped and whose approval I would've killed to win. That day I saw a huge man as though he were a child, someone totally unaware of the truth. Unfortunately, about a year after that conversation, I heard he was gunned down at a gas station. I hope my homeboy had made his peace with Christ before he died, for I believed in just how much Jesus loved him.

I had given my two weeks' notice at work, even though my bosses had already known well in advance of my decision to go to the ranch. They gave us a send off at their home with a barbeque. But that final week before leaving was very, very hard for me psychologically because of my fear that David would be the cause of my mother's eventual death once I was out of the picture. But in spite of my uneasiness, God wanted me to trust Him to take care of my mother.

And right at that time—shortly after the two-week program—Randall was informed that he should stay home for a while and spend more time with the ministry; unlike Alex and me, he had absolutely no background with World Impact. He was told that the ranch could still be a later option.

It was definitely hard to hear because I wanted him to go with me. I was basically his best friend and had led him by my example in turning around our lives. It was especially hard for Randall to accept, after having invested time in the two-week program.

The upcoming departure was also difficult emotionally because I had to leave all my homeboys, particularly Edward, Mousey, (and now) Randall, Patmite, and Wanky as well as my Uncle Carl. Further, I had to leave other family and a city that had become such a part of me. I tried to visit as many people as I could—from both the PJs and the Jordan Downs and many in between—to say goodbye.

Long ago, I had made a commitment to Christ that I would not take advantage of another woman because I had come to understand through my Bible studies that God loves women very much—fully as much as He loved me—and that He died for them too. I had dealt with this issue since Kim encouraged me to abstain from sex outside of marriage and to honor women according to God's Word.

I had become acquainted with another family after having been transformed, and the oldest daughter and I had discovered an attraction to each other several weeks before I was to set out for Kansas. The night before I was to leave, she and I were up in her room talking; and no one was at home but us. Things heated up between us, and we began to kiss.

I fell into the temptation of thoughts running through my mind: I would not be with another girl for a while, so I'd better get busy now! She was basically going along with it until I remembered I was going against God's command, and abruptly I realized this wasn't pleasing the Lord. I stopped before we went too far and maintained that it would be wrong.

She agreed and then apologized as well. We felt wonderful that we did the right thing, and the rest of the time went very well. At that time I reaffirmed a commitment that I would not have sex with another woman until I was married, and that was the end of that.

Chapter Twenty

The hour when Alex and I and several younger teens who were going to the ranch for what was called "Weekend Exposure" finally arrived. This program offered the young guys an opportunity to travel out with incoming students from various World Impact cities and to give them a feel of ranch life if they chose to become students in the future. Approximately twenty of us in all, including men on staff who had personally ministered to us from L.A., loaded up in two vans; and we set out for the sunflower state of Kansas.

Alex and Eric (in later years)

As we were pulling off, all I could think about was leaving my mother behind. I was totally submitted to God and had no other hope than to trust Him alone for the outcome. As we drove away, tears began to sting in my eyes as I reflected on all the years growing up in Watts—the good times and the bad. I considered the high degree of evil I had done and how God had kept me from death many times.

As I mused about my best friends—Edward, Mousey, Randall, and Wanky—the tears began to flow all the more. I felt especially concerned for Mousey because I had played a huge role in his life, having felt intensely responsible for his safety and well-being. He was truly like a little brother to me, and I didn't really know how he would make it on his own. With Edward and Randall, I figured they were big enough to manage without me.

The trip took us a couple of days because we stopped at several KOA campgrounds to enjoy the fresh outdoors and one another. Along the way we met other Christians at the camps and different people in restaurants and stores who were curious if we were a traveling basketball team or something.

I never imagined there were so many nice people—and complete strangers! Sometimes I would catch myself thinking, *"Boy, if they knew me a year or so ago, they probably would've steered away from me; and now these people are meeting a man changed from the inside out."*

The trip went very smoothly. The younger guys really helped loosen up my stress with their good-humored jokes and fun attitudes; I certainly grew to love them during those days. This was particularly true of the ones from Watts whom I had known since they were toddlers but had not been acquainted with on a personal level. These guys had watched my old life unfold and were familiar with the crooked values I had represented, but now they were also witnessing my transformation from Crip to Christ.

We reached Kansas on June 3, 1986. As we arrived from the west, all I saw were wide open flat prairie lands, cows and horses, tractors and diesels. I was all but gagging on the thought, *"What did I get myself into?"* When we got to Florence, Kansas, we whipped past it so quickly I couldn't believe it. I was shocked by how puny these little towns were.

Once we pulled up near the ranch, we noticed a huge sign—the one I had seen on the video—that read, "World Impact's Christian Leadership Training Center." The sign sat in front of the railroad tracks, and we had to cross those tracks to get to our final destination, a place hidden from us by trees.

A winding road took us past the barn where some pigs and a black and white cow called Bossie were eyeing us through the fence. We passed some grain bins, turned onto a bridge, and finally, the homes came into view.

Vans dotted the parking area everywhere, surrounded by other staff men and teen boys who were also coming out for Weekend Exposure. The five of us from L.A.—Alex, Glenn, Saul, Terry, and I—climbed out of the van and soon found that people were arriving from every city where World Impact had a ministry: Los Angeles, San Diego, and Fresno, California; St. Louis, Missouri; Wichita, Kansas; and Newark, New Jersey. In particular we met Phil Laurel from St. Louis.

Days earlier a graduation had occurred, and the five students involved were entering their second year. Those guys were the equivalent of seniors; and new students like my class—called first year students—were the equivalent of freshmen.

We met them privately to hear about their experiences and learn about the rest of the weekend's activities. One of those came on Saturday when we separated into different groups. The one I joined had to work in the strawberry patch, picking weeds or picking berries to sell to local farmers and families in the surrounding area.

On Sunday, at the end of the weekend, we all gathered for celebration, to worship the Lord, and to be encouraged as the newest class of students. It was a time of bonding and fellowship and, for me, a sense of finality as far as reality hitting home.

To be honest, my heart had really been torn since the moment we pulled up to the ranch on Friday. Emotionally, I didn't want to be there. I had tried to surrender to God's call in my life and had left L.A. out of obedience. But my heart wasn't in it, and it got worse as the weekend went on.

On that Saturday, Ken Silas, who was one of the Bible club teachers that had come out with us from L.A. and was my one-on-one when we stayed in the guys' house for those two weeks, was working near me in the patch.

While picking the strawberries, I kept debating in my mind whether or not I would return with the L.A. crew at the end of the weekend. My thoughts swirled back and forth, revolving the issue over and over again, setting out the pros and cons for staying or for going back. Emotionally, I was overwhelmed with the temptation to grab my bags in the final minutes of the weekend and not care what anybody said to try changing my mind. But at the same time, I knew in my spirit that God wanted me to stay.

I was in real anguish to the point of guilt, so I called Ken over to talk. I asked him to help me figure out what I should do because time was running out and I needed to make a choice. Ken was very gentle and inspiring.

He urged me to separate my personal feelings from what I knew God was asking me to do and then base my decision on that. Certainly I desired to obey God, but I guess He knew I just needed some encouragement. In tears I agreed to wait before jumping into a quick selection. Believe me, as a city boy, the thought of living on a farm with cows and chickens did not appeal to me.

Finally, on Sunday before the guys started loading up, one of the teens from the L.A. crew came up to me privately. I had known Ricky since he was about six or seven. He confided to me, "Clipper, I just want to say that I'm proud of you, man. You done changed, and if you can do it [sticking out the two year program], then anybody can do it too. If God wants me to when I finish school." In so many ways, Ricky was implying, "Eric, you are important to Watts, and we need to see you make it. Don't give up." Ricky didn't know I was considering going back with them because I had kept my thoughts hidden from everybody but Alex and Ken.

Shortly after Ricky and I finished talking, Devin walked over to me. We called him "Big D." He too had watched me gang bang while he was growing up and got to see the change in me now as well. Big D told me to "Hang in there" and that he was not only proud of me but that I was a great example to him. In his view, my transformation revealed the power of God so clearly in my life because he knew how committed I had been to the Grape Street Watts Crips gang. To my knowledge, no one had ever changed that radically from the hood and stayed with it. I sensed from my young buddy how important it was to him that I succeed. After our conversation, I ended it with, "D, I'm gonna stick it out, man. I know that God wants me here." Privately, though, I admitted to God, "I wanna obey you, but I'm gonna need help."

Unmistakably, God used those two teen guys not only to encourage me but to communicate His mandate for me—namely to be a living example of what He could do in all people's lives if they were willing to surrender to whatever He called for in their future.

I felt an immediate obligation to suffer for Christ so that my family—my people from Watts—would see with their own eyes what God had done, that Jesus Christ was being exalted as the Lord and Savior of my life. So by the time the vans started to load up, I had given up the plot to quit even before it got started.

We, the ranch staff and students, sat or stood watching as the vans pulled away. I fell into a sort of daze as I sat on the brick wall observing the L.A. crew recede into the distance, wondering what I had just gone through. Still, one thing was certain: my whole mindset had changed, and I was there to stay.

We new guys were assigned to a place of residence. Each home was marked with a different color of trim. They had the grey house or the brown house, the green house, the red house, and the blue house.

Saul and I were assigned to the grey house where we would share the space with two second year (senior) students, Kevin and Derrick, who would also be our house leaders. They had the responsibility of assigning chores and planning daily menus that covered breakfast, lunch, and dinner. The second year guys also had the task of buying the groceries.

Alex and Glenn were assigned to the green house with Jimmy and Samuel. Terry and Phil went to the brown house with one of the staff men, Dave, who was also responsible for our Bible curriculum, and Jim Elam.

Jerry and Ruth Peters and their family lived in the blue house; and Joe, our director, lived in the red house with his sons Lil' Joe and Chris. The staff had been living there from the time the ranch (Christian Leadership Training Center) was established in the early '80s.

The cool thing about the ranch and World Impact in general was that everyone had what they called a "one-on-one" partner, an accountability partner. So likewise, we too were assigned someone to meet with personally once each week at a minimum.

Our daily routine consisted of waking up no later than 6:00 A.M. Monday through Friday. Depending upon the particular house, next came chores, devotions, and/or cooking breakfast if it was your assigned day for that particular meal.

After breakfast, class began at 7:30 if you were a second year student and 8:15 if you were a first year. And work began immediately after each class. If you were assigned lunch duty in your particular home, you would come in about twenty minutes earlier to prepare your group's lunch.

Work would continue until about 5:00 P.M. But if you were assigned dinner duty, likewise, you would leave work a little earlier to fix the meal. Depending upon your home, you would do chores and/or homework. If your huddle with your one-on-one partner was scheduled for that day, then you two would meet for at least an hour to share how you were doing emotionally, spiritually, or with relationships in your home and to be encouraged or challenged. For the most part, free time occurred after that, from around 6:30 or so until whenever we decided to go to bed.

One of my first challenges came when my house leaders decided to assign our chores at 5:30 in the morning. That was crazy to me and Saul. We tried to persuade them to change it to the evening as the other guys did. But they would not listen. So we figured we'd make their job hard by not "jumping" when they said jump.

If it was time to get up for chores, we put it off as long as possible—just to irritate them. My plan was to force them to submit to our demand to change our chore time. However, this attitude began to spill over into other areas, and things began to fall apart in our home. At one point it got so bad, things took a turn for the worse.

One of the house leaders and I were talking about our particular cities and naming off different attractions they have to offer. He was from St. Louis, so naturally he mentioned the Arch and other things. And of course I was listing Hollywood, Disneyland, the Lakers, Magic Mountain, the Dodgers, etc.

At one point he began to put L.A. down. I started seeing that as a challenge as though it were gang related and felt like I had to defend the hood. And because of my speech impediment I wasn't able to out-talk him, and it felt almost like I was being smothered.

So I told him he'd better squash it or I was going to show him what the true L.A. was like. Of course, he didn't take me seriously, not knowing where I had come from. He kept it up, so I finally grabbed him, picked him up, and body slammed him. In retaliation, he jumped up, yanked out his pocket knife, and threatened to stab me; so I put him to the test and was daring him to do it. By this time, Saul had come in, after hearing the noise, and encouraged me to stop pursuing him.

My particular house leader, whom I had gotten into it with, and I both had the same one-on-one accountability partner. The time came when our situation was brought up. I didn't tell Jerry about our house problems, not wanting to be seen as a snitch, but my house leader did—and rightly so.

The conflicts in our home were becoming so obvious among the students that the issues could no longer be ignored. Jerry Peters, my one-on-one staff member, and I met shortly after the knife incident. He asked me about it and what had been my role in the dissension in the house.

My response was to be honest and not bite my tongue. I was struggling big time having house leaders, who were both younger than I was, telling me what to do—especially ordering me to get up at 5:30 in the morning just to do some chores. The other house wasn't doing that, and I couldn't understand why our leaders were unwilling to change. So I decided to rebel against them.

But the incident itself had occurred because I felt challenged and disrespected, and so my pride would not allow him to even think he could punk me and get away with it. That was the spark that ignited the bomb inside me.

God gave Jerry the wisdom and gentleness to deal with my real problem, which was disobedience to God's will. Quite simply, His will was that I obey Him and that I needed to submit to those in authority over me. Yes, my house leaders were younger than I was, and they could have been a little more sensitive to Saul's and my point of view. But I needed to obey God by following the house rules.

That was tough to swallow because I had to humble myself to be able to obey my Lord. God knew my struggle and where I needed to be in order for Him to use my life later on. But it would be just the beginning of a rough process of adjustment for me.

Jerry arranged a time for the three of us to meet and talk about our problems. I knew in my heart that I needed to take the initiative and apologize to my friend for putting my hands on him and for making his responsibilities difficult to carry out. He too apologized for how he handled things between us.

That marked a turning point in our relationship. He and our other house leader began to seek our input on different issues like chore times. Though our friendship began to grow, it didn't mean we were going to master everything at once. It would indeed be a process.

Chapter Twenty-One

Kevin and Derrick—our house leaders—were also good cooks, particularly Kevin, who really knew his way around a kitchen. He had jokes too, and kept us laughing at the ranch. Meanwhile, Jerry and I continued to deal with my temper issues through accountability, prayer, and Bible reading. And I sincerely made efforts to try getting a handle on it.

Our director Joe, a godly and good man, had a strong personality. He knew what he wanted from all of us; and when it came to work duties, he was a no-nonsense type of guy. Actually, he wasn't directly over the work duties; Jim Elam was—a one-time college football player who was as strong a man as I had ever seen. But occasionally Joe would work alongside us on a project if Jim was tied up with other things.

I always felt reserved around Joe because of his strong personality and had always anticipated a potential conflict with him. It was as if in the back of my mind I saw him as a threat to my own will. So I always avoided him if I could when it came to work.

Jim, a true man of the south, was not imposing unless he had to be; and at times he could reveal that side of his nature. His leadership style was gentle but firm. But in contrast, Joe's was firm first and then gentle if necessary. It was his aggressive nature that kept my guard up.

That anticipated conflict finally came—when I was not in the mood. We were preparing to go shopping in town. It was the only time we got to leave the ranch unless under special circumstances like visiting local churches or participating in activities with the Wichita, Kansas based ministry or something like that.

I was late as usual because I was making sure my hair was combed right. Joe and everybody else had been waiting for me on our small bus, but finally Joe came running up the stairs calling out my name. I walked out of the restroom, not aware that all the others were sitting on the bus. Joe tore into me for being late. I tried to apologize and explained that I didn't realize we were ready. He said that I *should have* known.

He kept on accusing me of always being late, and his harping was starting to bother me at this point. I told him to go on outside because I was coming, but he just stood there waiting to make sure. I said, "I know how to walk by myself, and I don't need you to babysit me."

Joe made another comment, so I swung my fist into the closet door beside us in the hallway. I put a fist-sized hole in the door to make a statement to him: *"Get away from me!"* He stared at me, then turned and left.

God later convicted me to the core: I felt that I was disobeying God Himself. At once I went to Joe and apologized for how I'd acted. He accepted my apology and advised me to watch how I handle my feelings. He recognized the negative way he'd approached me and promised he would work on his manner.

Back out in the sun, the work was never the same from one day to the next. We could be pulling weeds from the strawberry patch, picking potatoes, or hauling hay bales to the barn. We could never really get comfortable with one thing early on in that first year. To be honest, I was not used to physically working so hard; my perspective, of course, was from one of the biggest cities in America and a gang lifestyle to a rural setting and life on a farm. I know I wasn't the only inner-city kid who had come to or was currently on the ranch, but not everyone learns on the same level or grows at the same pace.

On one particular day, I had just finished an assignment and was basically standing around waiting for Jim to find me and give me something else to do. When he spotted me—being always the wise guy—he spouted, "Eric, what you doing standing around doing nothing? Well, I got an exciting job lined up for you."

At this point, my curiosity was growing. I asked nervously,

"What?" as I jumped in the truck with him. He drove me over to the barn and got me a shovel. "Move that cow manure from this pile—over to there," he smiled, pointing to a location about twenty-five feet away. I just about died. Each time I would break apart a shovel full, the light breeze would carry the smell with it. That was a tough job at first; but sad to say, I got used to it.

During free time, the guys would typically go out to the court and play basketball. They would invite me, but I had no real interest in participating in sports. All I did basically was stay up in my room and write letters to my family or call home. I must have seemed somewhat anti-social—not because I wanted to be that way but because I was having trouble relating to these people. I had nothing really to talk about.

It was during my first couple of months at the ranch that I discovered Dr. David Jeremiah's teaching program "Turning Point" and Dr. James Dobson's "Focus on the Family" radio program, including their children's series "Adventure in Odyssey." I really got into those Bible programs, and God began to teach me a great deal.

I really enjoyed the work crews that would come out from Salina, Marion, and other small Kansas towns. They would arrive there to help us build things, fix things, and pick weeds or strawberries. The women from those groups would bring all kinds of food to feed us. These times of fellowship and work really served as encouragement.

Local farmers would stop by to help us with different things as well, and I got to see those guys in action. I thought farming was boring, but these people intimidated me with a fierce work ethic. And their handshakes were always firm and filled with meaning; I learned to brace myself when one of them shook my hands. And to this day, I shake hands the same way to let the person know that I mean my greeting.

My favorite people who came out regularly to support us were a farmer named Jerry Cebers, who did our plowing and harvesting, and Jim and Agnes Farley. Mr. Jim was an elderly man who always carried around peppermints; when he greeted you, he gave you a peppermint. But beyond the friendliness, this man taught me so much about work. He knew something about everything; I was always amazed at his vast knowledge. And he was very patient with me—and with all of us—as he worked at our sides. His wife, Ms. Agnes, and their granddaughter, Alanna, would bring sandwiches and homemade cupcakes or whatever. Ms. Agnes always had a smile on her face to bless us. At our first meeting, she greeted me with a warm hug as though I were her son. She always spoiled us, and she did this with every class that came through the program. I loved these people.

Jim and Agnes Farley

The more I spent time with my one-on-one in his home, watching how he interacted with his kids David, Luke, Elijah, and later Jeremiah, I saw the love he had for them just as I had seen with Kim and his kids. These family units were inspirational, and I began to desire a family of my own. In fact, this had become one of our topics of discussion in our meetings.

Jerry would talk to me about staying pure in my thoughts and trusting the Lord to take care of the rest. During my first month at the ranch, the Wichita ministry visited with many of the teens and young adults and families for a baptism in our pool. One of the young adults in that group was Leah Steps.

I had seen her the previous year in L.A. when she came to help World Impact for the summer. She was the first black Christian young lady who had impressed me with how she carried herself. But that is as far as it went.

When I saw her at the baptism, I thought, *"I know her from somewhere."* It later dawned on me where I had seen her before. From that I began to ask myself *"What if?"* and a special feeling developed for her. She and her best friend, Andrea, were there together. The two of them looked so clean and fresh: not so much on the outside—though they were—but on the inside. I didn't know that young black women could be so impressive in that way. I had to introduce myself and remind Leah that I had met her in L.A. the previous year.

Alex and I became best friends at the ranch and spent much of our free time together, lifting weights, listening to oldies, and just getting to know each other better—even though we had both grown up in the PJs. I developed a certain little fantasy about the two of us getting together with Leah and Andrea. He wasn't exactly innocent either; he began to share the dream too, although I was probably more into it than he was. Still, such fantasizing became a fun pastime because it opened up our ability to dream.

I dared not give Leah any sign of how I felt about her. Whenever we would get around them for special outings, I would speak and keep my distance. I knew I was not in a situation to pursue her, but also I felt that she was too special for me because I saw myself as an ex-thug. What could I possibly offer her?

My first Christmas at the ranch was kind of bittersweet. Being so far from home, I felt pretty lonely since I didn't get any cards or other contact from my family; and that lack made me feel forgotten. It was kind of like being in jail; you always look forward to letters and packages, especially around the holidays. But on the other hand, I got cards from Kim and his family, Fred and his family, and from my bosses from the Trophy Shop; all those made me feel good. I was especially glad to hear from the latter because my boss, Bob—the owner and founder of Rex Trophies—had died of throat cancer a couple of months earlier.

The staff and different churches worked closely together to do special things for us at that time of year. In early December we were each instructed to write down three things we would like for

Christmas. I asked for an alarm clock, which I still have to this day, some stamps to write home, and something else. I also got a gift from Suzy Kriebel on staff in Watts. She always took care of me in terms of keeping me connected to home with letters of encouragement, post-cards, Laker T-shirts, and pictures of different relatives and friends she worked with.

Sometime after Christmas, we were invited to a certain church to share our testimony in a small town called Carbondale, Kansas. This church had organized a group to come out and assist us in our work, headed by a couple named Bob and Judy Cairns. I grew to love this couple and their many friends who helped to make our lives easier at the ranch.

Joe Graham, our ranch director, asked me if I would share my testimony. I had never communicated my story to an audience before, so I was kind of nervous—mainly because of my speech impediment. But I agreed to do so. By the time I finished, I was well past the time I had been allotted because of the grind I had to go through just to get out my words.

At the end I was in a daze, wondering if I had made any sense. People kept flocking up to me, thanking me for sharing my life as an L.A. gang member and how Jesus had brought me out of that life-style. I felt uncomfortable with their thanking me; I didn't want the credit because it was still so fresh in my mind who was responsible for changing my life. My response was, without any hesitation, "All because of Christ. Not me." I didn't want any praise.

Prior to this, the only time I had stood before an audience was when I traveled with World Impact to Jack Hayford's church back in California. The president and founder of World Impact, Dr. Keith Philips, was leading the meeting; and after his message he shared with the congregation—numbering in the thousands—how Christ had transformed my life and taken me out of the world of violent gangs. Dr. Phillips asked me to stand up, to my utter shock, and let the people at the Church On The Way meet me. The crowd gave me a thunderous applause, and I quickly sat down.

Joe began asking me to share my story more often with different groups. At times I would agree while on some occasions I would defer to others. But the Lord began to give me the desire to read the conversion autobiographies like *Born Again* by Chuck Colson, former counsel to President Nixon and now founder and president of Prison Fellowship Ministry.

I read his book about three or four times before having the privilege of hearing him in person in Wichita, Kansas. I read others' stories about survivors of prison camps where Christians were tortured for their faith and about guys who had come out of the mob as a result of Christ impacting their lives.

Through these demonstrations of God's transforming spirit, He was showing me the power of a Christian testimony. Up to this point I hadn't realized I even *had* a testimony because I didn't actually understand what a testimony was. But reading others' stories gave me a desire to share my own with joy because it would bring so much glory to Jesus Christ.

I had always looked forward to using the phone to call home to talk to family and my homeboys. But I hardly ever received a call from home when it wasn't about somebody dying and it seemed like it was someone I knew about or knew personally.

One phone call I got was about my homeboy Crow. I was informed he had gotten shot down at a gas station. I couldn't help but remember asking him shortly before leaving L.A., "What are you going to do when you stand before Jesus—claim Grape?" My heart sank when I heard the news; I could only hope he had made peace with Christ before he died.

So every time I was told I had a phone call, I wondered first if my worst fear had come true—that David had killed my mother. Fortunately, I never got that particular call. But over the course of a two-year span, word would come from home that more than fifty of my friends, enemies, or acquaintances had died. The majority of those received the final blow from gang violence.

Living on the ranch did have its advantages. It gave us all a sense of security, something that many of us had never experienced before coming to this place. Hearing about the many drive-by killings and the other gang related deaths of people I knew gave me the sense that I was safe. I could have very well been among the dead if Jesus hadn't given me a new heart. So, little by little, I grew to realize how God was using the ranch in my life.

Chapter Twenty-Two

As the different seasons rolled on, the ranch participated in various sporting events. We got involved in a variety of leagues around the community like softball, basketball, and even donkey softball—the same game except played on actual donkeys. I felt like a hillbilly to the core, but it was a great experience.

For a while, I would not participate in sports because I flat out didn't like them with the exception, as I mentioned earlier, of boxing and martial arts, which I had taken with a friend back in Watts who was a fifteen year experienced martial artist. These I found fascinating primarily because they inflicted pain, without the pads.

The guys on the ranch had always tried to get me out, but I would typically just refuse. Instead, I would go in my room and write or listen to several programs on the radio such as Dr. David Jeremiah or "Focus on the Family" or their program "Adventures in Odyssey." Meanwhile, Jerry Peters, my one-on-one, had been urging me to spend more time with the guys for fellowship reasons. One night I got tired of Jimmy and the other guys begging me to join them in basketball, so I decided to go out and surprise them.

The guys were glad to see me and quickly included me in the game. I had played with my Uncle Carl a few times but really didn't like the game personally; and I had tried it a few times back in the projects but not enough to warm up to it or to find enjoyment in it either. So I was kind of clueless and awkward out there. The only thing I had going for me was my will to win and my strength and raw speed.

Yet by the end of our time, I found I had actually enjoyed myself. That was astonishing to me: I really had fun! The pleasure might have been more in being with the guys and having a sense of doing my Lord's will to accept the invitation to enter the world of these people I lived and worked with.

But as time went on, my passion for the game itself took root. That first night out I felt embarrassed in front of the guys who were far more experienced at basketball than I was. But the event lit a fire under me; I said to myself, *"I'm gonna learn this game!"* A part of my past character rose up that wouldn't allow people to dominate me and get away with it.

Among the guys, I thought Jimmy and Terry were the two best players. Jimmy was silky smooth and smart. Terry was a raw athlete and a huge Michael Jordan fan. He could not be stopped out there. So I decided to pick their brains—especially Jimmy's—and sought their help to make me a better player.

This was around the time of the 1987 NBA playoffs. We only got to watch TV on Sundays after church, and on this particular day all the guys were tuned in to those playoffs. Out of the eleven students at the ranch, eight of us were from L.A.; so most of the guys were Laker fans while the rest, including the male staff, were Celtic fans.

I soon joined into the friendly rivalry, representing my home team—the L.A. Lakers—who went on to win the NBA Championship that year. It was during this time that Magic Johnson caught my eye. Watching him and Larry Bird battling for the basketball crown, willing their teams to the finals and leaving only one to celebrate the ultimate victory, gave me an insight into the nature of a champion.

I saw in Magic a general's heart and a passion second to none on the basketball court; I observed how he made his teammates better by his unselfish floor leadership. I chose to use him and James Worthy as my models, when it came to basketball, and tried from then on to grow in my game.

Still, along the way it wasn't pretty. I was so physical and passionate defensively that it started to frustrate a couple of the guys. I didn't mean any harm by my style of play, but I was simply expressing who I was. Just as when I was a Crip and felt duty bound to lead by example if I expected others to represent at the same level of intensity, so it was likewise in basketball.

Eventually it came to a point that relationships were being

affected. The guys began blaming me for fouling too much, almost to the point of mocking me. I certainly couldn't out talk them, and their laughing was like pouring gasoline on the fire.

Finally I told them, "If you say one more thing, I'm gonna slap you like a b----!" One guy in particular said something else that made me think he was testing me, so I walked over to him and slapped him with my right hand—just like I had warned.

At once everything went silent. Everybody there was shocked, even stunned, by what I had done. I advised the guy to put up his guards if he wanted to swing; I began daring him to test me again. But he looked at me sadly and said, "I'm not gonna fight you."

Immediately my Lord revealed to my heart how wrongly I had handled the incident. I was never more convicted. But then my mind flew into a rage because I realized Satan had won a battle and gotten me to dishonor my Lord Jesus.

I began kicking the gate repeatedly and kicking over the kids' big wheels and other toys. I started telling Satan to "F--- yourself! I hate you, you f---!" while thrusting my middle fingers into the air. I could almost hear him laughing at me.

My next reaction was to talk with Jerry before I went berserk. I stomped toward his house, furious with myself. If I could have stepped outside my body and faced myself, I would have slugged that jerk in the jaw—that's how disappointed I was with my behavior.

We kept our basement doors unlocked, a habit I thought was crazy when I first came to the ranch; so I stormed right into Jerry and Ruth's basement, picking my way through all their storage items, blindly knocking over big objects, and generating plenty of noise. The whole family was in bed when I stood at the bottom of the stairs yelling for Jerry to come down and talk with me.

He rushed down in his pajamas and slippers, startled by the strange racket and uncertain of what he would find. But he could obviously see that something was wrong with me. I described what had happened and how ashamed I felt for disappointing my Lord and hitting my friend in spite of how he had provoked me. I blurted that I was wrong in how I handled the situation.

Jerry calmly talked me down so he could get to the bottom of what was going on. I felt like the guys were testing my heart to see if I was a punk or not; it was like reliving my childhood. My immediate impulse was put them in check as quickly as possible. I came to realize it was pride to the core that drove me to put the challenge back on them.

He encouraged me not to let pride destroy my friendships and suggested that I needed to obey God above my own feelings. Jerry and I prayed that I could take the lead in making things right by apologizing for putting my hands on another man, a brother in Christ. I understood the real enemy was not the guys but the power behind what they had done to get me to that boiling point—Satan.

I repented immediately and begged God to help me with my anger and to not let the enemy win. By the time I was done, all the guys had gone back to the houses, so I went looking for my friend to re-establish our positive relationship.

By this point, I was nearly in tears. I asked him to forgive me for what I had done; and to my amazement, he did. He also apologized for egging me on and not stopping when I asked him to. We gave each other a big brotherly hug, and that night marked a turning point in our friendship. The joy from this led me to seek forgiveness from Alex, Glenn, and the other guys for example. And they gladly accepted.

In the spring of '87 a film crew came out to shoot us doing various work assignments as part of a new video about the ministry. Joe, our director, asked me to assist Derrick in milking the cow so they could get some shots of us doing that. For nearly a year, Joe and Jim hadn't been able to get me into that barn to save their lives. I wasn't going, period! But with this newly-found attitude of voluntary submission, I agreed to go in and help Derrick milk our Jersey Maid cow, Bossie.

Why had I been so against going into the barn? The place was crawling with rats as big as cats. I had been willing to put my life in harm's way to watch my homeboys' back or to stand up for Grape, but now that I was out in the middle of nowhere—rural Kansas—I couldn't stand up to frogs or rats.

As I look back, I see that my willingness to submit to authority, even when I didn't agree, was proof that God was indeed doing a good work in my life. And I think Joe was milking it for all it was worth, too, because after the filming, he told me that since I'd finally braved the barn, Derrick would be training me as his replacement. Joe had run game on me, and I bit it.

Chapter Twenty-Three

June was quickly approaching, and the second year students were getting ready to graduate. The remaining months would be filled with deciding what they would do after leaving the ranch and training us as their replacements as house leaders, tool room manager, and caretaker for the animals.

At the same time, we were preparing to host our first ranch banquet after the graduation. We were expecting about nine hundred people. The event was scheduled for the same weekend that the new students were coming along with the Weekend Exposure staff and teams from various World Impact cities.

The second year students—Kevin, Derrick, Bryce, Jimmy, and Samuel—had really become some of my closest friends in my Christian family. The year we had shared served to bring us closer together as God worked in our hearts. A bond was established among us, and our common denominator was Jesus Christ our Lord. It was a sad day for me to see them go.

But when they left, it gave our class (with the exception of Terry, who went home for personal reasons) two weeks to spend together. On the day that Kevin and the guys left the ranch for good as students, the five of us remaining—Alex, Phillip, Glenn, Saul, and I—called a students-only meeting.

We planned what kind of leaders we were going to be and what sort of examples we wanted to set for the new students coming in. We all agreed we would lead by our service to the new guys. We intended to learn from the mistakes of the outgoing students, to take those good things that we did learn and build on them. We decided we would not expect of them anything we ourselves were not willing to do. Each of us, one by one, committed ourselves to one another, to hold each other accountable to be in the Word of God and to allow ourselves to speak into one another's lives when we saw anyone slipping. And then we pledged all these things in prayer.

That period of time together—alone as a group—charted our direction for the upcoming year. We discovered our purpose as a collective class of individuals, dedicated to raise the level of what it meant to be ranch guys. I fully agreed and participated in all the subjects and felt very much a part of the core of it all.

God had given us a standard to shoot for with Jesus Christ as our center focus. But this didn't mean it would be easy because immediately I noticed a pressure to deal with different feelings that were stirred up in me even before the guys graduated.

Specifically, Alex and Glenn were made house leaders in the green house. Saul became director of the grey house; Phil was given management of the brown house; and I was placed in charge of the animals. I took offense to that because it felt like a demotion or something. In other words, the others were given responsibilities that dealt with *people* while I was stuck with a bunch of dumb beasts. I couldn't understand why I was "put with the animals."

With the exception of Alex, who had animal chores in the mornings, I couldn't see how my working with smelly pigs, chickens, and cows was going to prepare me to be used by God later on. It was as though I was the "black sheep" of the bunch, and that self-imposed image became a thorn in my side. But I knew I had to trust God through it.

The banquet/Exposure day finally came, and we had nearly a thousand people on our ranch. The new students were Marlon, whom I had known back in Watts and from junior high; David Neal, also from L.A.; and Mardell from Wichita, Kansas. They came with teens from their particular cities as well as the staff men from World Impact.

Our president and founder, Keith Phillips, attended the banquet along with Rosey Grier, the former NFL star who played for the New York Giants and later with the Rams where he was a core member of the famed "Fearsome Foursome" defensive line. After those accomplishments, Rosey became a bodyguard for the late Robert F. Kennedy and established an acting career in Hollywood. Finally, Rosey became a Christian and started his own ministry in L.A., ultimately joining World Impact's national board.

At the banquet Rosey sang some songs with his wonderful voice; and Dr. Phillips, whom we simply called Keith, gave a message. Alex, Saul, and I shared our experiences of our first year at the ranch and our hopes for the remaining year and beyond.

Standing there and looking out at the huge crowd, I was beyond nervous. I was anxious because of my speech impediment and its slow pace in a race against the clock. Certainly I was honored to be sharing my life and what God was doing in it but scared to death that people would be so fixed on my stuttering that they wouldn't hear or make sense of what I was trying to say.

In the end, it went off well; and I received plenty of compliments. Two of these were from the mayor of a small town called Marion, if I recall correctly, and the mayor of the largest city in Kansas—Wichita's Mayor Bob Knight. He and his wonderful wife, Jane, greeted me later. They expressed how much they had enjoyed my story and how God had worked in my life. They also suggested that, if I decided to move to Wichita after graduating the following year, I should look them up so they could introduce me to the rest of their family and get to know me better.

I was shocked that a major politician and his wife would

seek me out, actually wanting to meet me. I had always considered politicians to be selfish and phony. In those days I cared very little about governmental affairs, other than reading the autobiography of President Nixon's "hatchet man" and counselor, Chuck Colson, which sparked a beginning interest in the world of politics. But what fascinated me about Mayor Knight was he was a Christian. I didn't know that was even possible—a politician could be a man of God!

My first time voting was in 1984, and I voted for Reagan for President because he was not afraid to look the Soviet Union in the eyes without blinking. I liked that, but that was my only time tuning in to politics.

Meanwhile, the banquet was a success, and I was overjoyed at having had the privilege of taking part in the event. I had never stood before such a large group, and our testimonies were obviously a blessing.

After the banquet, Rosey Grier and I got to know each other a little bit. Both being from L.A., we had something in common. He was bigger in person than I expected; before that I had only seen him on the television show about Daniel Boone.

Over the course of my first year at the ranch, I got to know many people from all over Kansas. Among them, few stood out more than those from Salina—Bob and Judy Cairns and their companions from Carbondale—or a group of mostly teens from western Kansas out of a little church in a small town called Meade. From that company emerged the Hoddy family.

During the Meade company's visit, several of us were asked to share our testimonies and an explanation of a typical day's schedule at the ranch. When it came to my time to speak, I was quite nervous, not knowing how these kids were going to react to my stuttering. True enough, what I dreaded actually did happen. Several of them who couldn't have cared less about hearing descriptions of our work started laughing among themselves in the back of the group.

I figured out while I was sharing that they were laughing at the way I talked. A part of me wanted to march over there and slap them up-side their heads, but God gave me wisdom on how to deal with them. I said something to the effect, "You know, it's very hard for me to stand up here and talk to y'all. I can't help the way I talk. *Ask God why I talk the way I do!* But I'm up here because I want to glorify

Christ in my life. If any of y'all want to go ahead and laugh at me, do it now. You got the floor."

Those guys who were laughing stopped on a dime. They were stunned, not expecting to be confronted in front of everybody; yet I never pointed them out at all. I didn't embarrass them, but they knew exactly which individuals I was talking about.

In that amazing moment, of their own free will, each one spoke up humbly and apologized to me in front of everyone. I graciously accepted their words. Afterwards, they came up and greeted me and expressed their remorse once more. One kid in particular decided to reach out to me and wanted to keep in touch. His name was Todd Hoddy.

Todd was a white kid from a loving family, people who loved Jesus Christ and made family closeness a high priority. Todd and I built a solid friendship from that point on. He became one of my biggest supporters and friends; in fact, he became like a little brother to me. And even though he was a die-hard Celtic fan, I forgave him anyway.

In our second year at the ranch, we hit the ground running. Our desire for the truth of God's Word seemed to grow exponentially. We were memorizing lots of scriptures, holding one another accountable to practice excellence in our work, and putting a big emphasis on servant-leadership—making service an important part of our being leaders to the new guys.

I had reached the point where I was tired of worrying about whether I would ever get married and have a family of my own. I began to see that concern as a distraction in my relationship with Christ, so I decided to just focus on getting to know my Lord. And when I started to do that, the desires went away.

I began applying the word of God more and more in my life and adopted the standard I once had with the Crips—namely, to be loyal to Christ no matter the cost. Sometime I would be put to the test, even to almost the breaking point.

Winter was coming around that year, and Alex and I were still taking care of the animals. I didn't realize the cost of caring for them until after the previous class had left the ranch. Because my duties with the animals took place in the evening, I often had to miss going into town on Saturday afternoons. I tried to accept the situation, even though it was tough because it was the only time we consistently looked forward to each week. We got twenty-five dollars a month for spending, and I had finally gotten a handle on my phone bill expense, which had been averaging about $15.00 a month. Our clothing allowance was $10.00 a month. Nevertheless, it was something that we all looked forward to.

One day the ground was covered with snow, and the wind was blowing from the north. The temperature was probably around fifteen below zero. The rest of the guys were now in the houses, all nice and warm. After dinner they were planning to drive into Emporia for grocery shopping. I wanted to go into town very badly and was trying to finish with the animals in time.

But that day I had a problem: the outside water troughs were frozen on the surface, so I had to break up the ice and then fill them up. Everything seemed to be going wrong. I also had to feed the chickens in the coop and supply them with water. And then I had the cows to worry about. When you milk a cow by hand, you have to keep your hands lubricated with water so you won't burn the nipples when squeezing out the milk. But when the wind chill is below twenty degrees or so, sticking your hands in water doesn't feel too good.

My Bossie

My fingers were as cold as the snow outside; they were so icy they were aching. My blood seemed to be freezing them into popsicles as I tried desperately to warm them up by sitting on them or putting my hands under my jacket. Neither of those tactics seemed to help. So I decided to dunk my fingers into the milk instead because it was warm coming from Bossie's body.

The snow was coming down hard, and the wind was blowing it horizontally. I could hardly see in front of me. The walk from the barn to the houses was about a half mile, and I had to manage it all in the snowstorm.

Bossie and the other animals were fed, and I guess they were satisfied; but I was mad at life. All the way home—which seemed to take forever—I complained to myself, *"Why does everybody else (except Alex) get to go home and warm up, when I'm out here slaving? I hate this crap! Why did I get stuck with some dumb animals that make me miss out on trips to town and other stuff?"*

Out of nowhere, I could hear the Lord's voice in my mind just as clear as day, *"Eric, these animals need you more now than at any other time."* And then I recalled the verse I had recently memorized, "Whoever can be trusted with very little can also be trusted with much, and whoever is dishonest with very little will also be dishonest with much" (Luke 16:10 NIV).

That scripture shot through me like a bullet through a wet paper towel. I got the point, and I realized my job was probably more important than any of the others available at the ranch because these animals were totally dependent on someone to feed them and give them water, especially during the winter months.

I stopped my complaining at once and gave God thanks for not only encouraging me in that time of frustration but for giving me the awesome responsibility of caring for the animals. That moment in the raging blizzard turned out to be one of my greatest instances of growth, and I never grumbled about having to care for the animals again. Now I took joy in doing so.

Chapter Twenty-Four

I continued to grow in my relationship with Christ. He was indeed my hero of heroes. My love for the Word of God also continued to expand. In addition to Jesus, God used three other biblical characters in my life as examples of men who had tragedies but were still used by God. First, I was drawn to Peter the Apostle early on. He often said or did things without thinking first. For example, when Jesus told him and the other disciples that He would suffer and then be crucified, Peter jumped in and exclaimed "Never!" Understanding who was speaking through Peter, the Lord rebuked Satan for trying to stand in the way of His mission. Peter had no awareness of Satan's role in that moment, but Peter's compulsion caused him to act before thinking. Yet Peter had a leader's personality; out of all the disciples, he seemed to do what all the others weren't willing to do—he took risks.

Likewise, King Solomon impressed me because he was given the opportunity to ask God for anything he wanted, but Solomon asked only for wisdom. Wealth and power were not what he desired, but God's approval *was*. That had a profound effect on me.

But it was Solomon's father, King David, who attracted me the most. The God of heaven, the very creator of the universe, called David "a man after His own heart." How profound. That's what I wanted to hear from the Lord someday.

These three men, along with some others, became role models for me. Jesus Christ, of course, was my only hero; but on a human level, God used these characters to bring out something special in me—a desire to be God's man.

As the weeks and months went by, the new guys—Marcel Hill, David Neal, and Marlon May—continued to adjust to the ranch life. Marcel had a gentle personality, always eager to learn God's Word. David was the adventuresome type, ever the explorer of the outdoors. And Marlon seemed the take-no-prisoners man. He worked hard and pretty much minded his own business.

Actually, Marlon and I had much in common, having both grown up in Watts (along with Alex); he and I had very tough backgrounds. Marlon inspired me to think critically and not just feel my way through problems. He wasn't the mild type, but he challenged me in a number of ways to examine situations.

To be honest, I had never really done that. My issues were pretty buried until then, but God used Marlon to began that probing process. However, because we both had strong wills, this often led us into heated arguments. Marlon could be pretty intimidating to people because of his huge size and menacing face. Most weren't used to confronting that. But I had learned in the streets to show no fear and to stand up to anyone, believing I would ultimately win.

Marlon tried to intimidate me once, despite knowing me from back in L.A., though we had never hung out together. On that occasion, he tried verbally to cause me to shrink; but I stood nose to nose to him, declaring, "If you cross me, one way or another you'll lose. I'll catch you when you're asleep and do something to you, boy! Don't test me."

Eventually, he and I grew to respect each other, and our deep talks would sometimes go to 3:00 or 4:00 in the morning, only to have to wake up in a couple of hours or so. We often paid for it the next day, but unquestionably those conversations were worth it.

The fruit of our talks no doubt gave me access into his life to a degree that very few were allowed to enter. And to this day I believe God used Marlon to begin the process of my learning to go deeply into my own life. And for that, I'm grateful.

As the months went by, our class grew closer and closer together. We would continue to offer encouragement and hold one another accountable. We memorized scripture together; and collectively our Bible classes, under the sound teaching of Dave Zagunis, grew more solid.

I continued to be the emotional one in the group and often

got excited over the smallest of things I was learning from God's holy Word. He was definitely making a difference in my life. One of the ways I realized this was when my grandmother Mary died.

When I got the news of her death, I began to worry because I didn't have the money to go to Arkansas on the bus. But Jerry Peters, my one-on-one, and his wife were planning to drive down to Arkansas to visit her parents and siblings and offered to take me to Pine Bluff. And different Christians pitched in to buy me a one-way ticket back by airplane.

My reaction? "An airplane! Man, I ain't getting on no airplane. That thing might crash! And what's holding it up, anyway?" But through prayer and explanation, I decided to entrust my fears to the Lord, and I agreed to do it. It would turn out to be an exciting and memorable experience—and wouldn't be the last time, either.

Ruth and her sister took me to Pine Bluff after spending a night at her parents' home. I had the honor of introducing them to my father and stepmother Louise and to other family members.

It was great to be back in Pine Bluff—only the third time since I first left my other grandma who had raised me. It was the second since meeting my father and his family back in 1983. And both times had been to bury my two grandmothers.

Immediately, my family (mainly my cousins Wydale and Arthur) discovered a few changes about me. First, they noticed I wasn't sagging and wearing my pants below my hips. They also saw that I didn't drink beer or alcohol anymore. And finally, I was no longer using profanity in casual instances. God had been restoring my childhood mannerisms like "Yes ma'am" and "Yes sir," and I began answering my father in that way. He was somewhat taken aback by the change but appreciated it very much.

It was tough burying my grandmother, Momma Mary, because I wished I had gotten to know her better. But I stayed in Arkansas a few more days, enjoying my brothers and sisters—William, Jr., Dexter, Jackie, and Shawn—whom I had just met. They got a kick out of meeting me, their big brother from L.A., for the first time; and I got just as big a kick out of them as well as my baby sister Tia. We shared a lot of laughs speaking Pig Latin with each other.

But before leaving, my faith would be tested by my older cousin Wydale. He believed I was turning into a square because I had become a "religious freak." He thought having devotions from God's Word each day was boring. But I didn't care about his opinion. Finally, Wydale got mad at me because I didn't want to drink any alcohol, and he would not stop talking trash. I figured he was a little tipsy at the time, so I tried to avoid an argument. But he wouldn't let up. Finally, I'd had enough and told him to shut his mouth.

I was beginning to get agitated, and I felt the old me starting to resurface. When my father saw me getting angry, he told Wydale to be quiet and go somewhere else. But he wouldn't, pushing my father's hand out of the way. When I saw him do that—as if my father were the enemy and he wanted to get at me—I strode up to my cousin, face to face, and dared him to swing. At this point I was prepared to prove where I came from. My father quickly turned to me and advised me to let it go.

At that moment, inside my head I heard my Lord telling me to obey my father, and I did. I said, "Yes, sir." The pride in me was brought under control immediately; this pleased my dad and turned out to be a great testimony to all the family who had witnessed the scene.

They never heard a foul word out of my mouth, never saw my temper flare up. But what they did see was my willingness to obey my father. After that event, my cousin Wydale apologized to me and gave his reason for initiating the whole thing. I accepted his apology wholeheartedly; it brought us closer together, and my respect for him grew as well.

I was glad that I had started playing basketball with the fellows at the ranch prior to my grandmother's death and had developed my game quite a bit. My brothers William and Dexter, cousins Wydale and Arthur, and some of their friends found time to shoot some hoops at a local park. My father, who was a star athlete in high school, got out there and played with us. It was the first and only time that I ever got to do that with my dad. My brothers knew that wonderful feeling all too well, but I didn't.

After about three or four days with my family, Ruth and her sister came to pick me up. Leaving my father and these dear people was very hard to do, but in that little time God had sown good seeds in their lives and in mine.

I spent a night with Ruth's parents and family and then the

next day was taken to the airport. It was to be my first time flying; and needless to say, I was scared to death. I could not understand how that big heavy airplane was going to hold us up without cable wires or something.

Ruth and her sister had to pray for me before loading up. I didn't drink alcohol anymore, or I would have drunk up all of the plane's liquor from my fears. Fortunately, I brought my Bible and had the opportunity to pray. Never had I been so conscious that my life was not in my own hands. That overwhelming sense of my need for the peace of Christ was so evident that I couldn't stop clutching the Word.

Once we got through the turbulence, the plane leveled off; and it felt as if we were cruising along on a Greyhound bus or something. And the rest of the trip was fine as I came to realize that if we died, I knew where I was going anyway.

Though I had been gone for just under a week, it was good to see all the guys who couldn't wait to hear about my airplane experience because they knew how fearful I had been to get on board. I was glad to get back to the ranch and smell those farm animals and that freshly cut grass. I had come to understand even more just how much of an honor it was to be a student at that place.

Our second and final year was drawing to a close, and the time for making arrangements was being set in motion. Alex, Glenn, Phil, Saul, and I started making phone calls to our loved ones, inviting them to our graduation and allowing them plenty of time to plan ahead.

As graduation time grew nearer, the significance of all aspects of the ranch program seemed to take on deeper meaning. I savored everything I did and thanked my God for knowing more clearly why I had come to the ranch in the first place. I saw that my number one purpose for being there was to get away from all the distractions of the hardcore streets of L.A. and grow to know Christ and His Word better. And I had.

Second, I was to be an example of what Jesus can do in people's lives if their hearts are truly open. I hoped that had been the case. Finally, I was to be equipped for life and service to others, and maybe that was one of the clearest changes taking place in the entire two years and one week that I was there.

Our graduation resulted in one of the biggest turnouts in the ranch's history. But before the event itself, the time became one of the saddest in my life. One of the planned activities was that the graduates and their parents would go into town, Florence, KS, to have dinner. The guys' moms and other family members all traveled to Kansas to celebrate their sons' big day—except for mine. I had never felt so unloved. It was difficult in the sense that I was trying to do something right in my life, and it felt like my family didn't care. This was not really the case: it was more financial.

But nevertheless, it still hurt. Susie Kriebel, one of our World Impact staff members from Watts, was the first to notice the distance and the growing sadness on my face. She approached me at one point and asked if I was depressed about my mother not being there for my graduation because she had been trying to help my mother. I confessed "yes" and how I dreaded going out with the guys and their moms for dinner. But wise Susie offered to be my mom for the evening and went with us. Susie had been there from the time I first left L.A. two years ago, keeping me up-to-date with pictures, cards, and letters and even sending us guys from L.A. some 1987 and 1988 Laker Championship t-shirts.

Her stepping into that role as a substitute was quite the blessing to me. Even in that unhappy situation, God was there to encourage me and to help me to get through a tough time. I was able to enjoy the event with my classmates and their moms and have a great time after all.

From that, I decided I wasn't going to let my family's not being there spoil my time with my new Christian family. I concluded that it was not about me, but rather it was about Christ and what He had done in my life. *He* was to be glorified, not me.

I became aware of so many people whom I had come to know and love. I'd never realized how many people God was using outside of World Impact. In my two years at the ranch, I met thousands who were sold out for Christ and, through World Impact, saw the differences He was making in the lives of inner-city kids like me simply by loving us and reaching out to us in many ways.

The graduation was a success, and a few of us had the opportunity to share a little bit of our plans and how God had worked in our lives. It was a very bittersweet day because we were parting and opening new chapters in our lives. But on the other hand, it was a great moment for me because I had accomplished something I never thought I could do.

I had failed in elementary school, failed with junior high, and failed at high school as well. The thought of spending two years on a ranch in Kansas was scary, and I didn't imagine I would stick it out. In fact, it took me awhile to fully unpack my bags. But two years and one week later, I stood before hundreds along with four of my closest friends and classmates and received my Christian Leadership Training Center certificate and class ring.

I'm the one on the far right.

It was a great feeling being recognized along with these guys, but now I was going to face life without them—Alex, Phil, Saul, and Glenn, with whom I had lived, eaten, worked, and shared stages in our growth in God's Word. We basically came in as boys and were leaving as men.

As a sendoff, we were treated to a week's vacation at Raven Crest, a Christian retreat camp out in Estes Park Colorado, for hiking, basketball, Bible teaching, and fellowship. We were prepared to meet up with other staff members and young adults, representing the different World Impact cities where we were going to help minister to kids and their families.

I had chosen just a week before graduation to go to Wichita,

Kansas to join staff with World Impact there. Up until that point, I was firmly committed to going back to L.A. to work and help support my mother. But Joe Graham, Jerry Peters, Al Ewert (director of the Wichita ministry), and Bruce Gusterfurson (vice president of World Impact) all thought it wouldn't be wise to go back home.

They were well aware of my struggle with my mother's drinking problem. Whenever she would call me, it was usually to say that somebody I knew had just been gunned down or killed in some other way or to talk after she had been drinking. Never did I remember so clearly just how helpless I was as at those times in particular. It would send me into deep depression because it would remind me of my fear that David eventually would be the cause of my mom's death.

That's why I was so determined to go back home. Yes, I wanted to get a job and support my mother, but I also wanted to be by her side in case David tried to hurt her. That way I could be an instant threat to his life if he tried something crazy.

But my leaders didn't think it was a good idea to go back home at this time because Jerry and Joe specifically knew how down I would get after talking to my mother when she'd been drinking. So they advised me to go to Wichita since I already knew the staff there as well as many of the children whom I had become familiar with from camps and other programs out at the ranch.

Still, I rejected their suggestion because it threatened what I wanted to do—to go home and protect my mother. For about a month or so I wrestled with their advice, and I had no peace of mind. Soon I started to wonder, *"What if I go home, and then an old rival walks up to me and blows me away or something?"*

A fear began to set in. I don't know if it was my own doing or what; but I started to consider, *"What if Jerry's and the others' advice is from God, and I find myself outside of the will of God?"* There was no way I wanted to be apart from the Lord's desire for me.

My true motive became very clear at that point. That's when I came to realize I was pulling my mother out from under God's ability to take care of her and was trying to do it myself.

When I reached that conclusion, I decided to set my own will aside and continue to trust in His. Once I did that, peace of mind was restored; and I felt under my Lord's righteous command again. So I met with my one-on-one, Jerry Peters, and told him I was willing to go

216

to Wichita and to be on staff with World Impact. I made this decision about a week prior to graduation day.

My belongings were transported to Wichita before leaving for the retreat in Colorado, which was a good distance west of the ranch. The day we pulled out on the long winding road at the ranch, seeing the basketball court, the alfalfa field, the river, the barn and factory, and the famous strawberry patches, a flood of memories passed through my mind. It was hard to be leaving a place that had been my home for more than two years. I recalled the beginning struggles I'd had with anger, the inability to concentrate on instructions, the physical confrontations but, even more than that, the love I came to know and share with some of the greatest people on the planet. It had suddenly become a part of the ages, and I was now leaving as a man.

Guys at the Ranch, a reunion years later. I'm the third from the left in the front row.

We spent several days at Raven Crest, hiking, fishing, playing basketball, and hearing good teachings on the Word of God. It was a great time of fellowship and fun. We also took part in a men's prayer breakfast with businessmen, lawyers, judges, and pastors. It was a satisfying period, allowing us to unwind as we prepared to enter the next chapter of our lives. Included in this time, I spent each morning sitting outdoors near a cliff at the back of Raven Crest, doing my devotions in God's holy Word and enjoying the wonders of His creation—listening to the birds and gazing at the beautiful mountains.

At the end of our time, Alex, Phil, Glenn, Saul, and I got together one last time to encourage each other and to share our love and appreciation for one another. The staff at Raven Crest had been awesome and really helped to make our time there a blast. But one by one the vans loaded up and left for the various cities.

Alex headed off to World Impact in Newark, New Jersey. Phil went back to St. Louis, Missouri; Glenn returned to L.A.; Saul went to Chester near Philadelphia; and I headed back to Kansas to work with World Impact there. And three new students came up: Ed and Andre from Newark as well as James from Fresno, California. They were on their way back with us, to begin their two-year commitments at the ranch.

Chapter Twenty-Five

When I arrived at my destination in Wichita, I moved in with Al Ewert, director of the ministry in that city. Al had helped advise me to come and work with them in Wichita rather than going back to Los Angeles. He quickly put trust in me by giving me complete responsibility over the grocery shopping and the planning of menus. This is something that had eluded me at the ranch because I was not ready to lead people until I had dealt with some things. But now it was placed in my hands. Immediately, I was put alongside several men on staff to help them teach Bible clubs to the kids in our community and in different age groups. I worked with Andy Entz and Tim Ladwig, for example, with our high school people—the "Senior teen" groups. I also worked with Bob Engels in our fifth and sixth grade groups and with Jeff Davenport in our kindergarten group.

With many of these kids I had already established prior relationships, with the exception of the kindergarten group. So I got started in my new role as an inner-city missionary on a good footing. I was basically Andy, Tim, Bob, and Jeff's assistant. I wasn't comfortable leading the teaching times because of my stuttering condition; but my strength was relationships, being able to relate to the kids.

My schedule was full, and I had plenty of things to do. In addition to Bible clubs, I did the custodial work in our office and church building as well as grounds work. I was put under the leadership of Mr. Al Bergan, who reminded me a lot of Mr. Jim Farley, who had helped us a great deal out at the ranch.

Al knew something about everything, and he enjoyed teaching me things and spending time talking to me; and I gladly welcomed him. He was a very wise man whom God began to use to impact my life for the good. He and his wife, Ms. Helen, would every so often invite the staff out to their home for food and fun.

As I grew to be friends with the kids, I decided I would get to know the parents of each one I personally worked with. I wanted the families to be familiar with the man their children were meeting with on a weekly basis since I was the new kid on the block, so to speak.

And that I did. I made sure every available parent and/or grand-parent met me. I would sit down with them in their homes and basically share my testimony with them: where I came from, how I got to this point, and the vision I believed God had given me for the kids under my care. I also offered them my phone number, though they were already established in relationships with the ministry and its staff.

I never forgot what the Lord had impressed on my heart when I was contemplating quitting the ranch during my first weekend there, the Weekend Exposure. I was to be an example for the young, in speech, behavior, and mind. I was to be God's model for what He could do in a young person's life in the ghetto, especially if the heart were willing to trust Him.

Al Ewert told me once that he could see God using me in these kids' lives because of the advantage of my background as a gang banger with the L.A. Crips and the fact that I had come from a broken family without a dad present to love me and train me in how to be a man. These kids had to see the Gospel of Jesus Christ working for the good in my life. I knew that was true, and I did not take that lightly.

A Bible club for the older kids consisted of driving around the community on our ministry's bus and picking them up from their homes. We would then bring them back to what we called the "village," which was where our church, office, medical clinic, and Al's and my apartment were; and Andy and Lisa Entz and their family lived next door.

In these facilities we had a game room area in our church building, a basketball court, and an open field outside for softball, football, and other sports. We would let the kids play for about forty minutes and then break into our separate groups for a Bible lesson and snacks. It was during these times that my basketball game began to develop, playing with my senior teen guys who had serious games themselves.

Our leadership group consisted of Tim, Andy, James—(aka Bootchie) a volunteer and member of our church body—and me. The four of us had about ten to twelve high school teens in our group. It was often a challenge to get them serious and focused on the Bible lessons because, of course, at least two in the group always kept everybody from settling down.

Tico and Shelton were the particular two who had such comical influences on the group, the distractions making it hard to get things going. Naturally we had to get on these guys a lot. But when we could get them settled down, the guys did focus on the lesson, and we would get things done, even including Shelton and Tico.

I was a bit reserved to begin with because I was the new guy. But these fellows knew me from coming out to the ranch on special occasions and had heard my gang stories. They were fascinated by them and had asked a lot of questions. So I already had their basic respect and acceptance, but now I was in a new role of being a leader.

At first I would simply watch the more experienced ones and how they dealt with the behaviors and just the time in general because I didn't want to just jump in and demand the guys' respect in this new role. But the more I got used to the guys and earned their trust, the more I felt welcomed into their lives.

I quickly began to realize that even grownups experience pressures from groups to compromise the truth or to seek peace rather than respect. God was beginning to teach me how important it was to be a man of integrity and to learn to be these guys' Bible club teacher first; then the friendships would come later.

Bootchie had strong relationships with the boys and often spent time with them away from the club. They always seemed to seek him out to take them places or to hang out with him at his house, to make music in his studio or whatever.

At times the guys would be distracting to one another or talking back to Andy and Tim and sometimes even Bootchie. I would have to speak up and encourage them to pay attention. Sometimes I felt that my sternness was causing the guys to distance themselves from me, and that would cause me to question my stance. I wondered if I should loosen up, back off a little, and maybe they would like me more.

But the Lord would rebuke that thought, telling me that it is more important to stick with the truth and seek out their needs instead.

And it was better to be respected than liked. So the Lord kept me focused every time I felt such guilt. But over time, I noticed these boys would come to me privately with their different problems or would call me in the wee hours of the night when they were hurting inside for various reasons.

I didn't realize this until much later, that God had been meeting a need in my life for more than three years to this point. It started with Kim Seebach and Fred Stoesz, who were there at the beginning, helping me to transition into the world of Christianity and the work field. Then He placed me at the ranch under the counsel of Joe Graham, our ranch director, a strong leader who was always willing to tell me the truth. God further provided Jerry Peters, my one-on-one counselor; Jim Elam, who showed me the importance of work; and Dave Zagunis, who taught me so much about the Word of God.

Finally He put me in Wichita, under the graceful leadership of Al Ewert, director of World Impact in that city and my roommate and friend. I was further grateful for Andy Entz, my next one-on-one, who would help me lead the kids I now had under my care.

Ruth and Al Ewert

But God would also bring two more men into my life. First was George Fooshee, my godly friend who helped me to see the im-

222

portance of handling my finances wisely and of giving. George and his caring wife Marjean would invite me over for lunch or just to spend time with me.

And second was Bob Knight, Wichita's longest-serving mayor—he and his wife and my friend Jane along with their daughters Jennifer, Amy, and Kristin, who called me their adopted brother. We would regularly go out for lunch on Sundays after church, and the girls would ask me questions about my past life in the Crips.

While I was at the ranch, I had developed an interest in politics, mainly from reading Charles Colson's autobiography *Born Again* as well as from my love of biblical prophecy and how it shows that God is indeed working behind the scenes in the affairs of men. I had shared my fascination in these two areas of learning with Mayor Knight, and obviously he took mental note of them. So he started giving me, perhaps, a quiet lesson in politics just by simply introducing me to different associates of his.

Every time we were together in public or just hanging out with his family, he never failed to introduce me as his friend to judges, lawyers, councilmen, and women or just to different people who would greet us because he was our mayor. He went on to invite me to his campaign headquarters for his many re-election victories. I would later meet two governors through him—former Kansas governors Mike Hayden (R) and the late Joan Finney (D)—as well as former Drug Czar and Secretary of Education in the Reagan and Bush administrations, William Bennett. I also got to meet the President of Russia, Boris Yeltsin, and others through the mayor.

A few months after I came to Wichita to help minister to kids and their families, life for me would take another turn for the better. We had a solid group of young adults, who mostly came up through the Bible clubs with World Impact and who were now in careers of their own but had continued to support the ministry and fellowship in our church, which was called "Celebration."

These young people often did things together as a group—dinner, softball, or whatever—including having our own Bible studies. Some of them, such as Leah, Andrea, Bootchie, and Dorothy, even helped out in Bible clubs. I was assigned to ride the bus on Monday night pick-ups, to supervise the teens while Andrea drove the bus.

One particular night I was not able to ride the bus because I had come down with the flu. The next day Andrea brought over some homemade chicken noodle soup and other goodies just to be an encouragement to me during my illness. On another occasion, she baked me some cookies and created some little coupons that entitled me to another batch of homemade cookies, dinner for me and two of my teen guys, and one for a walk in the park with her.

That certainly got my attention, so I brought up the subject in my one-on-one meeting with Andy Entz. He and I met together each week to talk about how I was doing in my life and work. I told him about how Andrea had been taking care of me and how I felt she was treating me differently from the other single guys. I asked Andy how I should deal with it because I didn't want to assume the wrong thing and cause her to stumble.

Andy thought I should invite her out for a coke and ask her how she felt about me so I wouldn't be misinterpreting her true intentions. And that's exactly what I did.

I invited Andrea out for dinner and a movie. After we ordered our meals, I jumped right into it. I said, "Andrea, I kind of noticed that you've been treating me a little differently than the other guys, and it was making me curious about how you feel about me. I hope I'm not assuming something false about you. How do you feel about me?—so I won't have to wonder anymore."

Andrea explained how I had caught her eye at our initial meeting during my first month at the ranch; it had been when we had the baptism out there for somebody in the Wichita's celebration service. She said she also noticed how gentle I was with the kids and how passionate I was in sharing my testimony in spite of my severe speech problem. Truly, the love of Christ in me is what attracted her.

Andrea said that she just basically kept it to herself with the exception of sharing it with only her one-on-one, Aileen Ratzliff, one of the members of our Wichita's staff. She admitted she didn't want to distract me from what God had been doing in my life at the ranch but had simply prayed that if I was the one, He would reveal it by causing me to come to Wichita after I graduated. So when I *did* come to Wichita, she believed the Lord was behind it by answering her prayer; that was why she made the soup and coupons and offered me all that special treatment.

Unfortunately, I didn't feel the same way she did. I told her that in my first year at the ranch I had spent so much time worrying about whether or not I would ever have a family of my own that I allowed it to distract me from my relationship with Christ. I also shared that before my second year began, I committed my life and focus to the Lord: to learn about what He wanted for me and about who He is.

I was finally content with being single for however long it took; so, I explained, getting into a relationship at that time was not for me. Still, I told her I would be willing to pray about it and get with her from time to time over a coke to update one another on our feelings.

She went along with that, but I noticed she didn't finish her meal. After dinner we went to watch the movie "Tap" that had just come out starring Gregory Hines. After the movie, Andrea dropped me off at home. I thought we'd had a wonderful evening, but I found out later that it wasn't all great to her. She went home upset by how I responded, and meanwhile I didn't have a clue.

As time went on I noticed that she was kind of distant and not herself. Even still, the ministry activity continued on the same as ever, including my riding the bus with her on Monday evenings. One night after dropping off the teens, except for one, I was given quite the compliment. One of our teen girls started talking to me about one of my teen guys regarding their on again/off again relationship.

Kelli said to me, "Eric, if I ever marry a man, he is going to have to be like you." I was kind of taken aback by that because her comment was so unexpected. Andrea told me later that some of the teen girls had a crush on me; and when they found out about her liking me as well, they were a little upset. But at the same time, they respected the fact that a friendship between two Christians, who happened to be young black Americans, was something good for them to see. So Kelli's statement taught me about the need for black youth to see solid Christian couples—who also happen to be black.

I began to see Andrea differently and thought that God might be calling us together after all. In the summer of 1989, Andrea decided not to teach during that period but, instead, to go out to L.A. and help the ministry in their schools. I suspected she was basically just trying to get away from being around me, believing that I had no feelings for her.

After she left for L.A. that summer, suddenly I wasn't seeing her driving the bus on Monday nights. She wasn't at Celebration services anymore. The Sunday afternoon young adults' get-togethers were missing someone. Then I realized I too was missing that someone. I began to understand that I'd developed feelings for her beyond just a brother and sister in Christ relationship and felt there should be more. I was now missing her a lot.

Andrea

Chapter Twenty-Six

Andrea came home midway into the summer to take part in the wedding of our friends, Rich and Karen Ellsastrom, as Karen's bridesmaid. Although she was only there for the duration of the ceremony and then flew back to Los Angeles, I could not take my eyes off of her and couldn't wait for her to come back.

My teen guys knew something was up because they said I had a glow on my face. Meanwhile, I was making good progress with them. Our Monday night senior group was pretty big, and God had begun to lay an idea on my heart to invite those boys who really wanted to get serious with the Lord and with one another to get together on a separate night to meet as a small accountability group.

The guys responded. They included Bird (Terry), Shelton, Torrez, Junior, Donovan, Azrael, and me. I wanted the group to be ours so it could be a gathering that felt safe to let down their guards and just be themselves. I encouraged all of us to be open to accountability from each other and get out of the experience what God wanted to do in us and through us.

We decided on a group name that would eventually draw distinction. It would be called "The Covenant Group," meaning we had made a covenant to one another and to Jesus to grow in our Christian lives. Soon I started to see that the spirit of our Thursday covenant group was carrying over to our Monday night group. The jokes and distractions lessened significantly. God had indeed done a great work in our covenant group.

Eventually, I had earned these guys' respect and was invited into some of the most painful areas of their lives. They came to trust me—as I did with them.

Their families, the Molinas, and most of the others embraced me because they knew I loved and cared for their kids. One of the coupons that I got from Andrea entitled me to a home cooked meal with two of my covenant guys. They loved it because, by now, they were very supportive of Andrea's and my potential relationship.

When she got back from L.A., I began to pursue her, even taking advantage of another of the coupons. By now she was probably aware that my feelings had changed. After several meetings together, on November 18, 1989 I took Andrea up on the coupon that entitled me to a walk in the park with her. It was during this time that I moved in. I told her that if she was still interested, I would like to make our get-togethers official: I asked if she would be willing to date. She said, "Yes!"

My Gift

From that Thursday autumn night, we began to spend more time together. We even made our one-on-one mentors a part of it, inviting them to hold us accountable to be pure in our relationship. I did not want to mess this up but wanted to remain faithful to God's Word and not fall into sexual temptation, as I had done so frequently in my past.

I valued Andrea so much and wanted to treat her like God's princess. She was a godly woman, above reproach, who was a servant like no one I had ever known. She enjoyed giving of her time, money, or even her expert experience as a professional educator whenever a kid or someone else needed tutoring. I did not want to cause her to stumble, so I encouraged us to pray together often and to always abide by good boundaries.

We agreed to keep her bedroom door open whenever we were hanging out in there, with an open invitation to her roommates, Delrina and Dorothy, to come in freely if they so chose. Andrea and I wanted to do it right and to obey Christ as a young dating couple. We were also aware that we were role models to many kids in the ministry, especially because we were young black Americans. We believed that our kids, especially our teens, needed to see us doing the right thing and being responsible to God's Word to remain abstinent until marriage.

This was a tall order for two young black adults from the culture of the inner city. The relationship was indeed an answer to prayer for us both, though it came from two different directions. I had prayed at the ranch to have a family of my own someday with kids to love like I had never known. Andrea had prayed that if I were the one for her, God would cause me to come to Wichita rather than go back home to Watts. Both dreams had begun to unfold right before us.

However, the close intimacy that was ever growing was beginning to stir up deep hidden emotions in my life. Up until this point God had been dealing with my character as a young Christian and teaching me about Himself through His Son Jesus Christ and His holy Word. Before, He was teaching me how to deal with my anger, how I should treat people, and how I should respect authority, including those in authority over me and the law of society. He gave me a love for His Word and an eagerness to know Him personally.

But now something different was beginning to take place in the deepest recesses of my heart, something I had not dealt with before. Andrea was very proud to walk by my side and never missed an opportunity to introduce me to her co-workers and friends. I was frequently uncomfortable with her "showing me off" because I wasn't used to being that *loved*. Sometimes she would call up a friend from work and make arrangements to meet this other couple at a local ice cream shop or other location to just hang out and talk.

On such occasions, it never failed that the husband would ask, "So, what do you do for a living?" Of course I would tell him what I did—that I worked with a ministry called World Impact. I didn't really view our ministry roles as that of missionaries, but that was what we were. Still, since I wasn't a career missionary, I didn't see myself as an actual *missionary* to the inner cities. I had just seen it as the body of Christ loving their community through the gospel; to me, from a worldly standpoint, it wasn't a real job. The husband would then tell me what he did: "I'm a judge" or "I'm an attorney" or "I'm a doctor."

In the privacy of my own mind, I felt a growing shame. I was making hardly anything as a support staff employee. So I began comparing what these people were possibly earning—fifty to one hundred thousand a year, perhaps. Andrea's friends were usually women she worked with as teachers. So these couples, in my mind, were "stable." I believed the husbands must be good providers; but here I was, making less than Andrea. I worried that I wouldn't be able to take care of her or make her happy if we got married.

These growing feelings began to affect my speech greatly, causing my stuttering to worsen; that is, when my body is under tension or stress, the effect shows up in my speech. It got so bad that I would sink into a depressive mode around her friends, withdrawing from the conversations. I assumed they were laughing at her in private. The bottom line was that I felt Andrea deserved more than a retard like me who couldn't even talk right. More and more I felt like I was an embarrassment to her rather than a man to be proud of. My mind raced with thoughts. How would I take care of her? How could I be a leader in our family if God called us together in marriage? I felt that she deserved more. Maybe she even needed a way out.

Finally, one night while we were having our weekly visit at Spring Time burger restaurant, I decided I would go ahead and end the relationship so she could be free to find someone who could provide for her needs someday.

As we sat across from one another, I began sharing as best I could why we should stop dating. I told her she deserved more than what I could ever be for her. Tears began to fall down my face as I pleaded with her to get away from me. I told her that I was nothing, and that had been the story of my whole life. A nothing!

Instead of feeling sorry for me or rejecting me, Andrea responded exactly how I needed her to do. If she hadn't, I probably wouldn't have had the courage to continue the relationship. She said, "Eric, I'm not with you because of what you have or you don't have. I'm with you because of *who you are;* and if God wants to give you things later, fine. But that's up to Him. I love you, Eric, not your title."

With that response, she gave me the courage to allow our relationship to continue. Her acceptance of me was filled with such love that I decided she was worth the risk. God had brought such a good woman into my life, and to reject her because of my own insecurity would have been utterly wrong. That night, through Andrea, God communicated to me that He was not far from me, even in those private areas of my life.

I guess you could say the night gave me a greater bounce in my outlook, and I was now ready to trust not only Andrea but, more importantly, God Himself in a new and fresher way. God brought us closer that evening, giving us a renewed sense of respect for and intimacy with each other. Over the next several months and *many* conversations and times of prayer together, we grew to trust one another greatly. Our relationship had become an encouragement and model for other singles and children, and we took that very seriously.

But opening up too deeply can have its price. Before the summer of 1990, a particular conversation sent our relationship into a nosedive. Andrea was sharing with me some personal issues from her past; and as I sat there in my car listening, a picture of a little girl popped into my mind. She was sitting in a corner with her knees into her chest, and she was crying. I thought it must be Andrea.

I immediately shared that with her, and she was quiet for the remaining time we were together. From then on she became very distant from me, but I couldn't understand why. Eventually, probably within a week's time, she put a halt to our relationship. I thought I had done or said something that was wrong. I didn't know what was going on because she didn't give me an explanation.

I was speculating on everything from my having done something wrong to the possibility that she'd met someone else and had grown tired of me. I didn't know. I was basically devastated. I went from a state of shock to confusion, then from embarrassment to anger.

By the end of the summer of 1989, we had not had a conversation at all. I became even more angry because I felt I had torn down a wall that had protected me from women for years to be able to trust this awesome person, and now she had dropped me for no reason I could imagine.

I had to close my heart to her in order to get through the rejection I felt from her. Still, we saw each other at Celebration every Sunday and even went to a young adult retreat out at the ranch that summer called "Shine in '89." This was made up of former ranch students and young people who were a part of World Impact from the various ministries across the country.

It was pretty much after this event that I decided to give up; and by the end of the summer, I had. My attention turned back toward my ministry and the kids I'd been working with. But sometime after school had started—around September of 1990—I got a call from Andrea. She apologized for what had happened and explained that she was dealing with issues in her own life; and unfortunately those things had affected our relationship. I told her I understood and would have to get back with her soon. But actually I had reached the point where I'd finally let her go and was willing to move on with my life.

Growing up in the streets, you learn to cut off emotions so you can survive a broken relationship or some tough situation. And by this time, my survival mode was in full throttle because I had burned up so much energy opening my life to her, only to be dropped like a dime. So I didn't think I trusted her anymore.

I met with a fellow staff member and good friend, Tim Ladwig, whose counsel I valued very much, and told him she had called and what she'd said. Like everybody else, Tim was concerned with our break-up and prayed that the relationship would be healed. He said to me, "Eric, if you truly believe that God brought her into your life and if you really care about her, then you have to decide whether or not she is worth the risk."

I believed that was sound counsel. I also knew that God had indeed brought her into my life, so I thought about what Tim said and prayed the Lord would help me turn loose of my anger toward Andrea and help me forgive her.

Andrea called me a couple of days later from her grandmother's home where she was staying. She invited me over to talk, and I accepted. All the way there, I was asking God to help me forgive and trust Him with the outcome.

We talked for a while, and I was finally able to understand a little better about where she was coming from. *I* wasn't the issue. Andrea was dealing with things way beyond me, and I finally got that. I received the heart to forgive her and agreed to give the relationship another chance. Certainly this was to the joy of everyone who knew us, especially Tim and the kids whom we worked with.

Over the next several months, Andrea and I grew even closer than before. We continued to pray together and to make ourselves accountable to Andy and Lisa Entz, who had been with us throughout our entire dating relationship.

Andrea had been hoping I would ask her to marry me before the break up, if I recall right. But this was even more true since we'd gotten back together. Still, I was not going there unless I knew beyond a shadow of a doubt that God was giving me the green light. The thought of it scared me because I felt so inadequate.

Chapter Twenty-Seven

Meanwhile, I had grown to the point where I began questioning whether or not I could survive in society without World Impact. I realized that I wouldn't know what to do if I did leave the ministry because I had been under their wings since leaving the Crips gang.

Under their care, if I came to work late, I wasn't going to be fired. I didn't have to worry about not having a meal to eat or a place to lay my head. Medically I was taken care of, and I was surrounded by people who loved and cared for me. But what if I left and got out on my own? What would I do for a living? How would I make it on my own two feet, much less take care of a family? What skills did I have and could rely on? Could I survive in the "real" world with my stuttering condition, and would the world be patient with me?

These questions began to plague me because I realized I was trusting World Impact more than I was trusting Christ. Of course, it wasn't World Impact's fault at all. God had put them in my life since I was eight years old. They were the one group who had been there for me from day one. School did nothing for me. Jail did nothing. But Christ Jesus, using World Impact, had blessed my life in so many ways. Could I actually make it on my own without them? I really didn't know and was becoming increasingly afraid to take that risk.

Again, it wasn't their fault I was growing to depend on them. They pointed me to Christ as the source of all my needs. When I realized that I wasn't truly depending on God for my material needs, it was time for me to break away from that. During one of my one-on-one meetings with Andy Entz, I expressed these concerns and the fear that I had or anticipated if I ever left World Impact.

Andy encouraged me to pray about it and to search my heart concerning what should be done. Out of that conversation I decided it was time for me to leave the ministry and learn to lean on Christ alone for not just my spiritual needs but also for my material ones.

Several of the young adult men and I got together and decided to share an apartment. I thought I would help take the lead in finding us a place to stay. We found a five-bedroom condominium, and Scott, Marlon, Gitt, Moses, and I all moved in together to help offset the bills. I got a job at B & G Plating, owned and run by a friend and World Impact board member in Wichita, Brad Wells.

It was very tough to leave the ministry after having helped so many kids of all ages and their families. God had given me wonderful opportunities to share Christ's love in practical and tangible ways, and quite a few of them I personally led to Christ. It was like leaving my family.

I was taking many great memories with me as well. In such a short time, it seemed like I had spent a lifetime in the ministry. God had given me the honor of sharing my testimony briefly with President H. W. Bush's drug czar, William Bennett, as well as Oliver North. I had the privilege of spending an evening at the homes of former Chief of Staff in the Lyndon Johnson administration and then an executive board member of World Impact, Marvin Watson and his family. I further enjoyed a few meetings with Rosey Grier, famed NFL great and now minister, sharing our testimonies at a prayer breakfast. And through our former Mayor Bob Knight, I offered a little of my testimony to former Russian President Boris Yeltsin when he visited Wichita, Kansas during his American tour.

The Lord had done so much in my life and through my life in just a handful of years—even taking a few men into our home to help them get clean and turn their lives around. Al Ewert, who was my roommate at the time, trusted my judgment and gave me the freedom to reach out to these guys who needed someone to walk with.

But now it was time to get out and learn how to trust God alone, paying my own bills and basically co-managing a home with five young men in it. The thing that made it all work was our common belief that Jesus Christ was in charge. Talk about diversity: Marlon and I were both black. Scott was white. Moses was Hispanic, and Gitt was Asian. With our widely varying backgrounds, we should have had some difficulty living together; but Christ was the glue that made it work. We were brothers in Christ for real.

The Christmas season came quickly, and I had begun entertaining the idea of asking Andrea to marry me. By now, I was convinced God had given me the green light, and it was just a matter of gathering the nerve to ask her and figuring out how to do it.

I had talked with Andy, Al, and Tim about it first and prayed about the courage to make that next step. Our friends Rich and Karen—both on staff with World Impact—were going to their family's home for Christmas, so I asked them if I could use their place as a cozy setting because I was about to pop the question.

Of course they were excited about it and gladly said yes. I had bought Andrea a few gifts a couple of days before Christmas—including an engagement ring. The night before, I went out and picked up some salad, French bread, spaghetti, ground beef, and sauce.

Andrea's family was getting together as they usually did each year to open presents that morning. So we made plans to exchange gifts Christmas night, and Andrea was to meet me at Rich and Karen's for dinner.

I prepared the meal and spread it on a beautiful table set with Christmas trimmings and a few candles and put on a Kenny G Christmas album. When she arrived, I was just finishing up. We sat down and ate our meal, cleaned up, and then proceeded to open our presents. She had me unwrap mine first.

When it came time to open hers, I had the packages stacked on top of one another. The ring was buried in a big box filled with newspaper, and it sat on the bottom. When she got to that last one, all she saw was the paper. Puzzled, Andrea looked at me and said, "Where's the present?" I told her to keep looking. Boom! When she found the small gray box, she cried "Eric!!" as if stunned and excited at the same time. Before I proposed, I wanted to read her a poem I had written. Then I pulled out the ring and asked her to be my wife. With no hesitation whatsoever, Andrea said, "Yes!" and we hugged each other. I then led us in a prayer, asking God to bless our engagement and to keep us pure.

That evening we went around to family and a few friends to give them the news. A couple of weeks earlier, I had gone to her mom and stepfather, Earnestine and Johnnie, to ask for their blessing. They both seemed sort of shocked in the sense that a guy had actually respected them enough to approach them first. That's not common in the black culture, at least not from my perspective as a young black man. But I knew God wanted me to honor them in that way. Needless to say, everyone was excited for us that night, including my mom back in Watts, whom I called that night, and my father and stepmother in Flint, Michigan.

The next day Andrea and some of the women flew to Chicago for a conference put on by Urbana, a kind of Christian rally for young people. The trip was already planned and paid for, so it was tough seeing her go only a day after Christmas—the day I proposed!

Over the course of the next six months, we went about planning our wedding. Basically she did all the work; I was just learning from her. As with many men, I didn't have a clue how to go about it even though I had been a part of five or six weddings during the past year and a half and the best man in four of those. But I knew little about the ins and outs of all it took to plan a wedding for ourselves. My main responsibility was to make sure I had the honeymoon taken care of.

During those six months of planning and waiting for our special day, we grew closer in many ways; but it was apparent from our marital counseling that communication would be our top issue.

We had chosen Andy and Lisa Entz to counsel us, mainly because Andy had been my one-on-one during the last two years since leaving the ranch; and Lisa had been Andrea's one-on-one throughout our dating and engagement relationship. So we trusted their judgment and Christian counsel.

When we got very personal in some areas, it became harder for Andrea to talk about certain things. Up until this point, I had only been able to communicate the concerns I was aware of in my own life. I knew my stuttering would be an issue I would have to confront aggressively if I was going to be the husband I felt God was calling me to be.

All in all, we encountered some emotional moments in our premarital counseling, but we kept our focus and committed to spending the rest of our lives together as husband and wife.

As the wedding day grew closer, all the guests were invited to come; but again, none of my family was going to show up for reasons of their own. Just days before the wedding, I fell into a depression. I felt unimportant to my family. Even though that wasn't the case, I had no way to deny the way I felt. On two of the most important occasions of my life—graduating from the ranch and my wedding—none of my relatives would be present. So I had reasons to feel that way.

But once again, I decided not to let anyone or anything stand in the way of our special day. I made a point to enjoy my new family and my soon-to-be bride and to let God deal with the rest.

A couple of days before the wedding, Andrea and I were together in what would be our new home for the first year. Her stepfather was letting us live in one of his rentals rent-free during that time. We were just hanging out together, and things got a little heated.

We started kissing and were about to step over that boundary; but we both agreed that, since we had done it right this far and wanted to do it God's way, we should still be patient a few more days. We then prayed and thanked God for giving us the power to wait until our wedding and thanked Him for being our strength. And shortly after that I left and went home. That was a victory for both of us.

The night before our wedding at my bachelor's party, Alex White, my best man, along with my friends Lance Brown, Shawn, and others, went to A.J. Sports Grill. They had a basketball court in the center of the place. We played four or five intense games of hoops; at one point, somebody accidentally elbowed me below the eye, which caused a small swelling on my cheek.

Needless to say, I almost freaked out, thinking the photographer would capture rare photos of me and my bride that we would have to live with for years to come. But even more, having to face Andrea first with a swollen eye was not a pleasant thought.

Fortunately, I packed some ice on my eye and even put a pork chop on it, having seen that done on the Three Stooges or some such crazy show. By the next morning, my eye was fine: all the swelling had gone down completely. But choosing to start the marriage off on an honest and open note, I confessed to Andrea what had happened, to her satisfaction. However, I did get "The Look."

Finally the big day had come. One of World Impact's local board members at this time, Pastor Earl Burkhulter, let us use his church, Stranger's Rest, to have our wedding. We had about five hundred friends show up, including Andrea's family and a number of kids who were a part of World Impact, to help us celebrate our day.

I was still in a daze as I reflected back on how far I had come. I realized that if God had not given my heart a new birth, I probably would have been either dead or in jail for murder or some other serious crime. That's where my future had been headed as sin continued to harden my heart toward anything or anyone who dared stand in the way of running my own life.

But now look! I was about to marry the love of my life! I called her my "gift" because she was given to me by my Father in heaven who cares for us both. My best man, Alex, helped to relax me during the lead-up to the ceremony, but nothing could prepare me for the moment the music began to play.

My hands were sweaty, and I continued to wipe them with my napkin. I kept praying and asking the Lord to give me the courage to get through such a tense moment. I was even more nervous because of my speech impediment. We had changed my part of the vows to accommodate my struggle with hard consonant sounds. I didn't want my stuttering to spoil the ceremony, so I asked Al Ewert—our friend, my former roommate, and the director of World Impact of Wichita—to *ask me* the questions instead of my having to repeat after him word for word; all I would have to do was just say "Yes" or "I will."

But before that point, I nearly burned down the church. It was time to light the candles, and we took our places on the kneeling bench. With the candleholders in hand, we lit up the flames. My candle wasn't fully in place, and it started to tilt over. Hoping not to cause a scene, I tried to grab it with the opposite hand. Instead, the candle dropped on the floor. I thought the church was going to burn down; but fortunately, I was cool enough to lean over and pick it up before the carpet floor went up in flames.

Obviously I looked funny to Andrea because she started busting up laughing. I felt so silly that I too began to laugh sheepishly. After that, the ice was broken; and I was able to relax and enjoy the time. It really turned out like we intended it—to be a blessing to our guests, especially to our family. If it weren't for my friends, Bob and Judy Cairns, from Carbondale, Kansas, we wouldn't have caught the wedding on tape. I had forgotten to contact the person whom we wanted to film it, but Judy happened to have her video camera with her and was happy to capture the event. Thank God for looking out for us again.

I had arranged for us to stay in a bed-and-breakfast place on our wedding night. After riding around in a limousine that my new mother-in-law, Momma Ernestine, had rented for us, we were tired after a long day. After spending the night here in Wichita, we got up and set out for our honeymoon destination the next morning.

After I proposed to Andrea on Christmas, I had called my friend Rick Archibald from Estes Park, Colorado, whom I had met and gotten to know when we took some teens to cut down trees on his property that previous year. He was a businessman there in Estes Park as well as a godly Christian. At the time, Rick had asked me if I was dating anyone, and I told him about Andrea. He said, "If you ever decide to ask her to marry you, and if you spend your honeymoon here in Estes Park, I'll give you one of my cabins for a week." Of course, I remembered such a kind offer and decided to take him up on it.

We woke up on the day of our wedding as Eric West and Andrea Lamon, but the next day we woke up as husband and wife. It was an incredible feeling to realize I was now a married man. Still, I felt pretty lost as to how to be a good leader in my soon-to-be new home, and this caused me to depend on God all the more.

We spent about a week there in Estes Park near Rocky Mountain National Park. We purposely had not scheduled any activities for that time, not wanting to stress ourselves out with the demands of having to go, go, go. Instead, we wanted to shoot from the hip, so we did only the stuff that seemed fun on the spur of the moment. The engagement, the planning of the wedding, and all of the tension it included were enough to wear on anyone, so enjoyment was the goal.

We spent a day of hiking, an awesome experience with such amazing mountain views in every direction. Horseback riding was also a joy, and this time I managed to stay on the horse. The first time I rode one was around the age of ten or eleven. My friend had invited me to his dad's house in Compton where a parade was supposed to be happening. His dad knew some of the participants in the parade and had arranged for us to ride the horses. I chose a jet black horse, a massive and muscular one; I figured I would *conquer* that beast. Everything was going well until he started to gallop. In the heat of the moment, I forgot the instructions on how to bring the horse to a standstill; so I panicked. I leaped off the horse onto concrete, scraping up my hands and knees. I had my friends rolling with laughter, and it turned out to be funny to me as well.

Meanwhile, on the honeymoon, my friend Rich Archibald and

his family invited us to a picnic, and we had a great time of fun and fellowship. The rest of our time was filled with sleeping in, shopping, and touring. The adventure ended with a long drive home and an overnight stay in a hotel.

Chapter Twenty-Eight

We slowly began to ease into the beginning of the rest of our lives together. But soon that adjustment would be put to the test. My challenging schedule at work, often changing at a day's notice, began to take a difficult toll on our new marriage. Of course I felt the obligation to do something about it; but since my boss and I couldn't work out a compromise, I chose to quit.

Unfortunately, I didn't have a new job to cover the loss of my previous one. Even though Andrea agreed that my constantly changing schedule had put our marriage second and made life tough to plan ahead for things, she didn't agree with me quitting my job without having another one ready to replace it. That meant no paycheck from my end and that she would have to cover everything with her income. But after about a month out of work, I was hired on at Brown & Ferris, Inc. (BFI), a trash collecting company, probably the largest in the world at that time.

Although it paid well, starting at I believe ten or eleven dollars an hour, we had to put in very long hours. I used to have to get up at 4:30 each morning and had to be ready to work the routes by 5:30. Quitting time was determined by how soon we got our routes picked up, which usually meant around 4:30-5:00 in the afternoon.

I continued to work with BFI for a little over a month. During one route in particular, I jumped off the back of the truck and landed in a ditch, rolling my right ankle pretty badly. Because I had not gotten my commercial driver's license (C.D.L.) yet, I couldn't drive the trucks; and I didn't want to work in dispatch because of my speech impediment. Actually, I *turned down* the position in dispatch though I didn't share that information with Andrea. Since I was still on probation at the time and had not qualified for health insurance or other benefits yet, I decided to quit. This came as a shock to my wife as well.

Once again I was unemployed. With my two bad decisions in less than four months, I felt like my previous fear that I would not be a good husband and leader was coming true. Soon a small panic began to set in that Andrea would stop loving me because I couldn't provide for her. I could have taken the opportunity to do something else within the company until my ankle healed, but because the job involved communicating work-related information, I avoided it. So yes, the situation reinforced my belief that I was a failure—and stupid. This wasn't coming from my wife but from me alone.

As those self-destructive emotions grew worse, I started needing Andrea's approval of me all the more. I began acting out these feelings by trying to get her to tell me she loved me. I would hear it from her when things were going well, but I wanted to hear it also in the tough times. It got so urgent that, if she just happened to be quiet for a moment, her silence would trigger questions of my value inside my head. I would take those times of stillness as if she were saying, *"You're a disappointment to me."* I just wasn't sure: was she really thinking that, or were all those feelings of disappointment just in my head?

I would ask Andrea, "What did I do?" She would say, "Nothing." But I couldn't take that for an answer—or at least the answer I believed I deserved. So I would pester her over and over again until she gave me what I thought was the "correct" response. But that only made things worse. Naturally, she was frustrated that I wasn't believing her, and I would often react by jumping up in a rage, storming out of the house, and slamming the door.

By this time sex had become a very personal issue for me. I had always resorted to that outlet when I was in the streets, when I was stressed, or just wanted intimacy. I guess it was a type of validation, a way of finding out if a girl truly cared for me or not.

It was getting to a point in our marriage that when she wasn't in the mood or happened to have had a long day at work, I immediately took it as a rejection. What it said to me was *"I don't want to because you're not performing like a real husband should. You can't even be responsible, so why should I make love to you?"* In hindsight I can see this was all in my mind; Andrea wasn't telling me these things. I was just looking through the lens of my past, and my insecurities were beginning to show.

I remember on one occasion when this happened, I left the house in anger for some fresh air with the thought that if anybody came up to me and said the wrong thing, I was going to take out on him all the rage I had stored up inside. My disappointment with myself kept growing, and I felt like I had no outlet. I was not planning to intentionally go out and start a fight with somebody, but if a person gave me a reason, then it would definitely be on. Thankfully, nothing happened.

My emotional state was becoming so bad, I could hardly hold a job. I had gotten a delivery job with Pizza Hut in an effort to find something to help Andrea with the bills. I knew it would require confirming different orders from people when I would arrive with their meals. Every delivery was different. Some customers were very kind and considerate, but some were rude and impatient. Those would see me struggling with my speech and would interrupt by cutting me off, causing me to spiral out of control in my ability to make sense. I would finish the evening shift feeling burned out and stressed in the mouth and neck area because of the physical wear and tear.

The tips made up the bulk of my income, but the communication part of the job eventually caused me to quit Pizza Hut as well after working there for only a couple of months. It was a blow to me emotionally because it meant I wouldn't be contributing to the home once again. I was afraid Andrea wouldn't understand why I quit.

It seemed like I couldn't do anything right. How could I expect my wife to respect and follow me if I myself couldn't see where I was going? I made it harder for her every time I let a job go.

The first year of marriage was like a relationship caught in an emotional twister. I was struggling with feelings I couldn't understand and whose origins I couldn't trace. My wife was similarly facing issues I could not relate to. We were speaking different languages when it came to our personal problems.

Our approaches to dealing with those concerns were completely different as well. Andrea simply distanced herself emotionally from me while I wanted to actively find the answers to our problems. I was quick to quote scripture that talked about how husbands and wives should work together. Meanwhile, she was going to her counselor, Dr. Svoboda, or her best friend, then Cindy Moon on the World Impact staff, and pouring out her feelings to them instead of me. My insecurities were driving her away, and I just didn't get it.

Needless to say, I became jealous of those relationships because I felt she should have been coming to me first. I wanted to pray over our problems, but she wasn't interested. The more my wife distanced herself from me, the more rejected and lonely I felt. Sex was the one thing that somewhat convinced me that she still loved me. But the problem was that I was so focused on me and my needs—pursuing her at 3:00 or 4:00 in the morning—I never considered that she had to get up and teach the next morning.

Our communication had come to suffer greatly in such a short time, and my behavior was the cause of it. I later realized that, instead of drawing value from how Jesus viewed me, I had placed my wife on the throne of my life instead. What I couldn't see at the time was how much of a burden this placed on her to carry. I was expecting her to meet a need in me that only God Himself could do, and it was absolutely unfair.

One time she had left the house without telling me where she was going. This gave me uninterrupted time for my mind to launch into overdrive. Was she having an affair on me? Since she was no longer communicating with me on any level, Satan had a field day with my imagination, giving me another bout of depression.

Our basement was pretty much bare, and during the winter it could get down to 30 degrees. I can remember going down there in my shorts where we had a rollaway bed. I lay down feeling dejected and full of guilt, and I stayed there for a while without a blanket, even though it was very cold. It was my way of punishing myself for a couple of hours. I cursed myself the entire time, regretting that I was alive.

When she finally came home a few days later, I tried not to ask her a lot of emotional questions and just waited for her to do the talking. It was a very fragile time, and I did not want to lose my wife.

God later blessed me with a job at Boeing Aircraft, working in sheet metal. I was hired at the entry level, which meant that I needed no experience to work in the position. They started me at $11.00 per hour. I felt good about this new job, especially after getting hired after my first try, a rare occurrence when so many were wanting to work there.

At last I felt parallel with my wife, who had been teaching for several years at the time: I was now contributing to the home, which took a load off of Andrea. I had great benefits and was off on weekends. The only downside was that I worked second shift. So when my wife got home from work about 3:30 in the afternoon, I was getting ready to leave the house around 4:00; that gave us no time together except the weekends.

It was a bittersweet arrangement for a new couple. But I thought I had no choice. After awhile it caused strain because we didn't have time to deal with the marriage, and my working second shift made things that much harder.

Even still, the job did not put any communication-type pressure on me, and my work ethic was never an issue. God granted me much success at Boeing; and I was able to not only do a good job, but I won the respect of everyone around me. Even more, my Christian example of servant-hood and compassion for people allowed me access into their lives because they knew I cared.

But after only four months on the job, the layoffs began. Naturally, because I was one of the lowest employees on the totem pole, I was laid off in the first wave of cuts. It was very hard to go home and tell my wife that my time at Boeing was coming to an end. Thankfully she knew it wasn't under my control. Having my wife understand was very encouraging to me.

Andrea had always been a giving person; and I knew that when finances were tight, her lifestyle of giving would also suffer. But she saw me trying, and that's all she wanted. God was still in charge, and I had to remember that.

Unfortunately, my struggles with self-worth spun out of control during times when I wasn't contributing to the home; and briefly, that became the case again. Once again sex became the essential I depended on from my wife to make me feel I was whole and okay.

I had been more or less refusing counseling because I believed the problem was our lack of effective communication. Still, I agreed to meet with Andrea and her counselor a few times, but nothing in those sessions seemed to be helping me and my need; during those times my wife was primarily the focus, and I was simply there to understand how I could best help her to heal. The questions were usually directed toward me and what things I could do to make life easier for her. I felt like I wasn't being heard and couldn't help but think, *"What about me? What about my problems?"* This is not to cast blame, but I felt thoroughly neglected. It was like asking a blind man to be a tour guide. At that point I didn't have eyes to see what was going on inside me; people seemed to be forcing me to understand things I wasn't capable of doing at the time.

After awhile, I started raising the hard questions myself about what *she* needed to do for me as well. Eventually I got tired of going to counseling because my needs weren't being addressed in any way while my frustrations continued to grow. So I decided to quit.

I later agreed to try a support group. I went as promised and figured I would be open and honest about what problems were making me struggle in case anybody asked. One of the things I shared was that sex was an issue for me in our marriage and that I was causing my wife to stumble—but I didn't know why. I spoke openly, believing every participant in the group was safe to reveal whatever was on our minds without fear of criticism or rejection. For the most part, I felt comfortable opening my heart. At this point I was about two or three weeks into the group.

Yet at the following week's meeting, I was met directly at the door. The group's facilitator informed me that I would no longer be allowed to attend the meetings because I wasn't supporting my wife as I should, and she asked me not to come back! I felt like I was being punished for being open and honest. Or had I been too vocal about my faith in a secular group? Perhaps that was the real issue.

Whatever the case, I was simply stunned. The lady made me feel like dirt. Only my sense that God was watching me caused me to bite my tongue. I wanted to tell her something about herself, but I had just finished giving the Lord a lot of credit the week before; and I didn't want to drag His name in the mud. So I quietly turned and walked out to my car.

I did meet a few other times with Andrea and her counselor, trying to make it work. But eventually I dropped out again.

In the meantime, when our year was up in our free house, we decided to move into the Somerset apartments in Wichita. We had also started attending a different church. World Impact's Celebration service turned over its worship to the community under the leadership of a young pastor and his wife, Bill and Sherri Wilson. The church transferred into a different building at a local park, but we decided after awhile to move on.

We chose to move to Vineyard Christian Fellowship. I soon got a job there and was one of two employees on the maintenance staff; I became the lead guy. The new change seemed positive, and I believed it would bring a consistent income. I didn't have to worry too much about communicating with the public, and this gave me a measure of peace.

But even with these changes of jobs and churches, problems continued to emerge in our marriage. Again, at the core of it all was our differing communication styles, the way we dealt with things. Our difficulties simply weren't being addressed. My wife's approach was to talk to her counselor instead of with me. I continued to feel like I didn't matter to her. Once again, I wasn't getting it no matter how hard I tried.

My approach was to attack the issues head on, often blaming her for not opening up and blaming myself for the struggle she was having. It was a vicious cycle. My way of feeling loved was through sex. So when I heard "no" or "not tonight," it felt like the door being slammed in my face. The meaning I received was *"I don't love you"* and *"I'm not interested in you."* That's the way my mind was interpreting the situation. We weren't talking about our problems; neither were we praying together or spending time in God's Word. I believed it must have been my fault, and much of it was.

One of the things contributing to my mounting stress was that we were doing a lot of good things for other people. We were constantly helping others with food, money, and our time. Even though I was no longer on the World Impact staff, I continued to work with kids; my heart had never left those I had helped in the past. I continued to spend time playing basketball with them and talking about their lives. But in my own marriage, problems weren't being dealt with.

I hated that I felt tempted to live a lie, to pretend like everything was going well in our home. I was ashamed that in my own marriage I couldn't solve our problems. I pleaded with God to teach me how to handle my married life and how to keep it separate from my public life—without being phony. I was not willing to sacrifice my integrity just to make a good impression on those who viewed us as a good Christian couple. So I needed desperately the wisdom to balance the two.

My mission was to be different for Christ. I felt like I was carrying the load for not only my personal marriage and the inner-city kids that I was ministering to but for family and all of those gang members in L.A. from my past. I believed they needed to see the convincing power and love of God to change broken lives. That meant perseverance on my part, not giving up.

All I had ever known were broken or nonexistent marriages and divided homes. Everyone around me was like that! So I did not want my marriage to fail. Neither did my wife; she was the example in her family. Our success would speak volumes about the love of Christ—but what would our failure say? I worried about what others might think because I cared about how my behavior would affect them, whether for good or bad.

But Satan also knew how much I loved my Lord and continued to play on my emotions and on my past. He seemed to prod at me so I couldn't settle for any unexplained answers but needed to be constantly wearing on Andrea to open up and be honest with me. And it was always her silence that got to me. Horribly, I didn't realize I myself was causing the silence to some degree: I had lost her trust and respect. Satan used that against me as well—to grind me into the ground with guilt for how badly I was causing my wife to stumble. I simply didn't know what was going on beneath the surface.

Chapter Twenty-Nine

Our one-year lease soon ended at the Somerset Apartments. We were faced with having to renew—knowing that our rent was going up— or start searching for something else. We looked around at different houses, but nothing fit our budget or our preference. My wife explained to me how taxes work, how renters are not able to write off the rent onto their taxes and that all the money we'd spent was totally lost. Once that clicked in my head and I calculated all the money we'd paid in rent in a twelve-month span, I became open to the idea of buying a home. At least we could write off the interest on our taxes. That was the survivalist in me, not wanting to let anyone take advantage of me.

We decided to begin exploring our options. My wife had outstanding credit and a very good name as a professional educator and as a person. She had knowledge about how to start the process; I didn't have a clue, so I basically trusted her judgment.

Still, nothing clicked with us. We considered that we didn't want to buy anyone else's problems, so we determined to build our first home. Both incomes together would be enough to take out a mortgage and provide living expenses. We qualified for a home loan and soon began the process of building our first house.

For a while I had held off from such a commitment because I was afraid if I lost my job, we wouldn't be able to afford the payments and other expenses; I asked myself—then what? I certainly didn't want to bring embarrassment on my wife. I had been afraid of failing, but I knew it was Andrea's dream to have her own home. I wanted to make her happy after all the turmoil we had gone through in just two years of marriage. So now I was willing to step out "in faith" and trust God in the matter. I felt she deserved it.

We had also begun pursuing foster care. I was content to live without kids if that's what she wanted. But adoption had come up earlier in our relationship as a possibility. We wanted to begin a family, perhaps feeling that it would help gel us together. We both enjoyed children and wanted to love some little one out there who was alone for whatever unfortunate reason and needed the love of a mom and dad.

Although I had held off on major commitments such as a new home and children until I felt our marriage was stable, now I had agreed to both owning a home and adopting children; but we could never agree on the timing. However, when I got to know her eighth grade student, Serena, who was in foster care at the time, my heart turned toward bringing her into our home and making her a permanent member of our family. Serena adored my wife, her teacher, and often confided in her. The two had grown close, and eventually I grew close to her as well. I also had the honor of leading her to Christ. And after going through part of the foster care process, we were given the honor of having her spend the weekends with us.

But suddenly things hit hard between me and my wife; they were pretty much the same issues. My wife left one evening and was gone for almost a week. She had gone to her mom's to stay.

During that first night alone I wanted to kill myself. I thought going through the foster care process and the possibility of building our first home were enough to please her. Those shared realities made us smile. I had basically given the green light to fulfill her dreams—even before our issues were straightened out—just to make her happy. I believed these things would cause her to feel confident in my ability to care for her and make good decisions. But somehow, the need for sex and communication, though not in that order, were still buried core concerns, problems grumbling below the surface.

Once she returned, we merely coexisted until after our home was built and completed on August 3, 1993. We continued to live in the apartment on a month-to-month basis until we closed on the house. We finally moved in, and all seemed to go well for a while. But before Serena was set to join our family permanently, my wife called me at work and asked me to move out.

I immediately jumped on the defensive, stating that my name was on the mortgage too and that I had just as much right to stay in my own home as she had. Andrea then said, "Fine, then. I'll move out, and you pay the bills." A part of me wanted to fight back and force her to put her money where her mouth was. But I realized I had a critical choice to make: I could let her leave but would risk losing our brand new home because I couldn't afford the mortgage and all the bills alone, or I could move out and deal with feeling defeated. I felt I heard God whisper to me, *"Don't fight her. Trust me."* So I obeyed and told my wife that I would move out.

When I hung up the phone, I was devastated. I just knew something had to happen; problems could not continue to go on and on while being ignored. But I never imagined it would come to a sudden separation. I fell into a deep depression almost immediately.

My mind was flooded with questions like *"Why?"* and *"Where am I going to stay?"* and *"God, are you going to do something?"* All I could think about was the embarrassment I would have when our families and close friends found out about the separation. *"What am I going to say?"*

It became too hard for me to remain at work and do my job. I didn't want to stay there and struggle to separate from my feelings, to pretend like nothing was going on. So I decided to leave and figure out what I was going to do next. I grabbed my things, shut the door to my maintenance office, and walked out of the church.

On my way out, our church receptionist, my friend Sue Lynn, asked me what was wrong because to see me upset was a very rare sight. I blurted out that I couldn't talk at the moment and just had to go. At that point I didn't care if I lost my job or not because all I could focus on was the problem at hand.

I jumped in my car and just started driving, not knowing what to do or where to go. Everything was a blur, very confusing, while I was being hit with a variety of intense, agonizing emotions. I grew more and more angry with my wife, feeling betrayed by her. I even felt bitterness toward God for supposedly not answering my prayers concerning my marriage. Despairing thoughts suggested He had abandoned me since He was not providing the results I needed.

Once again I questioned if my Christian transformation was worth all the heartache I was going through. But I still had that element of fear of leaving God. I was driving on the highway feeling all this and debating whether or not to drive off the overpass. Only my reverence for the Lord kept from acting on my suicidal urges at that moment.

But after awhile I stopped at a store and bought a large Big Gulp soda and some rat poison. Then I checked myself in a local hotel room. My plan was to dump out about a third of my drink and then fill up the rest with the poison. I would swallow the "death drink," lie back on the bed, and just fade away into the pages of history.

That was the easy part. The hard part was getting past the Lord. I tried to look for excuses to end my life because I was simply tired of struggling aimlessly. It was like that game show, "Let's Make a Deal"—every door (escape) I picked to run through, God was there waiting behind it, giving me a reason why I should live.

The Lord did convict my heart because the bottom line was I really didn't want to die. I didn't want to disappoint God or hurt those I cared about, so I decided to obey Him. As soon as I made that choice, I thought to call my friend Al Ewert from World Impact. Apparently, Sue Lynn—concerned about my wellbeing—had called my wife and told her I had left work very disturbed. Andrea, in turn, had called Al Ewert to see if he'd heard anything from me. When I called Al, he was very excited and concerned about my safety. I admitted what I had been planning but assured him I wouldn't do anything stupid. Even still, I didn't want to give him my number and location because I just wanted to be alone to rest.

The next day I called in to work, and Sue Lynn was happy to hear that I was okay. The staff had been asked to pray for me, and I was promised that my job was not in jeopardy for walking out. I had proven myself faithful in my duties and attendance, and they were aware of how I had such a heart for people. So they were very supportive and wanted me to come back when I was ready.

Later on I made the difficult decision to face my mother and stepfather David (who were then living in Wichita) with what was happening in our marriage but without going into a lot of details. I didn't ask them for advice, and they didn't offer any either. They simply made their home mine.

I had hesitated about asking them if I could move in with them because of the alcoholic environment and how my mother's drinking problem, along with my stepfather David's, had always caused me anguish. But now I had no choice but to accept that I needed my mom's help, especially because without knowing what my wife would do to work this out, I didn't want to sign a lease that would bind me to an apartment for six months to a year. So moving in with my mother was a big help. They didn't ask any questions but simply allowed me to bring up the subject if I was so inclined. They not only loved me, but they loved Andrea as well and respected our marriage. My niece De'Essence was kind enough to move out of her room for me, giving me some privacy.

This all took place in early December between two of the biggest holidays in our country. Thanksgiving and Christmas can make people feel very good about God, family, and country; or they can make them feel extremely lonely and dejected. Of course, I felt nothing but those negative emotions, making the timing of the separation even more miserable.

A counselor was recommended to me by my wife's therapist, Dr. Svoboda. She referred me to a clinician by the name of Jim Dyer. I was kind of skeptical about meeting with him because I didn't want to go through secular counseling again. Dr. Svoboda assured me that the man was a Christian, so I decided to go just to please my wife and her doctor. We met in his office, not far from my mom's; and the first thing I asked him was, "Are you a Christian?—because I won't be coming to these meetings if we can't include the Bible in my counseling."

Jim said enthusiastically, "Yes, I am! That's fine with me." Then I added, "I want us to open and close our time in prayer at every meeting." And I wanted him to hold me accountable as well. Jim was cool with that, and we hit it off immediately.

I had always held to the ideal of being absolutely real, no matter the cost; and this would be no different. Our first meeting went well. It was basically an introduction to his philosophy and approach. The second half began with my sharing details of my current situation and how I felt about things.

But as the time went on, he began to delve into my past to find out how deep my scars went. For example, "Eric, when your stepfather called you a sissy for running in the house after you were chased by some gang members, how did that make you feel?" I would reply something like, "It made me sad." Jim would prod me further, "Yeah,

I know, but how did that make you *feel?*" I would say again, "It made me feel sad." But he would push harder, "Yeah, I know, but how did that make you feel way down deep inside?" He had stopped preaching and gone to meddling, as we say in the south.

By then I was getting frustrated because he was badgering me with the same question over and over again. I thought, *"Why is this man asking me the same thing? I've told him I don't know—how many times?"* After awhile, he moved to another question. Finally, I got so anxious that I started standing and pacing, asking this man again what he wanted from me. I couldn't give him a better answer than the ones that I was already giving him! And by that time my stuttering was getting worse as I continued to tense up inside.

I pushed chairs away from me as if I wanted to tear up something. So picking up on that, Jim stopped the session and asked me to step outside with him. I didn't know what he was up to, but I thought, *"I know this guy isn't calling me out, because he'll lose."* But when we got outside by the dumpsters, Jim told me to kick one of the trash bins—just to give it a good blast with my foot. I looked at him like he was crazy. But he was actually serious.

Jim reminded me that I had asked him to hold me accountable to deal with my past, no matter the cost; and that was what he was attempting to do. And as I slammed against that can, I could hardly keep a straight face because Jim loked so funny trying to look tough; but I finally got it. I felt that *my stepfather didn't care about me.*

It became a turning point in my counseling because he was right. I *did* want him to hold me accountable in Christ, and I decided to submit to his authority and help from that moment on.

Having a Christian counselor proved helpful to me. He was not only my therapist, but he became my friend. We did not leave our counseling relationship as the only means of help. He kept the balance. When it was time to advise me, he was the counselor; but when the session was over, he became the brother in Christ I needed. We often played basketball at the YMCA together, and I got to know his wife Debbie as well. This began about a two year counseling relationship.

During our sessions, I was free to express my heart—sometimes even in tears. It became the primary hour of my life, a time that I came to depend on. Jim had me go far back into my past just by asking me questions, some I'd never had to answer before. Often I didn't have immediate answers for him. We frequently began our time in prayer, asking the Holy Spirit to open my eyes as I looked into my childhood and to show me things He wanted me to see and understand. And, at my request, Jim always applied the Word of God in our hours together.

And because of God's faithfulness, I was able to recapture early memories of me and my grandmother as we sat on the front porch in the evening, wrapped in one of her hand knitted quilts, eating cookies, and talking about her early years, slavery, or God. She was very funny as well as kind.

The more I described my childhood, the clearer the past began to appear. I soon started talking about events I hadn't thought of in years, such as the time when the three brothers pulled a pellet gun on me, pointed it at my head, and forced me to perform oral sex under threat of my life—at the age of seven.

These discussions began to crack open deep feelings of anger and shame. During those times I felt dazed because the experiences didn't seem real or like they had actually happened to *me*. I had let them slip away because, in my mind, my past was over. I had learned to repress those memories because revealing emotion in the streets was a form of weakness—and I wanted no part of it. And now, God Himself was calling me to face the suffering all over again, only this time in a more open and honest way. He was actually giving me the power to go deeper than I ever had while He helped me trust in the promises of His Word.

The more these troubles began to surface, the harder life got for me, being separated from Andrea. The Christmas season was almost unbearable to go through while I had to witness my mom and David's drinking again on a daily basis. They would argue and curse one another out; and sometimes they would physically fight, and I would have to break them up. Back in the day I probably would have choked David to death or something, but now I tried to be open and realize it wasn't his fault all the time. These memories compounded everything, but they were necessary.

This environment made it tougher to cope with my separation, and I longed to be home. I could think of little else: I needed to be in my own home, not living with my mom or anyone else. Those feelings turned up the intensity, if you will, because it made me press Andrea all the more to work on our marriage with continual messages on our house phone and notes on her windshield. But I could never persuade her to do so. She held to absolute silence about where things were headed, and it was driving me crazy. I felt helpless. My counseling sessions were my only safe haven, my only outlet.

During this time I tried to stay as focused as I could and maintain other relationships while I went through my own problems. For a while after I got married, I had lost contact with some of the kids I had befriended years earlier. I wasn't able to spend as much time with them as I had before.

One in particular, De'Angelo Evans, had become a star athlete at his high school in football and basketball. He was the state's top tailback and was being compared to pro athletes like Barry Sanders and Emmitt Smith. In spite of his busy schedule, he found time to reach out to me again, and we rekindled our friendship. He became a source of encouragement to me as I had been to him as a child through World Impact. He also got me on a weight lifting program called "Bigger, Faster, Stronger," and it really helped me get my mind off the tough issues facing me.

God was so faithful to me in many ways. Now He even sent a couple of my Bible club kids, from my World Impact days, in whose lives I had once invested. They were Darae and Oscar. By this time, these guys had become teenagers and were trying to find their own identities and deal with girl questions. The three of us began to hang out a lot. I had to set aside my "teacher" hat and just be their big brother. This turned out to be a real blessing for me because I got to know these two, as well as De'Angelo, as young men. I couldn't be too consumed with my own problems around them because I wanted to set the example for what it means to trust the Lord, even in the tough times. God seemed to be using them and their issues to remind me of that.

We played a lot of basketball in local parks and gyms, and they knew they were needed and appreciated during this time in my life. But tragically, our growing friendship was cut short when Darae, as I understand it, was accidentally shot and killed. His passing was a devastating loss to his family, including Oscar, who was his cousin, as well to me. My young buddy was supposed to ride along with me the next day to take Oscar to live with his brother Dayton in Kansas City, Missouri; but he never got to make that trip. Instead he made a greater trip to be with his Lord Jesus Christ.

At the same time, Dee was busy preparing for the close of his incredible high school football career as our state's all-time leader rusher and, I believe, number nine in the nation, behind Emmitt Smith, who was ranked number one. He was heavily recruited by Division 1 schools but would finally decide to attend the University of Nebraska.

Their departures left me with nothing to do, aside from work and being at my mother's home. Eventually I fell back into the rut of worry about whether or not my wife would reconcile with me. The depression got worse, and then thoughts of suicide began to surface again.

I asked my friend and co-worker at Vineyard, Mark Olze, who was an associate pastor and licensed counselor, to help me find a place where I could go to get some help. I realized it was critical for me to work on myself, or I couldn't be sure of my future. The guilt was beginning to mount up even more. Certainly my counseling was great and was helping me unlock my past, but God was calling me to go even deeper still.

Chapter Thirty

Mark helped me find a Christian clinic called Brookhaven in Tulsa, Oklahoma. The money issues were worked out, and Pastor Tom Rozolf allowed me the necessary time off to do what I needed to do.

I drove down there alone, a couple of hours' distance. During my first night in the clinic, they put me on suicide watch, a pretty typical procedure, I'm told. And they made all the patients go to bed around 9:00 or 10:00 in the evening. That was difficult for me because I'm a late night owl; I've usually gone to bed around midnight, even to this day. But I guess rest was the issue.

I began a ten-day stint, consisting of about twelve scheduled sessions a day. The whole person was dealt with, and the information was very specific. They discussed nutrition, medicine, generational sins, and much, much more. They even included some speech therapy at my request. And at the center of it all was God's Word.

In these classes I had to open up my life to total strangers all over again. Emotionally, the first couple of days were more than draining. But I had gone there fully prepared to suffer until God gave me a breakthrough. So I allowed myself to be held accountable.

One of the great features I enjoyed there were the times of group sharing. Those present included people from just about every walk of life: we ranged from businessmen, country folks, and blue-collar workers to big city people like me.

In our own individual ways, we all had something to offer. Each of us shared openly, and that kind of honesty gave every person the confidence to probe his deepest fears and longings. One kid in particular had been sexually abused by his father, and God used my testimony to capture his trust. I witnessed my young friend having a breakthrough after he watched my willingness to struggle against my stuttering problem, fighting to get out every word. He told me he wanted to be as courageous as I was and, after that, allowed the group to walk with him through his attempt to deal with his pain.

But the Lord used this kid to work in my life at the same time. My heart broke for him as I watched the love of Christ move in his heart. My own problems became less important to me when I realized that feeling sorry for myself was not an option and as I felt led to walk closely with him through our time together there.

At one point I was asked to name every person who had hurt me or sexually molested me while growing up. One by one I had to forgive them as God had forgiven me. This powerful verse was the absolute key: "For if you forgive men when they sin against you, your heavenly Father will also forgive you. But if you do not forgive men their sins, your Father will not forgive your sins" (Matthew 6:14-15, NIV). I was beyond grateful to God for His forgiveness, so it wasn't an option to deny forgiveness to those people in my past; it was completely clear to me, and I followed through wholeheartedly.

In one of our sessions, we watched a video series on knowing your value in Christ by Malcolm Smith. He talked about how our sense of self-worth must be rooted in Jesus Christ and not in our titles, such as a doctor, lawyer, mechanic, secretary, or whatever. This included, for me, even my stuttering because I had always based my value on my performance as a stutterer, which was very poor. After that, I had turned to my performance as a member of the Crips gang, which had given me such a false sense of security for a short—but not lasting—period of my life.

For the first time I realized I had been searching for unconditional love all the years since being forced to leave my grandma. I'd tried to be the most fearless gang banger that I could be, even to the point of putting my life on the line for my friends. It hit me that I was actually willing to take a hit or a bullet for one of my homeboys and for what I believed in as a Crip. I had built that false image to find a sense of meaning and purpose in my life. But I wanted my identity back; I wanted true meaning again. That little boy inside me had died, and I wanted him to live again—because *that was the real me.*

Yes, I had knowledge of God's Word by this time. And yes, God had given me a great taste of His love and forgiveness, and those around me really saw a genuine change in my life. But now it had all come to a standstill. I understood that my wife had accepted me, and her love had been covering much of the shame I felt for myself. She had enabled me to enter into the relationship and come out from under my protective rock.

But along the way, I had placed her on a pedestal, putting her in that unfortunate position to fill the void in my life. I began to understand the weight I had placed on her and how unfair that had been. But God knew I couldn't see this, and it occurred to me that maybe He was behind this whole separation situation just to get my undivided attention and that my hospital stay was being directed by Him all along.

This new insight gave me such a fresh perspective on where my focus needed to be: I should be finding my value in Christ my Lord. I also had to confront the possibility that I might not ever get back with my wife. I had to understand that if she decided not to love me enough to stay in the marriage, I still had to draw my love from Christ alone, the only source capable of filling my deepest needs. This was my long-awaited breakthrough, and I embraced it with all my heart.

Nearing the end of my stay at Brookhaven, my assigned counselor and I began developing a plan for me to follow after I left. Until I learned what my wife would decide to do with our relationship, I needed to show her that change was underway and that I was indeed working on me.

I would have to maintain a job for more than a year to consistently provide my wife with financial help. My counseling with Jim was necessary to continue, something I was planning to do anyway. The constant calling and leaving my wife messages—trying to persuade her to make the marriage work—had to end. The only contact allowed would be to mail her a money order or check. If we eventually got back together, I had to stop pressuring her for sex. These were just a few of the areas of concern that I needed to work on. My counselor and I committed these changes to prayer, and I stated my motive for making them: it was to obey the Lord.

I also had to start seeing my wife as my sister in Christ and to pray regularly that she would grow closer to Him as well. I had never specifically thought of her that way before because I was too attached emotionally in the role of husband. This concept became a key element of my whole healing process and helped me begin praying for her without resentment.

I had come to Tulsa seeking help just ten days earlier without understanding or direction, but now I was going back home with my eyes opened. Leaving the clinic was very hard to do because I felt I was saying goodbye to family, but I was excited to get back home and begin living again.

God had given me victory over two temptations to have affairs with two different women during the first several months of our separation before going to Tulsa—leaving my integrity intact. Anger had driven me to the borderline of both of them, but obedience to Christ won out. A part of me wanted to rush back to Wichita to tell my wife what God had done during my stay at Brookhaven, but I knew I had to stick with my plan, and I was determined to do exactly that.

Chapter Thirty-One

I went on to hold my current job one year, accomplishing one of my goals. My financial support became consistent—as long as my wife agreed to accept it. I quit calling her and leaving begging messages to work on our marriage together. I cut off all attempted dialogue with her but was leaving it up to her to initiate communication when she felt ready.

At first this restraint was emotionally hard to do, but I had to stick with it. As time went on, I came to a point of peace that felt prepared to lose my wife if she so chose. I was beginning to see my future as a single man as the joy grew of knowing I was finally letting Andrea go while trusting the Lord to continue to work in her life and praying earnestly for her as my sister in Christ. Slowly my desire for what was best for her became more important to me than our getting back together.

In 1994, several months after my Tulsa trip, having been faithful to my goals, I got a call from my wife. She wanted to tell me that she had scheduled an appointment with a divorce lawyer that week. She was letting me know she was through with the marriage and that I could come to get the rest of my stuff.

For the first time, I was in total peace of mind. I said to her, "Andrea, I meant it for life, and I love you. But if that's what you want to do, then that's between you and the Lord. I'm sorry it has to come to this, but all right. I gotta go. Bye." And I hung up. The best part of it all was that I didn't have a panic attack or desire to call her back and beg her not to go through with it.

264

That day I knew I was free in Christ; the bondage of the past was finally broken. The little boy inside had begun to heal. *This* is how God blessed my obedience!

But several days after talking with my wife, I got another call from her, courageously telling me she had cancelled her appointment with the divorce attorney and wanted our marriage to work after all. She suggested a slow transition back together and back into our home. Of course I agreed to her terms with great joy and without objection. One of my goals, if we got back together, was to allow her to set the pace; and I was committed to doing just that.

We began seeing each other for dinner once a week along with our foster daughter, Serena. As time went on, I began to spend a night on the weekends; and eventually she said, "Come home." Now I saw clearly that God had taken me from my family to demonstrate my need for Him alone to be the fulfiller of my deepest longings. And I believed the same was true for Andrea. Since we were bringing Serena into our fmaily, we needed to be equipped emotionally and spiritually to be a blessing to her. It was necessary for Serena to see God's hand in my life if she was going to learn to see God as a good Father as well.

One of the positive things about living at my mom's for approximately fourteen months was that I had the privilege of teaching my nephew Omar and my niece De'Essence about Jesus Christ and His love as well as a host of other biblical truths.

My mother Marie and my stepfather David ("Dave-Bo") were both still heavy drinkers and would often get drunk and argue. Those times gave me the opportunity to be a stable influence and sow seeds of truth in the kids' lives while they were still young and while I was there. I would have them in the room, answering any questions they had concerning the Bible; and I had the honor of leading them to the Lord. Our times together also helped calm them from the sometimes hostile environment of their home; though the alcoholic binges didn't affect them personally, life was stressful while not knowing what would happen to Momma and David when they started drinking.

I jumped right into parenthood when I went back home. I was suddenly the father of a teenage girl whom we had come to love as if she were our very own. Andrea and I had talked about possibly adopting someday, but I had always held off because I wanted us to get a handle on our marriage first, and I needed to feel like a provider.

But our affection for Serena grew. She was Andrea's student in her eighth grade algebra class, and the two of them had become close as Serena opened up to my wife more and more. Andrea related to her very well; and together, God gave us the desire to bring her into her home as our very own.

Serena would occasionally spend time with us as we went through the foster care process. Eventually, we were awarded custody once her previous foster mom supported the transition. She was an older woman who had been a nun, and the time seemed right for both of them.

Even still, we only had her for about a year. The situation didn't work out as we all had hoped, but the memories we did have together will last forever. Our whole extended family grew to love Serena and gave her a place in our hearts for all time. Serena would go on to finish high school and college and get a master's degree. She married her high school sweetheart, Justin Hansen, whom we had also grown to love. They both re-dedicated their lives to Jesus Christ and became active members in our church. They have four beautiful children. Today we count them as friends, and we still consider her our daughter.

But after Serena moved out, Andrea and I were left with an empty nest. It was the first time we had been alone together since our separation nearly two years earlier. Things went well for a while, and I stayed pretty much consistent with all my goals. But eventually Satan began to test me with the past—the same issues, the same problems. Finally, Andrea asked me to leave once more. I certainly didn't want to go through that again, but what do you do? Rather than resorting to slamming doors or socking walls—as I had done in our first several years of marriage—I chose to quietly agree. But this time, I wasn't driven by fear and panic because I knew where my value comes from.

But on August 22, 1995 our lives were about to change in a big way. At approximately 10:00 on a Tuesday morning, the phone rang. I was in the process of packing some of my clothes for about a two weeks' separation. At first I didn't want to take the call, not being in the mood to talk to anyone. But a thought entered my mind, *"Better answer that phone!"* I was going to let the answering machine catch it; but instead, I followed the suggestive thought.

The caller was a social worker from Social Rehabilitations Services (SRS). I was thinking it was about one of the kids I was working with. I had been involved with a contracting group for teens called TKC, headed by my friends Mike and his brother-in-law Daniel, teaching kids how to work and be responsible in school and in life. I had also gotten on board with USD 259, serving as a para-professional in Special Education (behavior-disordered and learning-disabled kids). So I was expecting the worst.

But the caller turned out to be a case-worker whom my wife and I had met some time back in regard to adoptions. At the time, SRS had not been pursuing homes for adoptive infants; rather they were trying to find homes for teens, who were going through huge problems themselves. But we weren't ready for more issues.

The lady asked to speak with me or my wife. She said that she was sitting at her desk and trying to figure out what to do with a baby girl who had just been born the previous night (Monday). Apparently, we "popped" into her mind first, and she just happened to have kept our phone number in her desk. She was giving us a call to see if we were still interested. Immediately, I felt I heard God urge, *"Say yes."* So I said, "Yes! Definitely!" I asked her to let me call my wife and talk with her about it, knowing what Andrea was going to say anyway. By now, I too was ready to have a baby.

I made that call and gave Andrea the case worker's phone number. Andrea asked me to stay home and not to leave because she believed the phone call had been from God and that He chose to use this child as a means of keeping me in the home and forcing us to work together.

As an independent contractor working with kids who are under the protection and/or services of the state, I was responsible for paying my own taxes. I had about five hundred dollars set aside for that purpose, but that day I had to use the money to buy a crib, changer, diaper disposal, and various other baby items. I figured I could make up the tax money later, which I did.

We arranged to pick up the child the next day—Wednesday, August 23, 1995. She had been placed at the Wichita Children's Home, a haven for abused and neglected youngsters. When we saw the baby, we fell madly in love with her.

Ashley weighed 5 pounds and 11 ounces. I was scared to pick her up, afraid that I was going to accidentally drop her on the ground and watch her splatter. But I soon got over it. The night we brought her home, our dear friends Didi, Leah, Donna, my mother Marie, Andrea's mom Ernestine, my sister-in-law Carolyn, and others all came over to meet Ashley and give us friendly parenting advice.

Our whole world had changed literally overnight. Andrea had asked me to leave for a couple of weeks on Monday, and on Tuesday we were back together and expecting a brand new baby girl. She lit up our home, and her life gave us a renewed dedication to work even harder on our marriage.

We bought a rocking chair with an ottoman and some Christian lullabies for infants. We soon found Ashley had her days and nights mixed up: she would sleep in the day, but would stay awake at night. Andrea and I would switch off and take turns rocking her to the music—for hours. When she would fall asleep, we would gently lay her down and try to sneak out of her room. If we accidentally bumped our shoulder or something against the wall, she would wake up screaming.

As every parent does, we would go back, check to see if she was wet, and then rock her some more. But these moments, even though they were tough physically, were times of great joy. I started praying for her nightly, holding her close to my chest. I would think of old Bible club songs and songs of worship and just sing to my baby.

I dedicated Ashley to the Lord nightly, constantly whispering into her ear, "Ashley, you were made in God's image. He made you for a purpose, and you are His. May He guard your heart, soul, mind, and spirit; and may He make of you what He has made you to be." From day one, I decided to whisper such blessings into her life. And over time she would develop into such a beautiful and healthy child.

That first month, however, was hard on the body because Ashley was very demanding. One night I got up with her around 11:30 and stayed up with her until about 6:00 the next morning. She would fall asleep, and I would just hold her thinking, *"Lord, I'm tired, and I have to go to work here in an hour."*

Our baby's late nights were beginning to take a toll on us physically until a dear friend gave us some great advice. In the past, a family had taken Andrea into their home while she did her student-teaching in the small town of Ellinwood, Kansas. Over the years Mr. and Mrs. Hood came to be our spiritual parents who love us as if we're their own. They would often invite us out to their home at least two or three times a year. On one of these weekends Mrs. Hood suggested we bathe

Ashley, make sure she was fed and changed, pray over her like we usually did, and then turn on her music and lay her down in her bed. Then we were to leave her alone. When she cried, we should just let her cry for a while.

We decided to try it. When we got back home, we put her advice into practice that night. Ashley cried and cried and cried. We could barely take it. It was as though we were abandoning her, and that hurt. As her father, I felt like I should rescue her, but we were committed to sticking with it.

Finally, after about an hour of crying at the top of her lungs, she fell asleep. I can remember creeping into her Winnie the Pooh room to see if she was still breathing—I was just that scared. But she was sound asleep. We had to repeat this several more times before she began sleeping about fifteen hours a night. That was our introduction to the world of babies, up close and personal.

Bringing Ashley into our family was the beginning of the rest of our lives, and we were and still are very thankful to the Lord for being such an awesome God. Out of all the people on the planet, He chose us to be the parents of our baby girl. It took us about a year to go through the adoption process. We were blessed with a good lawyer, Eric Commers, who helped us manage it. The judge assigned to our case allowed Ashley's biological father the right to have supervised visits with her, but he would voluntarily give up those rights later on. We did not have one obstacle in our way; all we had to do was go through the standard procedures.

After the adoption was finalized, we asked our friend Don Davis from World Impact to dedicate Ashley formally to the Lord. Many of our closest friends were invited such as Will and DiDi Scott, Tim and Leah Ladwig, Maurice and Gwen Douggins, Glenn and Peggy Bossler, the Drs. Svoboda, and many other friends and family. And then the three of us stayed in a hotel in Kansas City, Missouri for the weekend to celebrate. We also changed her name officially to Ashley Nicole, leaving the name "Ashley" in honor of her biological mother.

Over the next two years, Ashley continued to bring us extreme amounts of joy. We were so close that rarely was I not there to tuck her in at night and pray over her. At one point, though, the school district sent me to a weekend workshop in Kansas City for para-professionals. It was the first time I had been out of Ashley's routine for that amount of time. She woke up the first night, got out of her crib, and went and got in bed with Mom. And for the next year or so, she got up every single night.

Naturally this new arrangement took a huge toll on our bodies, but what can you do except deal with it? She was the happiest baby I had ever seen. I began investing in Christian videos like "Psalty's Praise," "VeggieTales," the "Beginner's Bible" series, and Focus on the Family's "Adventures in Odyssey." I also bought her Winnie the Pooh. I loved watching them with her; they brought out the kid in me a little bit.

Ashley was two years old on August 21, 1997, and we thought our lives were complete. But she was about to have company. Once again, God chose us to be the parents of another bundle of energy and sweetness. Around December of that year, we got a call from our neighbor and friend Dee, who was an official at Lutheran Social Services at the time. She called to tell us about a two-month-old baby boy who needed a home. But one other thing about him: he had a brother who was a year older, and the agency wanted the two to be placed together. That would mean having three babies under the age of two at the same time, so I was automatically closed to the idea. It was hard enough finding a babysitter just for Ashley, although our friend Donna White had offered to keep her during the day. Andrea started to feel opened to the idea but wanted me to make the final decision.

I felt so bad for these two baby boys; it wasn't their fault they were in this unfortunate situation. About the time I agreed in my mind to go for it and to trust God for the details, another couple with two kids already had agreed to take John, the older brother, into their family.

With that problem solved, we decided to go and visit the baby at the Children's Home where his foster parents would be waiting to let us see him. One look at that child and I fell in love with him. I knew in my heart of hearts that he was to be my son.

Andrea told the case-worker that we wanted him; and at our next visit, I believe, we took him home with us permanently. We began to call him Isaiah immediately to get him used to hearing it before the adoption was finalized. He was only called that within our family because the State didn't approve of any changes until the adoption was final.

Once again we hired Eric Commers, a Christian man, to be our lawyer because he had represented us so well with Ashley's adoption. As with Ashley's process, it took about a year, and we faced no obstacles as if God had specifically chosen Isaiah just for us.

The judge assigned to the case read my autobiography that all adoptive parents had to present and became fascinated by my story. He wanted to hear it again personally from me. It was sort of amusing: we almost thought he'd forgotten why we were in his chambers because he so enjoyed learning what an impact Jesus Christ had on my life.

The grandfatherly judge eagerly signed the adoption process as complete, truly believing that Isaiah was in good hands. We took pictures with our lawyer and the judge; the judge played with the kids for a while; and then we left, rejoicing that God had made us a family. Ashley Nicole and Isaiah Maurice West will forever be our gifts from God. We then set off to Kansas City as a family to celebrate for a second time.

We gave our son the name of Isaiah after the prophet in the Bible. He took on my middle name, Maurice, the name my family calls me. My son was a good little baby, one that smiled and laughed a lot and loved to be tickled. Ashley had begun walking at nine months, but Isaiah took his time and didn't really get going until he was about a year old.

Watching him develop and his little personality unfold was awesome. He could always entertain himself, but he did love watching Bible videos with his daddy. He could memorize those videos!—reciting all the characters' lines with ease, especially from the VeggieTales. He loved the way I would mimic his favorite, squealing "Daddy, sing the hair brush song!" as he prepared to be tickled. He could never get enough of it, and those times are fun, fun memories for me today.

I felt blessed to pray over Isaiah as I did with Ashley. Holding my son reminded me of the father who never held me. That's why cuddling him close was such a joy, knowing that he was mine and that I would raise him with a love I had never had. As he grew, my son loved to pray, and I looked forward to that each night.

I don't have the words to describe to you what a blessing I feel from the privilege of being called "Dad." One of my promises has been that "My kids are going to know their father, never having to question if I love them." And with God's help, I've been able to fulfill that to this point—seventeen years later.

My kids know I'm not perfect and have never pretended that I am. But they do understand that I'm real. When I need to say "I'm sorry," I'm not too proud to apologize to them or their mother or anyone else. From their earliest years I've tried to model what a genuine Christian looks like: a human being who makes mistakes but is under the same authority I've taught them to respect, the Lord Jesus Christ.

They say that kids spell love T.I.M.E., and from their infancy I was snuggled with them nightly eating popcorn and watching our Christian videos on the couch before bed. These were simply aids to help me introduce truth into their lives and to form memories that would last a lifetime. Ashley and Isaiah knew that regardless of what happened during their day, I was going to be with them before bed; it was our special time.

And for thirty minutes to an hour each night I would lie on the floor beside their beds (they traded off whose room we would use each night), and they would choose a few Bible songs to sing before we prayed. This was the most important part of the day when we would thank God for our blessings and one another, and I would ask the Lord to guard their hearts, souls, minds, and spirits.

To me, those were the instances that shaped memories that will serve as anchors God can someday use in their lives as my grandmother did for me. Truly, God has provided her influence in my life to serve as a model for me in my own kids' lives. Even today, when I remember those times, I will tear up if I don't cut it short. What priceless memories! Those times are irreplaceable.

During those years, I worked nights in addition to my day job with USD 259, involved with children in special education. I had committed to one year of part-time evening service in our church's maintenance department; but when a full-time position there opened up, Andrea asked me to leave the school district as well as the part-time job to take advantage of this new opportunity. I had enjoyed both jobs very much, but the full-time maintenance position offered the benefit of a tuition break for my kids, who were attending the church's Joyful Noise Academy, so I chose to think of my family first. Besides that, Andrea didn't want me having to restrain the special needs kids any more because of my recent heart attack.

My part-time boss, Bob Hingst, had been encouraging me to join the maintenance staff full time because he thought my hard work and Christian witness added much to the department. I agreed and have held that position for the last fourteen years. How great that I got to work where my kids went to school, both Joyful Noise and the church's Central Christian Academy. Both are now in high school.

From my kids' earliest years I've realized that I didn't want to miss out on their lives. I decided at that time that I would no longer work at night or on weekends if I could avoid it. I would always see athletes on TV after a game-winning basket or touchdown peering into the camera and spouting "Hi Mom!" Something always seemed wrong with that picture. I wanted my kids to remember, no matter what they decide to do with their lives, that both Mom and I have *been there.*

God has kept me very conscious of my responsibility as a father. I did not have a father to love me, teach me, or walk alongside me as I grew into manhood. My stepfather Charles, the only father-figure I ever really knew, was never there for me. In my view, he hadn't abandoned ship in my life; he was never in the ship to begin with.

During the most critical period of my life—what I call the bridge between childhood and adulthood—I ran my own life. For me, that transition was a flirtation with death, a life of risk and survival, a time of understanding nothing of who I was. O'G Clipper from Grape Street Watts Crips? That was not me! It was a protective shell I had built around me because I was frightened and vulnerable and needed to feel like I *belonged.* Sometimes I've wondered what it would have been like with a father who cared for me through it all. Personally I will never know the love of an earthly father. But I've made my peace with that: the sting is no longer there because my Father in heaven has met that need and more.

And because I've been given the privilege of being a father myself, that cycle—that old way of doing things—has been broken. Now I'm in charge of beginning a new cycle. With God's help, my kids will never have to face what I had to face; they will never question my love.

What do I want to leave for my kids? I hope it will be that Jesus Christ is who He says He is, the One who died in their place because He simply loved them that much. I want them to know that He made

274

them for a purpose—to know their Creator. I hope I've been faithful in pointing them to God, the one who loves them most. This is the legacy I want to leave them. Everything else is secondary.

My family with the kids growing up.

Chapter Thirty-Two

Before I applied for the full-time maintenance position at my church, the school where I worked, Greiffenstein Elementary, was demolished by a tornado in the spring of 1999. Fortunately, it took place on a weekend, so no one was in the building at the time. Afterwards we used another facility until our new school was built. I wanted to finish out my one year part-time commitment in the maintenance department at my church, so I put off leaving that second job where I had worked for almost a year.

Before the end of the school year, on May 23, 1999, I was to have another brush with death, but this time it wouldn't be at the hands of a bitter gang rival. I was playing in a basketball tournament in Haysville, Kansas—just south of Wichita—on a Sunday afternoon with my good friend Lance Brown. We were trying to advance in the playoffs when something went horribly wrong.

That morning my wife had gone on errands while I was at home with the kids. Andrea hadn't made it back yet, so I was growing impatient and sweating to leave for my game. Finally, unable to wait another minute, I got our friends' niece to watch the kids. I was anxious to reach the gym early to shoot around and warm up before the game. Shaneen was able to help me, so off I went.

We had finished the first half of the game, and it was now half-time. Before the bell sounded to start the second half, we had gotten in our huddle for some team direction and motivation. Once it sounded, we did a quick huddle and game plan and yelled out "Defense!"—at least that's what I was told. As I later learned, when we started to walk out onto the court, all of a sudden I collapsed. They thought I was kidding around at first, but that assumption soon turned into fear.

I knew nothing of what happened that day, and I still have no personal memory of my ordeal. It was a complete shock to wake up in a hospital bed and see a room full of people—my family, friends, teammates, and even the paramedics who had brought me in—standing around and staring down at me.

In that strange moment Lance described my collapse: how I had made some "snoring" sound; I'd taken a deep breath; my eyes had begun rolling back in my head—and I was gone. My wife said I had gone Code Blue three times. Our buzzer keeper told me that before the game had started, she'd been running around in a frenzy trying to get everything ready when something told her to grab her cell phone. She'd brushed off the thought because she never really needed it during games. But the voice persisted until she gave in and slipped it in her pocket.

In that same conversation our score-keeper, who was trained in C.P.R., admitted she had freaked out when she saw me collapse. Her mind had gone blank, and her training—which she'd never had to use in a real life situation—simply vanished. She had watched me lie there unconscious, feeling a tremendous weight of anguish at not being able to recall her training; but out of nowhere a sudden calm rested over her, and she remembered everything. She jumped right in, and while she was giving me C.P.R., her friend was calling 911.

And the paramedics shared before they had to leave how they were on their way back to base heading west; but when they'd reached a street called Seneca, they decided to turn right instead for no particular reason. They got the call about my situation and suddenly realized they were *about to pass* the Haysville Recreation Center where we'd been playing, where I was currently dying. They swung into the parking lot at once and rushed to my side. They thought God's hand was in the situation too.

Was it a coincidence that someone with a cell phone on hand (long ago in the days before everybody and everybody's kid had one) and another person trained in life-giving procedures were present at the moment I was dying? Was it a coincidence that the paramedics turned toward the scene of my collapse even before they got the call and happened to be in front of my building when the call came in?

What the secular world normally calls a coincidence, a soul focused on God sees as the unmistakable movement of His hand inside time. At such moments God's intervention seems so obvious and remarkable that the concept of coincidence appears almost silly.

While that devoted group of people were describing all these wonders, I kept slipping in and out of consciousness; but I did remember these amazing details. Still, my wife said the first question I asked was not if I was going to live or how the heart attack happened but "Did we win the game?" I guess that makes me a true warrior, most concerned about the game and my teammates, and we had a good laugh about it when she told me this later.

It turned out that I was diagnosed with a condition called cardiomyopathy, where the walls of my heart muscle are thicker than normal, which alters the electrical rhythm. The heartbeat speeds up too fast, and the body's natural defibrillator isn't able to provide the therapy that's needed to slow it back down, so it results in a cardiac arrest. For the rest of my life I'll have to wear an implanted defibrillator that senses any dangerous changes in heart rhythm and shoots an electric shock to my heart to restore a normal heartbeat. The doctors think I probably developed it as a child and it took years to manifest itself. I heard that one out of some crazy number even survives this type of heart attack. I still don't understand it all fully, but God has given me great and caring doctors and nurses to look after me over the years. I like to think of my heart situation as another opportunity to bring God the glory that He so richly deserves. It's just another chapter to the story, if you will.

When I heard the diagnosis initially, it didn't really bother me. I took it in stride with a sense of calm; maybe I felt like I was just hearing a bunch of big words. But when my cardiologist/electrophyisologist, Dr. Ashok Bajaj, mentioned I wouldn't be able to drive for six months, the reality of my health set in big time; and I realized my life would be changing from that moment on. Throughout, Dr. Bajaj and his staff were awesome as were the other doctors who assisted in saving my life. Dr. Bajaj didn't approach me as if I were number but consistently took the time to know me, his patient, never failed to ask how my family was doing, and allowed me to ask him anything regarding my condition.

Our relationship lasted for years until he and his wife passed away in 2008 when their plane crashed. His patients lost a fantastic doctor, a caring physician. His staff lost a wonderful boss, and his family and friends lost two loved ones. I will forever be grateful to Dr. Bajaj and for the way God used him in my life.

Chapter Thirty-Three

Present Time

The three men who have stood as the father figures in my life have each died now. I miss them all. I am most grateful for the way God closed the pages of history on each of these relationships. Each one had its own story of how we got from point A to point Z, and I give God all the credit because He loved us just that much.

My wife and I had separated during the Christmas season in 1993. Later, in 1994, Andrea called me with news that I really didn't want to hear. I was with my friend Lance, watching the Holyfield-Bowe fight, at the time. Naturally, I wasn't thrilled about being interrupted during the fight; but because it was from my wife, I was thinking she wanted to talk about my coming home. But instead, she needed to tell me that my stepmother Louise had called to say that my biological father, Big William, had just died. I went into an immediate daze; I just couldn't believe it.

Soon the shock turned into guilt because I had not returned his many recent calls; I was ashamed to tell him about our marital separation and have him be disappointed in us, so I always tried to avoid talking with him. He had grown fond of his daughter-in-law and had often talked about wishing to meet her in person someday. He had mentioned on numerous occasions how proud he was of me and of the huge changes I had made in my life, and now I was messing up my marriage! How could I admit such a thing? In some ways I even felt like I would be communicating that Jesus Christ had failed to bring harmony to our marriage, an unthinkable idea.

He had gone in for a routine checkup. My dad had fought in

Vietnam and was one of the first of our American soldiers to be affected by the chemical Agent Orange. The substance was supposed to harm only the vegetation and was used because our troops needed to spot the Viet Cong who often conducted guerilla warfare while hiding in the jungle trees and bushes. Unfortunately, that wasn't the case; and my father, along with many other American warriors, fell sick from this chemical. He was shipped to Saigon and eventually home where he was given an honorable discharge.

Because of this illness, he would spend the next twenty-plus years going in and out of the V.A. hospital and clinics for treatment and check-ups. Apparently at that last visit something went horribly wrong—he had a bad reaction or something and took a turn for the worse. As I understand it, he suffered for that entire evening while the hospital team tried to treat the agony he was experiencing. He couldn't communicate with his family except with tears.

I was told that around 4:00 the next morning, his suffering abruptly stopped. My family said a certain peace settled over him, and he began to crack a smile. Not long after that, he slipped into eternity. When I heard this, my first thought was, *"He made his peace with the Lord!"* I honestly don't believe that was just wishful thinking on my part because *something* has to explain how a man who had been suffering all evening could suddenly communicate a joy from the privacy of his own heart and mind. I wondered if *"Maybe God reminded my dad of our talks about Jesus, and He accepted His offer of salvation?"* Only God knows, but the possibility gave me comfort.

For nearly the first eighteen years of my life, I didn't even know if my dad was alive. But God heard a little boy's prayer to find his daddy, and He did. Even though we didn't communicate right at the end, we did get to share some heart-to-heart moments over the years; and for that I am grateful. I will continue to miss my dad until the end.

Big Charles has been gone since the early years of this century. He was the only father I knew for those first eighteen years. To his credit, about a year before he died he made a conscious effort to contact me, even going through a number of channels to get my phone number. He called to say he had left Los Angeles, had cleaned up from drugs, and was living back in Hot Springs, Arkansas.

He mentioned that he'd gotten down so low in life that he was through with living. But at that time, he said, *I* popped into his mind; and he remembered watching the enormous changes Christ had made in my life. He recalled the dramatic difference in me, and God used that memory to open his own heart to call out to Him. Big Charles said that he surrendered his life to Jesus Christ and sometime after that felt a need to ask my forgiveness for not being the father he should have been.

I responded, "Pop, I already have, and I want you to know that I can honestly say that I love you. You're my dad." For the next year or so we kept in touch with each other faithfully until I got a call from my Aunt Ruthie, saying he had been hospitalized and was being kept alive on a machine. She wanted to know what I thought about possibly pulling the cord because the monitors were showing no more brain activity. He was basically gone already; we just had to wrap our minds around that fact.

That was a sobering moment for me. I thought about the past year when we had gotten to really know each other, and I remembered the years long ago as well. I considered the courage he had shown in asking my forgiveness and the bond we'd developed as a result of his conversion to Christ. In my heart of hearts I knew he was now with his Lord and Savior and all that was left here on earth was his shell. So I added my consent to the family's, and we let him go. I knew at that moment, as I do today, that death is *not* the end for the believer and that I will see him again.

It seems remarkable that he didn't die until our relationship was totally healed, and that was because of the absolute love of a forgiving God. I miss Big Charles very much and wish he were still around for conversations. Looking back, I understand that people don't always express their love in a transparent way. Many raise their kids in the same way they were raised, no matter how wrongheaded. Perhaps I judged him too hard. But whatever the case, we ended with a very good understanding.

In 2000 my mother and David, along with my nephew Omar and my niece De'Essence, moved back to L.A., after having lived in Wichita nine years. Before I learned that they were moving—which stunned me to say the least—"Poppa David," as my kids called him, asked me if he could attend a traveling play that was going on at our church called "Heaven's Gates and Hell's Flames."

I was both surprised and excited by his request. For quite some time I had been encouraging Poppa David to visit our church, Central Christian, during various events; but he would always come up with excuses to stay away. So after awhile, I felt that God was telling me to just love him and not keep asking him anymore.

That's what I began doing. I stopped putting pressure on him to attend church or church-related events with me because, frankly, I was feeling a little discouraged. Still, I knew only God can change a person's heart and that I needed to trust Him to work in Poppa David's life. So I backed off and just tried to enjoy his company, especially with our spirited talk about guy things, politics, football, and so on. And on many occasions my wife and I had the honor of helping him— along with my mother and the kids—and just being there for them.

The traveling play called "Heaven's Gate and Hell's Flames" came to Wichita and was performed for several nights at my church. I took my nephew and niece to see it; and that night Omar gave his life to the Lord when they gave the invitation to come forward. Then, stunningly, on the last night of the performance, Poppa David asked if he could go. I just about blew a head gasket! I wasted no time saying "YES!!" At the end of the play, they gave the alter call and asked us all to bow our heads. I had been praying silently that the Holy Spirit would reach his heart.

While my eyes were closed, I felt Poppa David move as he brushed up against my left leg. So with one eye shut and one opened, I peeked and saw that he was preparing to walk toward the stairs. Sure enough, he went all the way down to the front of the stage and gave his life to Jesus Christ. My heart burst into joyous praise to God and His power to reach any willing heart. I couldn't help but marvel how very far we'd come. God is simply amazing.

Not too long after that, Poppa David told me they were planning to move back to Los Angeles. I was both shocked and sad but had to come to grips with it. I wished them God's best. But little did I know that when they pulled off in that U-haul truck, it would be the last time I would see him alive.

About a year later, I got a call from my mother saying that he had just died. Evidently, David had fallen asleep on the couch the previous night; and the next morning when she went to wake him, she discovered he had passed. Death has a way of sneaking up on you, even though you know it will eventually come. Certainly it was tough news to hear, both for me and my family. He had been battling diabetes for quite some time and had not taken care of his body—with all the drinking he had done for decades. Although after receiving Christ in his life, he was beginning to cut back significantly on the alcohol, perhaps the damage had already been done.

I was disappointed that they left Wichita because I wanted them to get involved with our church so they could grow with other Christians and have the support they needed. But my letting them go was another opportunity to trust God; I just hadn't realized the move would include David's death.

Perhaps it was the case that God knew his time was up, and the timing of Poppa David's accepting Christ in his life was preparation for that. Again, I had to marvel at God's amazing grace at work. And I find comfort in knowing that I will see him again.

These three men who filled the role of dad in my life have all passed away, but I'm so thankful to my Lord for giving me opportunities to bring a certain closure between each of them and me. All three of them manned up as far as I'm concerned. Case closed!

Today my mother Marie is back here in Wichita close to me. After David's death, she decided to return to Kansas. So my family and I drove out to L.A. in our van, rented a moving truck, and transported my mom, along with my niece and nephew, back to the sunflower state.

It's been a joy having my mom back. Here she has a son and daughter-in-law who will take care of her as she ages, and she knows she's surrounded by our love. My mother, too, has given her life to Christ, and she's been alcohol-free for about thirteen years. Today my mom and I are real friends, and I honor her. I thank God for our relationship and for making her to be my mom!

Andrea and I have gone through a lot of turmoil, but we are still standing. Both of us brought problems into our marriage from childhood and had no idea how such things could nearly destroy our union. Even today, life is not always easy. We still have our moments; but as in other marriages, because Christ is the Lord of our lives, we continue to stick it out even when things are tough.

Still, much healing has been accomplished, and the credit belongs to God alone. As long as we remember who is in charge, the marriage will continue to recover and grow. It is always my prayer and hope that healing will continue and the joy of Christ will replace the terrible pain of the past.

Personally, I have feared dealing with the public because of the impact of my speech disorder on my entire life—emotionally, physically, mentally, socially, and even spiritually. Unfortunately, Andrea has had to bear much of the weight of taking care of various business situations for me such as calling the plumber and explaining the problem or whatever the case may be. Although I've felt guilty, I've let her do much of that because I've shied away from struggling to get out my words, especially when I didn't understand something thoroughly. I always feared blowing up under the pressure of the person asking me question after question while interrupting me in the process.

I often ask myself why that is. While, secure in my Lord, I no longer depend on people's approval of me, I still have that desire to be accepted in the public arena. Sadly, this is the world we live in, and I'll continue to get hung up when people think I'm a prank caller because I can't get out what I want to say fast enough or when I can't place my order in the fast food drive-thru before the guy on the intercom blasts me with "Excuse me—I can't understand what you're saying! Could you drive around to the window, please?" I know this will continue to happen on occasion; I'm having to come to terms with that fact. It's no one's fault. It's just that it is what it is.

All in all, as I continue to walk in the confidence of my Lord, I will keep on growing as a man, a husband, and father. I hope to increasingly win my wife's trust and respect as she sees me taking on more of that responsibility. God has put her in my life for a purpose, I have no doubt. And without question, I'm very thankful.

As I look back over my life, I can only shake my head in amazement at how far I have come. Years ago society would have written me off as merely another sad statistic if God hadn't reached down and rescued me from a life being drained by overwhelming guilt and blindness. I spent so many years trying to find my place in the world, but the world had no room for me because I had nothing at all to offer.

What did I have to give? Nothing! As you have seen, I spent my first six years with my grandmother, Maggie Sue, who loved me with such a purity of love that I never had to question it. She did her best to protect me, care for me, and equip me for life. But our time on earth is like a book, and we won't always get to write in it what pleases us—as in the case of my early sexual abuse. But nevertheless, I remained a happy child with her.

They say that death is simply a separation from something as when the spirit is separated permanently from the body. If that's the case—and it is—then the day I was separated from her at age six, I died inside.

But the final death blow, if you will, came when I thought God had abandoned me as an eleven year old on the day I was humiliated in front of Jill because of the way I talked. In tears I decided to figure out how to survive without Him. Certainly I had few options. I turned my attention to what I thought was real power: the Crips gang. I lost my identity officially at that point and sold my soul to the gangster world where I saw clear and unmistakable power that *worked*. At least while it lasted.

I went on to fail in school from that moment forward with no one in the home willing to prepare me for real life. I became so ashamed of my speech disorder that any confidence I once had in the arms of my grandmother was utterly destroyed. I absolutely feared the "real world," so you can imagine the kind of dreams I had as a child. I had no dream! In my view, life held only two kinds of people: those who talked right and those who didn't. You know into which camp I placed myself!

Survival became the only game. The confidence I acquired was fueled by my anger, and that allowed me to accept the challenge of becoming the hardest Crip I could possibly be. Might makes right in the streets because, if you can prove yourself, the guys who used to punk you had to give you respect. The constant bullying and mocking and ridicule stopped because I had earned that respect. To many in the streets, I became known as Clipper from Grape Street Watts, and I lived it to the fullest.

By the end of those eight years of gang banging, I had gotten to the point of wanting to kill myself because all the values I had built my life around had lost purpose and meaning. I had been just chasing after the wind. Meanwhile, I tried to stop my mother from drinking, not wanting her to die like my Aunt Faye as a result of alcoholic damage to her liver; but what I didn't realize at the time—and what

I couldn't apply to my own life as well—is that if the human heart chooses not to change, no one on the planet can make that change occur. Without that understanding, I slipped into a depression that nearly brought me to the point of suicide.

I spent all my teenage years trying to gain control of my circumstances, only to lose control. Once again I was in a powerless position as when I was taken away from my grandma. I had sold my soul to Grape, yet what did I have to hold on to? Nothing! I was left spiritually bankrupt.

A time comes in every person's life when he starts asking that most important of questions: "Why am I here?" This one inevitably leads to the others, "Who am I?" "What is my purpose for living?" and then "What will happen to me when I die?" These were the hard questions that hit me during that time, but no one around me had the answers. I didn't even know where else to look. And suicide seemed to offer at least a solution of those questions in my head, though a false one.

The greatest battlefield on earth is the human mind, and whatever (or whoever) gains the most ground in that most private of places will usually win the battle. But my Lord had plans that I could not see! It was Jesus Christ who provided the answers I needed to hear—not just what I wanted to hear. It was He who took over the fight and cut through the darkness of my mind so I could see His wonderful truth. I was falling into a pit of my own digging. I had been searching for answers in all the wrong places and had been trying to fill up a God-shaped hole that is reserved for Him alone to fill.

I knew God was calling me that day when I walked down to Kim Seebach's house. The eternal Creator of the universe was asking me to give up my life and surrender to His Son! I needed to understand that I was in rebellion against Him, to acknowledge it, and to seek His forgiveness so He could save me from an eternity in hell. When Kim confronted me with the truth that day in his office, I suddenly realized my need for the Savior. God knew how inadequate I felt, how much of nothing I could offer Him in exchange except to receive His free gift through the shed blood of His Son. God's amazing grace *placed in me* the desire to repent from my self-destructive lifestyle.

That day I became so convicted by the Word of God that, after weeping bitterly for some time, I bowed my heart and life to Jesus

Christ. I stumbled into Kim's house a broken young man, but I left there a restored one, convinced that God had *not* abandoned me as I had once thought. And from that moment on, I have never been the same.

In reality, it hasn't been an easy ride since that mid-day in February of 1985, and I've had some very trying times. I've been suicidal, separated from my wife several times, self-admitted into a Christian hospital for deep counseling, and I've had to heal hard. I've come close to death from a heart condition and will have to wear a defibrillator for the rest of my life. But over and over again, God has proven Himself faithful, sustaining me in every step of the way.

God has built such a track record of faithfulness through all the turmoil in my life, how could I *not* trust Him? The world seems to think Christians are supposed to have perfect lives and be flawless beings all of a sudden, just because they become Christians. I discovered that certainly isn't the case. If anything, the One who is perfect, Jesus Christ, turns your life inside out, uncovering all the dirt from your former way of living and showing you just how much you need His aid day in and day out. This is called Sanctification, which for the true Christian can be a tough, tough process.

As a gang banger, I had radically suppressed my past because in the gangster world, you learn to show no weakness if you hope to survive in the streets. That's absolutely what I had to do. But God has used my marriage—and continues to do so—to turn me inside out. Many times I've wanted to give up because I've had to humble myself so much. But He gave me a love for truth and a hunger for His Word, and He's used these to support me through the troubled times.

No, Christians are not perfect. The difference, though, is that we have trusted in the Savior who *is* perfect, and He has given us the Holy Spirit who has promised to keep us until we see Christ face to face. "And you were included in Christ when you heard the Word of truth, the gospel of your salvation. Having believed, you were marked in Him with a seal, the promised Holy Spirit, who is a deposit guaranteeing our inheritance until the redemption of those who are God's possession—to the praise of His glory" (Ephesians 1:13-14, NIV). It is because of Jesus Christ that I know who I am and in whom I believe. I thank my Savior for who He is and for coming to earth to pay a price that no mere human could ever pay. Jesus has placed the highest value on all our lives; truly, we don't need self-esteem but His-esteem.

To sum up—mine is a story about the Creator's personal interest in a boy with no hope, about a God who decided in the counsel of His will that I was worth every drop of His son's blood. This is a story about the God of hope and His desire that no one should perish and about my enduring gratitude to Him for rescuing me. With all my heart, I encourage you that, if you don't know Him personally, you will open yourself to His call, to trust Him with your eternal future while you still have time. Jesus Christ is the greatest love the world will ever know, but He alone is also the One to whom we will have to give an account.

I want to thank you, the reader, for giving up some of your time to read my book. I hope you've enjoyed the ride. It has been an absolute privilege to share with you what God has done in my life; and it's my hope that in some way you've been blessed through it. And after some twenty years of putting off the completion of this book that God called me to do, I can say—I'm finally done. May the Lord bless you and yours.

Reader Testimonials

• Why do so many young people today join the lawless, savage gangs now infesting our inner cities' neighborhoods to make them hells of crime and murder—and is there a cure? Both answers are given in Eric West's totally honest, deeply moving story of his life From Crip to Christ. You will never forget it.

Ellen Myers grew up in Nazi Germany, the daughter of a German doctor who had served in the German army and in parliament and of a Jewish mother. She became the official interpreter of the American military after the war and later worked for General Lucius D. Clay, successor to Eisenhower as European Theater Commander.

• The city can steal hope. Brokenness, violence, and alienation lead to despair. This has a profound impact on the lives of the people living there. But God looks into the darkest corners—the places of greatest need—searching for His instruments of change, then reaching and rescuing those who would lead others to hope. Eric West is one of those. He not only survived the despair but now stands as a man of faith who gives hope to a lost generation. Eric's story is a triumph of the grace of God. And it can change you as well.

Al Ewert, Vice President of Ministry Development of World Impact, Inc.

• Even when Eric had no interest in the Almighty, the Almighty had already chosen Eric to be His child and spokesman. In this book Eric reveals his very misdirected life and how his only interest was to satisfy and glorify Eric. Yet at a certain time in his childhood, Eric had heard a missionary explain God's ability and desire to forgive sin as well as His grace, purpose, and overwhelming love; this experience so influenced Eric that he could not forget—though he did try to run. As his sins mounted up through the years, at last Eric was convicted; and he wanted to know and accept the only pure and forever love and salvation available for him and all sinners. As you read about Eric, your heart will break for his misguided life. Then you will glorify God for His calling of Eric and for this man's acceptance of God, his Son Jesus Christ, and the Holy Spirit to rule his life. Eric is an example of how God is able to give us a life that is miraculously new. To God be the glory.

W. Marvin Watson, former U.S. Postmaster General, White House Chief-of-Staff under Lyndon Johnson, former president of Dallas Baptist College, and a member of the World Impact's national board.